THE ESTATE

THE ESTATE

My life on the front line
of Britain's housing crisis

CHARMAIN BYNOE

WITH ELIZABETH SHEPPARD

GALLERY BOOKS UK

First published in Great Britain by Gallery Books,
an imprint of Simon & Schuster UK Ltd, 2022

1 3 5 7 9 10 8 6 4 2

Simon & Schuster UK Ltd
1st Floor
222 Gray's Inn Road
London WC1X 8HB

www.simonandschuster.co.uk
www.simonandschuster.com.au
www.simonandschuster.co.in

Simon & Schuster Australia, Sydney
Simon & Schuster India, New Delhi

Certain names and identifying details of people portrayed in this book
have been changed to protect their identities.

A CIP catalogue record for this book is available from the British Library

Paperback ISBN: 978-1-3985-1660-1
eBook ISBN: 978-1-3985-1661-8

Typeset in Palatino by
Palimpsest Book Production Ltd, Falkirk, Stirlingshire

Printed in the UK by CPI Group (UK) Ltd, Croydon, CR0 4YY

Dedicated to Southwark housing officers and all UK local authority officers, past and present, who have gone that extra mile to try to make a difference in their residents' lives.

To Clive Woods, RSO and Unison steward: Rest In Peace.

To my mum and dad, your strength made me who I am today.

To all my friends who have always supported me, especially Sharon, Gillian, Patricia, Noreen and Ramatu.

And finally,

Indya, Isaac and Lloyd, your love gives me hope.

CONTENTS

INTRODUCTION

'So what *do* you do, then?'

That's what tenants often say to me when they ask for something they can't have: a bigger house to move into *right now*, a repair guy to fix their leaky pipe in the next five minutes. They don't always understand that Southwark Council has a tight budget. It's public money, and we have to justify every penny we spend. That's why we sometimes have to tell them 'no', or explain how to apply for what they need themselves.

There's not much sympathy for housing officers. People imagine us sitting at our desks, drinking cups of tea and plotting how to evict people. They think we're faceless bureaucrats. Pen-pushers. But we're nothing like that at all.

In 2019, Channel 4 made the TV show *Council House Britain*. It highlighted the work of Southwark Council's housing department, and it gave us housing officers a chance to put the record straight. My colleagues and I worked with the producers and camera crew for months, sharing the challenges we face and how we try to help and support our residents. It was very exciting to take part, but just as we were wrapping up the filming, the Covid-19 pandemic turned everything upside down. Eventually, in October 2020, *Council House Britain* was broadcast. It felt unreal to sit in my living room and watch myself on screen, but I was really proud of what we'd achieved.

A few weeks later, I got an email asking if I would like to write this book. Straightaway I said yes. The TV programme was great, but it could only show snippets of what we housing officers actually do. I wanted to tell the bigger story – and here it is.

As I write, there's another pandemic going on: a crisis in public housing that spreads right across the country. It's not just my borough in south London where we have limited space to build, limited funding to use and there's always a cry from some family in desperate need of help. In every borough, in every city, in every part of the UK, it's no different. Housing officers work very hard to deal with the challenges that are brought to us. Too often we'd like to do more, but our hands are tied.

As well as shedding light on these problems, there's one more reason I wanted to write this book. When I was born, my family lived in one room in south London. Later on, we moved to a house on a council estate, so I empathise with my residents and the challenges they face. I'm also very proud of where I come from. Growing up, I felt like part of a community, and I strive to keep that community spirit alive. And it really is alive. It's just as strong as ever;

I know because I've felt it. In the lockdowns of 2020 and 2021, it's what kept people going.

I'm proud of my residents and the way they struggle through their situations, how they make the best of what little they have. I don't want readers to think that all of them have – or cause – problems. Most of the tenants on my estates are living a good life. No matter what their income, they're still proud. We've got kids there who go on to university, who get good jobs, who do well. Not everyone who comes from a council estate is a gang banger, whatever you might read in the newspapers.

Even when I can't change the world, each little thing I do as a housing officer can help someone from the community I'm working in. Every tenant's problem is serious to them, and we deal with each one to the best of our ability. Of course, we make mistakes and things go wrong sometimes, but we always try our hardest. I hope, if nothing else, that this becomes evident in the pages that follow.

Charmain Bynoe
March 2022

CHAPTER ONE

ONLY WAY OUT

2002

I'm hurrying to the address in Clifton Crescent, close to the Old Kent Road. I'm running late today, but as I turn the corner, I still notice how attractive it is around here. The Georgian houses on the well-maintained green are a pretty far cry from many of the flats I'm used to visiting as a housing officer in this part of inner London.

I'm here to assess a man who's applied to Southwark Council for a flat on the grounds of homelessness. Right now, he's sleeping on his sister's couch. As I knock on the front door, I straighten my clothes after my speed march and gear myself up for another routine appointment.

A young Black guy in his thirties answers the door. I give him my usual quick once-over. Visiting a person in their home always carries some degree of risk, but five years as a council housing officer have sharpened my instincts. My life experience has taught me to be wary, and this job's made me more so. If there's a threat to my safety, I'm quick to spot the signs.

He's a bit rumpled and sleepy-looking. Calm. Nothing here to cause me concern.

'Michael? Hi. How are you doing today?'

I hold out my hand but he ignores it. He doesn't say anything. I go on.

'I'm Charmain from the housing office. I'm here to confirm the details from your housing application.'

'Finally!' He sounds annoyed.

'I'm so sorry I'm late. I had an emergency this morning,' I say. I know that it's important to explain – to make clear to a tenant that their time matters to you – but my apology doesn't quite work.

'I thought you was coming at 9.30!' Michael says.

Now I start to notice an edge of real aggression in his voice. I'm immediately a little more alert. I smile at him, not showing my concern, keeping things friendly and relaxed.

'I do understand it's frustrating to wait,' I say to him. 'So let's go through the form now and see if we can get your application in.'

'I already done the form!'

'I know you did,' I say, 'but I have to check your information.'

He still looks angry, but he moves back into the darkened hallway. I hesitate before I step inside. Michael is upset with the council, but I don't see any real red flags here. I've had no advance warning that he might be a problem. There are no signs of substance abuse, no seriously threatening behaviour. His assessment will only take five minutes.

Calculating risk like this is just a part of my job. We housing officers find ourselves faced with drug addicts, gang members, situations of domestic violence, or just frustrated and angry people who feel they've been kept waiting far too long. One Southwark officer was chased across an estate by a bunch of men with knives. Another was stabbed in the hand in an altercation. In the local authority next door, a colleague was shot – and thankfully not seriously hurt. He'd been conducting what should have been a simple eviction of a man who wouldn't pay his rent.

So we know we're in harm's way, but safety in the workplace in 2002 might just be a note on the cover of a file: '*Do not visit alone*' or '*No female officer to visit*'. It's better than nothing, but in an emergency or a rushed situation, a warning like that can get missed – and today I'm in a rush. I should have been here two hours ago. But I got called to an emergency that is still not fully sorted. Now I'm trying to make up for lost time. Perhaps that's why I miss the warning signs I should have seen. My assessment of the situation isn't up to the mark.

'Come in, then,' Michael says to me.

My training is to always stay behind him so that at all times I can easily turn back and reach the door. But now he holds the door open and I automatically step inside. As he follows me into the kitchen, I instantly realise I've made a big mistake. There's no other door in this room – I've let him get between me and my only way out. Experience tells me that my best bet to keep things under control is professional confidence. I'm holding a copy of the housing application form that we will go over together and I glance down at it, eager to get the visit done.

'So, Michael. You were living with your mother but she asked you to leave in...' – I turn the form over – '...in November 2001. Is that correct?' I ask him.

While I'm talking, I'm taking in the details of the kitchen. That's another skill I've picked up on the job – the ability to suss out someone's living situation without staring or asking too many questions. I see at once that it's a family room, welcoming and warm. There are breakfast dishes waiting to be washed up in the sink. There's a pile of clean tea towels folded on the side. Children's drawings and a star chart for good behaviour are taped to the fridge.

'My ma was on my case,' mutters Michael. 'Always on at me to get a job. It ain't that easy!'

'No, it's certainly not. So you moved to this property belonging to your sister?'

'Yeah. When can I get my own place?'

'First I have to check that you qualify,' I explain to him. 'That's what this visit is for.'

He doesn't respond. As we stand there, I'm becoming more and more aware of the silence around us. I realise uneasily that there's no one else here.

'Is your sister at work?' I ask him, making sure.

'Yeah. Early shift. The kids are at school.'

My heart plummets, but I carry on. 'Three kids. So there are five of you. Where do you sleep?'

Instead of answering, he glares at me suspiciously. 'Why you askin' all these questions?'

'It's my job to assess your living situation,' I tell him. I notice that he's becoming more agitated, starting to breathe heavily.

'I sleep through there. On the sofa.' He jerks his head towards the hall. Seeing an opportunity to escape from the kitchen, I ask as casually as I can manage, 'Can you please show me?'

'What you want me to show you for?' His voice drops to a growl. 'You work for the council! You know what the sitting room's like!'

I understand how all these questions must sound to him, so I try to explain.

'I have to check how many people sleep here,' I say. 'If this place is overcrowded, it will help you get a flat of your own.'

But Michael is still glaring. 'It's a waste of time!' he mutters. What's bothering me most now are his hands. They've started clenching and unclenching at his sides. *If I'm too assertive*, I think to myself, *then he might get really nasty*. I look for a way to take the aggro out of this situation.

'Okay,' I say quickly, 'we'll check that in a minute. You've been staying here for five months. Is there anywhere else you could go? Friend's place, maybe?'

'Nah! I told ya! I need my own flat! When—'

'Michael, I promise, we'll do this as quickly as we can.

I just need to confirm the information that's on the form. Can you please show me your original documents? Your birth certificate and passport number?'

'My sister done the form! She got all the papers and she filled it out!' The housing application form is lengthy and detailed. *Michael's sister must be busy with her job and her family*, I think to myself. *If she did all that, she really wants her brother to leave.*

'You seen my forms! You know I need a flat!' He's shouting now, squeezing his hands into fists.

Unfortunately there are important reasons for these checks, so I am going to have to insist. We've recently received a number of housing applications using false identities. Fraudsters have been looking up the birth certificates of children who've died, then using their details to claim benefits.

'Michael, it's important that we follow the procedure here. I need to confirm a few things.'

He narrows his eyes, then bangs his fist down on the sink. The metallic crack is sudden and very loud. I make an effort not to flinch. I realise that I'm extremely unsafe, just one mistake away from this situation getting out of hand. 'For fuck's sake!' He's really angry now. 'What's your problem? Why you givin' me grief?'

I do have one bit of personal protection. A few weeks ago, all Southwark's housing officers were given personal alarms. They're little silver boxes with a pin release – pull the pin and your eardrums are blasted by a siren. I wonder for a moment whether I should use it, but I'm not sure how it's meant to help me get away from a perilous situation like this one.

Perhaps if I threw the box at Michael, he'd go down like a sack of potatoes and I could jump over him and run. Nah, that's not going to work... The thought's just a product of the flood of adrenaline that's racing through my body.

'When – can – I – get – a – fuckin' – flat?' Michael demands through gritted teeth.

I keep my voice level. 'It's a bit long-winded, I get that. But I'm afraid this is how the application system works.'

'So how much longer?'

'I don't have a computer in front of me,' I say, 'so I'm afraid I can't tell you right now.' I'm edging towards the kitchen door as I'm speaking. Unfortunately, Michael's noticed this. He sticks out his foot and kicks the door shut. It's an unusual response I know, but when anyone tries to intimidate me, I can feel myself getting angry. *I ain't showing I'm shitting it right now,* I think to myself. *You are not going to look in my eyes and see fear.*

I draw myself up to my full height and say, 'Why are you standing in front of the door, Michael?'

'You got a problem with that?'

'Yes, I do.' I speak the words firmly. 'You are stopping me from leaving.'

'I just wanna know how long it's going to be with my flat!'

I've dealt with scary, out-of-control people before. If he sees that he's intimidating me, this situation will get worse. I give him a smile, making an effort at normality. 'So before

I can tell you,' I say, 'I need to go back to my office and put your details into the computer.'

'Well, that's not good enough!' he yells into my face.

'I'm going back to the office now,' I tell him. 'We'll have to finish this another day.'

'Nah! You're not leavin'!'

'Yes, I am, Michael.'

He slams his fist against the sink once again, using much more force this time. A scary amount of force. 'You're not leavin' 'til you give me an answer!'

I don't know what to do. I'm trapped inside the flat with an angry, unpredictable applicant, with no way of contacting anyone. For the first time since I started this job, I'm in danger. Real danger. Welcome to the life of a housing officer.

CHAPTER TWO

YOU'RE LEGAL, BABY!

Our reception desk at Southwark Council's housing office in Meeting House Lane is always packed and busy. This desk is where our frontline team deals with everyone who walks in through the door – all our residents' requests, their problems and crises: everything from leaky radiators and noise complaints to domestic violence and serious anti-social behaviour. There's always a named duty officer and named duty rent officer available in the building for them to refer cases, but it's the customer care officers on the desk who work out what to do and who to get in touch with. There are often dramas here; staff have to deal with people venting and they take on a whole lot of issues.

Our interview rooms are all along one side, with walls of coloured glass to make the whole place feel brighter and less stressful. Keeping aggro levels down is the intention but it doesn't always work, so there are panic buttons underneath each table and CCTV is always watching. Our reception desk has already been raised to discourage irate residents from trying to climb over it, and a visitor once brought a car battery along with him and threw it against a glass door. Fortunately for us, the glass was shatterproof. A security shutter has been installed on the desk, but it comes down rather slowly. Once, while it was being lowered, someone gave it a kick and now it sticks halfway.

A couple of years ago, Gloria, a young mum at the end of her tether caring for her three kids in a one-bedroom flat, arrived here with her children and a bag full of nappies, toys and snacks. Silently she placed them and all their kit in the waiting area, then she turned round and left. The customer care officer that day, Kaarima, instantly realised that this was an emergency.

'Charmain!' she called. I was standing behind the desk, finishing dealing with another resident's query. I heard the urgency in Kaarima's voice. 'That woman,' she pointed. 'Can you get her, quick? Can you stop her leaving?'

I looked up and saw Gloria heading out through the sliding glass doors into Meeting House Lane. I could also see her pram in the waiting area, its net underneath stuffed full of carrier bags. Her baby son was sleeping in the seat but her two daughters, one a toddler and the other about four, were holding onto the handlebars, looking really confused and anxious in this noisy environment.

I'd met Gloria before and I knew that she wasn't coping well with her situation. My heart went out to her struggles as a single mum on a low income, suffering all the stress of sharing a one-bed flat with three tiny children. Their dad wasn't part of her family unit and it's not always possible to ask a man for help, even if you'd like him to take responsibility for his kids. Gloria didn't want him around and there had to be a reason. We didn't pry into it but, for all we knew, their relationship could be abusive.

But Gloria just wasn't helping herself. She'd got into rent arrears, so although she badly needed a transfer to a bigger property for her three under-fives, she couldn't have one yet because no one who's behind on their rent can be given a larger place by the council. The last time I saw her, I'd told her that she had to make a payment plan for her arrears and stick to it. We'd make sure the amount was affordable, and then she could be offered a larger property. Until she did that, though, we couldn't help her.

But I could see she wasn't listening. Each time I mentioned her rent arrears and how to pay them, she just switched off. She'd come in to see us twice in the past few weeks to chase up her transfer request, but still didn't seem to understand why she couldn't get one. It's really hard to help someone who just won't engage with what you're telling them.

'Gloria!' I ran after her, outside into Meeting House Lane. 'Gloria! Stop!'

As I caught up with her, I grabbed her arm. I was shocked by the blank look of exhaustion on her face. 'Gloria, what d'you think you're doing?'

She stared at me.

'Gloria. Look. You can't leave your kids here. Whatever the problem is, we can sort it out. But you've got to come back inside.'

'Nah.' Her voice was very low. 'I can't do nothin' more. You have 'em.'

I didn't think she wanted to leave her kids at all – this was just her desperate cry for help. She was completely at the end of her tether.

'Gloria—'

'I can't stay in that place,' she told me flatly. 'I've had enough. I got no space. I got damp. I got no room to breathe.'

I knew I had to get her back inside. 'Gloria, I know how you feel. We can find a way to help you. But—'

'And how long that take?'

'I'm afraid I can't tell you exactly. Let's not talk about it here on the pavement. Let's sit down inside.'

'Charmain, these kids ain't gettin' smaller! They gettin' bigger!'

'I understand,' I said. 'I get how stressful it is for you. But—'

'So you gotta house 'em! I can't do it!' Gloria was shaking her head adamantly.

'Listen to me,' I said. 'Really listen. You mustn't leave them here. If you do, I will have to call Social Services. It will count as abandonment.'

This time she heard me. She looked completely shocked.

'Abandonment?' she said.

'Yes. I won't have any choice. It's the law. I will have to report it. You might have to go to court to get them back.'

'But I can't go on like this!' Gloria cried. 'I can't. Not every single minute, every single day. My kids need better than this. How would you like it in a one-bedroom flat?' She shook her head and clenched her hands together in distress. Passers-by were starting to glance at us.

'I understand,' I said. 'I can imagine how you feel. Kids just take over, don't they? There's no room for you.'

Once she knew that I got it, that I understood the way she was feeling, she seemed to become a little calmer. She stood there looking totally defeated. When I reached out to gently guide her by the elbow, she walked back inside. Kaarima had already taken the kids away into our play area along with their buggy and the bags, and I could see her distracting them with games so that they wouldn't notice that their mother was in crisis. They were giggling and playing peekaboo. At least they seemed okay.

Gloria sat down. The dazed, blank look had begun to leave her face. Suddenly she burst into tears and cried for twenty minutes. I fetched her some tea then just sat there alongside her. It gave me a chance to think about finding a solution to her problems, but there was no use saying anything until she could listen.

'I wouldn't abandon them!' she finally managed to say.

'Of course not. You're a good mum. They're well looked-after, they're well-fed – you're doing a great job.'

Following our procedures, we did manage to find a solution for Gloria. We referred her to a charity that could award grants to buy clothes and necessities for her children. They also gave her help with her debts. Then we solved a problem she was having with her housing benefit, and the backdated benefit payments cleared her rent arrears. Gloria and her children were living in a property that was counted as overcrowded, so we completed a statutory overcrowding proforma for her. That in turn made her a higher priority for transfer, and she could move within six months. But that was back then; nowadays, her wait for help would be far, far longer.

So, in a way, her extreme actions worked. She was given the chance to make a fresh start. But she'd stepped out on a precipice, just seconds away from losing her children. Although I felt relieved that we had managed to help her, I was terrified just thinking about it.

• • •

2003

The first time I meet Pleasant, it's just routine: I'm doing a quick tenancy check. Everyone's at home and they seem like a nice little family. There's gruff Samuel in his mid forties; shy, polite Pleasant, at least twenty years younger than her husband; their five-year-old son Isaac and baby daughter Ama. I notice that Samuel does the talking while his wife seems slightly wary. But the house is well kept and the children are happy. I don't have any cause for concern.

The second time I meet Pleasant, Samuel is under arrest. He has battered her so severely that her eyeball has been dislodged from its socket.

The police phone me early one morning to tell me that

Pleasant's in hospital. Little Isaac ran and banged on a neighbour's door in the middle of the night screaming for help – a really brave thing for such a young child to do. Their neighbours were already awake because of the sounds of a fight – and it wasn't the first one they'd heard between the couple. The wife rang 999 while the husband went round to intervene. He found the kids hysterical, the kitchen table smashed to bits, blood splatters on the walls and Pleasant almost unconscious on the floor. Samuel was extremely intimidating, ordering the man to leave and yelling that this had nothing to do with him, but the horrified neighbour refused to go. Then the police arrived and Samuel was arrested.

When anything like this happens to one of my tenants, I go over what I've seen and what I've done again and again in my mind. Should I have spotted that something was wrong when I visited? Were there signs of abuse? Was Pleasant's little son too well-behaved? Too quiet? Did he seem frightened of his father? Should I have seen that his mother was being intimidated? It's awful to think that I might have missed a chance to protect a vulnerable woman.

Social Services step in quickly to arrange emergency fostering. Then, after a few days, friends from Pleasant's church who know the children well agree to take them. That gives Pleasant some peace of mind. But she's still scared of Samuel – terrified that he'll be released from custody and come looking for her.

It's the early 2000s and domestic violence isn't treated quite as seriously as it would be today. But there's been such extreme force used in this case that Samuel hasn't been charged with battering his wife, but with grievous bodily harm. With a charge of GBH, he's held in prison on remand.

We always contact the charity Women's Aid in cases like these. They can provide emergency refuge if it's needed, plus specialist counselling not just for the woman who has suffered the abuse, but also for her children. Women's Aid gives legal advice too: they put survivors in touch with solicitors who are experienced in family and housing law and assign a case worker to each woman.

Pleasant's new social worker phones me quickly. She's completely on the ball, and asks me all about Pleasant's legal position in her council house. I've checked already: right now, the place is in Samuel's name only. I explain to the social worker that this can be changed: Pleasant and Samuel are married, and that gives her an automatic right to half the tenancy.

'Great,' the social worker replies, 'so Women's Aid will get started on that. But right now, Pleasant's so frightened of everything, it's hard to get her to talk.'

'When the Non-Molestation Order's in place,' I say, 'surely that will help?'

The Non-Molestation Order will set limits that Pleasant's solicitor can request. It will specify that Samuel can't be within a certain distance of her, or of her home. Women's Aid will act as her advocates to make sure that she gets what she needs.

'Yeah, I think so,' the social worker says. 'I'll see her and explain how it works. What she needs to know is that even if they do let him out, he can't go near her.'

• • •

It's a warm May afternoon in Meeting House Lane, and things seem pretty quiet. I can't believe it's going to stay that way. Then I see Mr Youd at the enquiry counter. He's a tenant from the Cloister estate, a very small, slight man with short black hair and a permanently worried expression on his face, as though he's waiting for the sky to fall in. He's always scratching his head as though he's deep in thought. Behind him in the queue are a man in his fifties and a woman holding the hand of a fidgeting toddler. They're both shifting from foot to foot in that restless way that tells me they've been waiting for a pretty long time. I can't say I'm surprised: whenever Mr Youd comes in to speak to us, the same thing seems to happen.

Kaarima's at the desk, trying to deal with him. She catches my eye and I can see she's pretty stressed. I walk over to the counter and stand next to Mr Youd. 'So please can you tell me when is my appointment?' he's asking her. Kaarima gives him a reassuring smile.

'Next Tuesday, Mr Youd, like I said. At half past two. Somebody will—'

'Please can you write it down for me?'

'I'll do that straightaway, Mr Youd.'

Kaarima picks up a slip of paper from the counter and writes down the date and time.

'And they will deal with my repairs?' he asks her anxiously.

'Yes, Mr Youd, they will. Now if you could please just stand to the side—'

'But have *you* written it down?' Mr Youd enquires.

'Well,' says Kaarima patiently, 'I don't need to, you see. When I make a booking, the computer records it automatically.'

The older guy in the line behind is getting tired of waiting. He lets out a huge, noisy sigh. Mr Youd glances nervously over his shoulder.

'Did the computer record the right time?' Mr Youd asks.

'I'm sure it did, Mr Youd. It works really well.'

'But please can you check?'

I really admire Kaarima's patience, given the amount of work she has to do. But I decide that I need to intervene. 'Hello, Mr Youd,' I say to him. 'How are you doing? Is everything okay?' He jumps when I speak, then looks at me worriedly.

'Hello, Charmain! I'm just checking that – I need to check that my appointment time is—'

'That's fine. We can certainly check for you. But can you stand over here while our staff serve other customers, please?'

Kaarima smiles at me gratefully. As Mr Youd shuffles along the desk, she apologises to the older guy for keeping him waiting.

'Charmain! I need to check the time of my home visit!' Mr Youd tells me. He sounds panicky – and that's exactly how he feels. He has obsessive-compulsive disorder, and one of his symptoms is this continual checking. He goes over everything we tell him again and again until he's quite worn out. He's a sweet and well-meaning man and I've never heard him say anything that isn't respectful and polite. But his visits to the enquiry counter rob the customer care team of their will to live.

'So I just heard Kaarima tell you that your appointment is 2.30 next Tuesday,' I tell him, as reassuringly as I possibly can.

'Well, yes. But can you check?'

'I'm sure it's right, Mr Youd. She won't have got it wrong.'

He wrings his hands in anxiety.

'*Please* can you check?' he asks again. It's really sad to see him going round and round again in loops of such dreadful anxiety.

'Okay,' I say, 'Just wait a moment.' I step around behind the counter and scan the appointments schedule on one of the screens. 'Yep – that's definitely the right time, Mr Youd. Please don't worry any more. You've got the right information. It's all fine. Why don't you go back home now?'

'Yes. Yes.' He nods uncertainly. 'I – I will. I'll go home. I definitely will.' He turns away from the counter. I still stand and wait. A few seconds later, he's back.

'It's okay, Mr Youd,' I say again. 'Your appointment is booked.'

'Right.' He nods. He seems all right for a moment, then panic flickers across his face.

'Definitely?' he asks me.

'Really, definitely.'

Reluctantly he walks towards the exit.

'Thanks, Charmain,' Kaarima says to me.

'Don't thank me yet,' I tell her. 'I don't think this is over.'

I head towards the door into the stairwell to go back up to my office, but before I've got halfway, I hear Mr Youd's voice once again. He's shuffled anxiously back up to the counter.

'I'm sorry – um – sorry – this won't take a minute – uh – can I just check – um – what time is my repairs appointment next week, please?'

The older guy in the queue has been served now, but the woman with the toddler is still waiting. She's not looking happy. Her little daughter is dragging on her arm and beginning to whine. This time it's Anthony, the other adviser on duty, who's speaking to Mr Youd.

'Your appointment is fine,' Anthony tells him firmly. 'It's all booked. Somebody will definitely come around to see you.'

But Mr Youd looks distraught. He twists his hands together. 'But – but – please can you check that the computer has—?'

'Mate, you've been seen,' the woman with the toddler tells him sharply. 'It's my turn now.'

I don't want an argument to start at the counter, so I walk back over to them. Anthony is yet again writing down the time of Mr Youd's appointment on another piece of paper.

'Mr Youd,' I say to him, 'it's okay. It's all done. You can go now. The staff need to deal with other people.'

'But—'

'Honestly. It's fine. Your appointment is fine.'

This time, Mr Youd actually leaves the building. Just for a moment, the counter is quiet. The moment he's out of sight, I say to Kaarima and Anthony: 'Come with me!'

'Come where?'

'Come in the back office! Quick – we need you out of sight. He'll be back in a minute.'

Anthony gets it right away. Kaarima hesitates.

'If you stay standing here,' I say to her, 'he's never going to stop coming back. He'll still be here in an hour. I know it seems mean, but none of this is helping him at all. All it's doing is making him more and more upset. He'll feel better when he can get away from here, but as long as we keep answering his questions, he'll be stuck.'

'Okay, then.' Kaarima nods in agreement, and the three of us dodge quickly into the back office. There's a glass panel in its door.

'We'll just have to stay here 'til he leaves,' I tell them firmly. Mr Youd is an unwell and vulnerable man, but his obsessive-compulsive disorder is making him almost impossible to deal with.

Sure enough, two minutes later, a quick peer through the glass panel shows him coming back yet again into Reception. He's clutching the slips of paper that Kaarima and Anthony have written on. He stops at the empty desk and looks anxiously up and down. We all keep out of sight.

'I'm going to report this to his social worker,' I tell Kaarima and Anthony. 'I think the poor guy needs more support with his OCD.'

'He does, Charmain. He really does.'

A minute later, Kaarima decides to risk a second peep. Finally, Mr Youd has left. But I know he'll be back another day. I wish that this vulnerable tenant could find some peace of mind. Unfortunately, however, we know that his endlessly circling anxieties are bound to bring him back to us.

• • •

Once Pleasant gets out of hospital, she comes to see me at the office. Her face is still a mess and there's a gauze pad covering her eye. Her cheekbone is broken and her face is badly swollen. But although she's bruised and gashed, she's been lucky that her eyesight has been saved. Isaac's back at school and baby Ama is with her, fast asleep in her pram. I feel really relieved.

But she's still terribly on edge. She speaks softly as she nervously answers my questions. I hear about how she came to London from Ivory Coast after Samuel's family put pressure on him to get married. Their families arranged for them to meet, they got on well and he told her relatives that he'd help her to get an education. That was just what Pleasant wanted, and she put her trust in him. But when they got to England, she found she was alone. Her family couldn't afford to come and check up on her. She wasn't sure how things worked in this country, so she went along with everything Samuel said. His promises about her education didn't amount to much and pretty soon she was pregnant. Since then, her family has taken up all her time.

It was during her first pregnancy that things began to change. Samuel became very controlling, wanting everything to be a certain way. Pleasant tried to do as he was telling her, but he flew into rages if she didn't follow his exact instructions.

'When did he first act so angry?' I ask her gently.

She sighs. She's thinking hard. When she answers, her voice is low and flat. 'I can't tell you when it started, Charmain. I don't know.'

I understand what she means. I get it. Before I started working for Southwark Council, I was a project officer in a domestic violence refuge for over a year. It was a crash course for me, and I've never forgotten the women who lived there or their stories. I've had close friends, too, who've been through something like this. And one thing I've learned is that violence doesn't just start out of the blue. There isn't a big turning point, or a day when someone suddenly hurts you very badly. Domestic abuse is a gradual thing, almost like a kind of grooming. Without you realising what's happening, the abuser drip-feeds you into their control. Then, once you're ingrained in the relationship, the nastiness happens.

Pleasant's been brought up in a traditional way. She doesn't question the head of her household. Samuel has taken advantage of that. I try to take down the details of what happened on the day that he was arrested, but Pleasant can't pinpoint what started the argument that led to his violence.

'He just came home angry,' she tells me. 'I don't know why he was. He's like that.' She can't get to the memory. Perhaps she's blanked it out. I remember that he injured her head – that might have something to do with it as well. 'I shouldn't even be talking to you now,' Pleasant says anxiously.

'Is that what Samuel told you?'

She bites her lip.

'It's – the problem is – I – the – the UK authorities...' Her voice peters out.

'Did he tell you that the police would take the children away if you reported him?' I ask.

'He told me what is British law,' she replies simply.

'What exactly did he say was the law?' I ask her. There's a very long silence.

'He said – he says – I – I am not legal here!' Pleasant tells me at last. She clasps her hands together tightly and looks really afraid.

'What do you mean – you're not legal?'

'I shouldn't b-be in England.' She stammers as she speaks. 'He t-told me I'm an illegal im-immigrant. So I have to stay quiet. N-not draw attention to myself. If the – the authorities find me, they will s-send me back to Ivory Coast. But – but Isaac and Ama, they are English – they were b-born here. They have different passports

28

from mine. He told me this! If I was sent back, they would have to stay.'

Samuel's told her so many lies. It's as though he has been holding her hostage, using the children as his weapons. I feel so immensely angry that it's hard not to show it. But right now, my anger won't help Pleasant. It's my knowledge of housing law and my practical help that she needs.

'Pleasant,' I say. I look straight into her face. 'I promise you that what Samuel said isn't true. You are married to a British citizen. That means you have rights. We need to look through your documents. The papers are in your house, right?'

I see her hesitating. Samuel's had her believing for so many years that she's just one step away from being thrown out of the country. He's made sure that she hides away from everyone. And Pleasant also sees me as authority – a frightening authority that might take her kids from her. It's going to take some time before she trusts me.

'I understand this is very difficult for you,' I say to her. 'But next time you come to see me, could you bring the papers with you?'

'Ummm… they're in his briefcase,' she tells me. Her voice drops to a whisper. 'At least – I th-think that's where they are. But, Charmain – I c-can't go in his case. I can't touch it. He never, ever lets me.'

Even though she knows that he's in prison, it's as though Samuel's still listening somewhere. I see how completely she's internalised his power. He doesn't even need to be present to force her to obey him.

'Yes, you can, Pleasant,' I say to her. 'He's not here. You can decide what you should do. He can't stop you.'

· · ·

When Pleasant can't find the key to Samuel's briefcase, she breaks into it. When she tells me what she's done, I'm really impressed by her bravery. Somewhere inside this stammering, frightened girl is a steely young woman. At her next appointment, she hands me the open case.

'I h-hope he never finds out about this, Charmain.'

I look straight at her. 'Babes,' I tell her firmly, 'remember: he's not here.'

Pleasant takes a deep breath and nods.

'So,' I say, 'you are giving me permission to look through these documents?' It's important that we follow this procedure legally, stating that Pleasant is okay with what I'm doing.

'I give you permission, Charmain.'

I start looking through the case. It's all in good order, with passports and legal documents in files. Samuel has organised his paperwork well – it's just a shame he never told his wife what she needed to know. The children's passports are British and Pleasant's is Ivorian. Then I spot what I'm looking for. I knew it had to be here. It's a letter from the IND, the Immigration and Nationality Directorate. I quickly read it through.

'Pleasant,' I ask her, 'do you remember going with Samuel to the big immigration office down in Croydon?'

She nods.

'You had an interview there?'

'Yes...' She looks doubtful.

'Do you remember what questions they asked you?'

She shakes her head.

'No, I'm sorry. It was – it was hard. Samuel was there and I – I was worried that – I didn't want to give the wrong answer.'

She's been so afraid of making her husband angry that she's gone through this whole legal process without really understanding what's happening to her. 'Well,' I say to her, and I can feel my face breaking into a grin, 'well – did you know that you have indefinite leave to remain in Britain?'

'What?' Pleasant looks completely shocked.

'*Indefinite leave to remain.*' I point to the words. She flicks her one uncovered eye across the document, too fast to really read it.

'It's right here, Pleasant. You're legal, baby!'

'Really?' she asks me.

'Yes, really!'

And then her eyes light up. There's so much relief in her face. Although she's only in her twenties, I suddenly see how the fear and stress she's been living through have aged her. She looks so young and free. At last, she giggles. It's the first time I've ever seen her smile. Just for a minute, we properly laugh together.

'Oh my God, Pleasant!' I say to her. 'The world's your

oyster now, hon! You can do anything you want! We can get your name on the tenancy for your house. Then it will be just yours. And did your social worker tell you about the Non-Molestation Order?'

'Y-yes, yes, she did. I think I understand.'

'You'll have to go to court – Women's Aid will help you with that. The police will back you up. There's lots of evidence against Samuel. Once you've got the order, he won't be able to come near you or your house, or contact you, or get anyone he knows to contact you. He'll have to leave you alone.'

Pleasant hesitates. 'He'll have to?' she says softly. Again I see the shadow that falls across her face. I can tell just by the tone of those few words how completely her husband has ruled her life with fear. As far as she's concerned, he's in charge. She can't imagine that anybody could make him do anything.

'Pleasant, Samuel is hopefully going to prison,' I tell her. 'When he comes out, the Non Molestation Order can be renewed. The police will keep you informed about it.'

I can see how much she wants to believe this. For the first time, there might be some hope.

'Pleasant, we'll help you. Please trust me. You can make your house into a safe home now – just for you and Isaac and Ama. Your new life starts right here.'

CHAPTER THREE

CUCKOOS

2017

'There's bad stuff going on in this building,' my tenant tells me.

My ears prick up. I've heard about some problems in Stonewall House, but up until now there's been no one who will go on the record. The tenant who's ringing me today is being very brave – it's scary to report what you know when there are criminals involved. People worry about what will happen if they find out it was you who grassed them. He sounds pretty stressed out and I'm not at all surprised.

'Thanks so much for getting in touch,' I say to him. As I listen, I'm starting to make notes. 'It means we can do something to help. Can you please tell me what you've seen?'

'So – erm – there's ladies – er – sex workers in one of the flats here. Definitely. I seen guys hanging round on the staircase all hours of the night. They're dealin' in there too.'

'Do you know which flat they're using?'

'Other side of the building to me, third floor. And, um...' He hesitates. 'Yeah, now they're workin' in the garden as well.'

'The sex workers are doing business in the garden?'

'Well, they're using the dustbin cupboard. Two girls in there together.'

'Really?' I've seen some things in my time, but I do find this surprising. The dustbin cupboard isn't the most fragrant place.

I contact my manager Denise and tell her what I've heard. It turns out that she was just about to raise this problem with me. 'Yes,' she tells me, 'I drove by late on Monday night and I could see a load of men lined up outside the bin cupboard. No prizes for guessing what was going on.'

'Did you see a pimp?' I ask.

'I didn't want to stop and take a look. But it all looked pretty well-organised.'

When the estate's cleaners start work early in the mornings, the evidence is everywhere. There are condom wrappers all over the floor and sticky streaks up the walls where they've been chucked away. The place is in a horrible state, stinking of piss where the punters have been relieving themselves while they're standing in a queue. There are even human faeces. Our cleaners are wearing PPE but they shouldn't have to deal with this.

Nowadays, it's harder than it used to be for housing officers to supervise our patches. We work at a distance, referring issues to other agencies rather than dealing with them ourselves. But back in the noughties, we managed our own local areas directly. That meant we had much more control and we could order anyone we saw up to no good to just leave. I've done it myself. If I thought someone was dodgy, I'd ask where they were going. 'Visiting a friend!' they'd always say. I'd immediately ask them the name of this friend, and their address. Then I'd watch the cogs turning while they tried to make something up. Finally they'd mutter an address. 'You're going to No. 15?' I'd say. 'To Mrs Ellison's flat? But she's 96! I don't think you're her friend!' After that, they'd scarper. The best way to stop trouble is to get onto it before it starts.

I get padlocks installed at Stonewall House to keep the prostitutes out, but forced entry to buildings is a huge ongoing headache. It's especially difficult in winter when drug users and rough sleepers break doors again and again to get inside and out of the cold, jamming locks apart with nails and damaging magnets by repeatedly pulling them open. People who aren't entitled to get inside manage it by tailgating – quickly following someone who has opened a door on their way home. Or they just press random intercoms and hope that a resident will buzz them through without asking questions.

The sex work has been going on round here for quite a while. No one should have to put up with that so close to their home. I'm going to find out who's responsible and put a stop to it.

• • •

I carry out some checks and what I learn is pretty puzzling. The tenants in the two third-floor flats on that side of the block don't seem likely suspects at all. There's a Polish family with two young daughters – I met them when they moved in not long ago. They can't be involved. And then there's Lewis, a gentle, quiet Rastafarian in his forties. He's lived there for years and given us no trouble at all. I can't see Lewis suddenly deciding to run a prostitution racket.

When I make a visit, the Polish family answers the door straightaway. They're having breakfast and getting the kids ready for school. I explain I work for the council and they're really pleased to see me and tell me everything they know. They didn't know how to get in touch with me, they say, or they would have reported the problems in the flats already. The mother, Marta, is terribly upset about all this – she's been trying to make sure that her girls don't see the sex work going on around the corner.

'Don't worry any more,' I tell her. 'Now we know, we can do something about it.' I make sure they have my number in case anything else is bothering them.

Then I ring on Lewis's door. No reply. There's a strong smell of weed, but nobody seems to be in. What I do see are fingermarks and scuffs on the paint around the doorway, as though people have been coming in and out. I call back again later the same day. Still no answer. What on earth's going on?

• • •

Two days later, when I try the door for the third time, some-one answers. He's a young white guy with a buzz cut who I've never seen before. He definitely doesn't look like he'd be a mate of Lewis's. But he's wearing a T-shirt and looks pretty relaxed in the flat, like he's hanging out at home.

'I'm from the council,' I say. 'Come to do a tenancy check. Is Lewis in?'

'Er – I'm his friend,' the man replies.

'Okay. So is he in?'

Another man appears in the hallway behind him. He's older and dressed in a leather jacket. There's something here that's making me wary. But it's part of my job to go inside and talk to them. 'I need to speak to Lewis,' I tell the men. 'Is he in?'

Buzz-cut guy hesitates.

'Uh – he's not available right now.'

'But he's in?'

The two of them exchange glances. The younger guy looks worried, then the older one takes charge. There's an authoritative vibe about him – you can tell he's the boss around here. 'Come inside,' boss guy says to me, 'Miss—?'

'Bynoe. My name's Miss Bynoe.'

'I'm Donald. I'm Lewis's cousin. This is his mate, Mark.'

Donald shows me into the living room. He tries giving me some chat, but I don't respond. The smell of weed is even stronger in here. No sign of Lewis. 'I need to speak to the named tenant, please,' I say to them. 'Where's Lewis?'

'So I'm his carer, see,' Donald explains. 'I been sorting out his place. You know – paying his rent. We help him claim his benefits 'cos he can't work any more. He's got health problems, see.'

'What kind of problems?'

'Pretty serious. Poor old Lewis. He had a stroke.'

I'm upset to hear this. Lewis is only in his forties. 'When did that happen?' I ask them.

'Ummm…' For someone who's supposed to be his carer, Donald doesn't seem too sure. 'Last year some time. I'm his next of kin, see. So I get his carer's allowance.'

I can tell at once that this next-of-kin story isn't true, but I act like I believe what he's saying. If he thinks I'm suspicious of him, he'll clam up and tell me nothing.

'Okay,' I say, 'so then I need to do the paperwork. It's part of a tenancy contract that each tenant needs to notify the council of the name of their carer. Can I see your ID?'

'Er, yeah, okay,' says Donald, not sounding at all pleased about this.

'You got anything with you? Driving licence, maybe?'

'Er – I'm not sure.' He sounds really evasive. 'I might need to look in my car.'

'No hurry,' I tell him. 'If you can bring it round to the housing office in the next couple of days, that would be fine. So I'd like to see Lewis now.'

Donald and Mark exchange another glance.

'Well, um…' Donald says, 'he's asleep. Needs his rest. He's not well, see.'

'Just tell him it's Charmain. He won't mind waking up to say hello.'

They *umm* and *ahh* some more, but there's not much

they can do. We walk down the corridor and Donald pushes open the door of Lewis's dingy bedroom. Both of them follow me inside and stand very close behind my shoulder. I know that they're trying to intimidate me, so I turn back towards them, using my street sense. I need to show them that their tactic won't work.

'You all right there?' I ask them. I don't smile as I say it. It tells them I'm aware of what they're doing.

The smell of weed in here nearly knocks me out. It's early summer and the sun is shining brightly outside, but the curtains are drawn and it's chilly. Until I open the grubby curtains, I can barely make out Lewis. He's lying on a bare single mattress on the floor, covered with a sheet that's not been washed for a very long time.

'Lewis?' I say gently. 'It's Charmain. How are you doing?'

I crouch down next to him. He's wearing a vest that doesn't look too clean either, and when I touch his thin shoulder, his skin feels icy. He mumbles something, but I can't make it out. Alongside him there's a big metal mug. But no one has made Lewis a warm drink. The mug is full to the brim with joint butts and ash, and lying on the top is a huge half-smoked head. Lewis is a dread and he was puffing long before he had his stroke, but I really don't think he should be smoking like this now.

'Lewis?' I say again. 'Can you hear me?'

'He's confused, see,' says Donald. 'Ain't he, Mark?'

'Yeah, yeah, very confused,' Mark replies.

I look at Lewis again. He stares right back at me. I don't think he can talk – whether that's the stroke or because he's stoned I'm not quite sure. I'm shocked by his expression – the given-up look that's in his eyes; a dull, hopeless stare. This monochrome Lewis is so different from the chill, funny guy I know. But the look is still intelligent. He understands that I'm here and he wants to tell me something, but he can't.

'Lewis,' I ask him, 'are you seeing the doctor? What about physio, to help you get better?'

'He's got physio soon,' says Donald instantly. 'We're just – er – getting it arranged.' He's obviously lying.

'Thanks,' I say to Donald, without turning my head, 'but I'm talking to Lewis.'

I touch Lewis's shoulder again and look straight at him. His so-called carers are keeping him stoned while they help themselves to money and get up to God-knows-what in his flat. I want him to know before I leave – without saying it out loud – that I've seen what's going on and I'm going to do something to help him.

Lewis is a victim of cuckooing. It's a callous practice where the home of a vulnerable person has been taken over by criminals to do their business. It's not the first time I've seen it, and it makes me so angry that before I stand up and speak to Donald and Mark, I have to pause for a moment until I'm calm. Then I take a deep breath and ask them about any repairs that might need doing in the flat, as if this is just a normal housing officer's visit. They reckon they've fooled me so of course they look relieved. I let them think whatever they like, and we talk for a few minutes about a blocked drain.

· · ·

The minute I get back to the office, I make a safeguarding referral for Lewis. This means I've seen something that's caused me to believe that a vulnerable person is being exploited. In my referral, I explain in detail what's going on. Southwark's safeguarding team will now appoint a social worker to monitor him.

Then I contact the Southwark Antisocial Behaviour Unit – SASBU – to report what I've been told about Stonewall House: the drug-dealing and sex work. We were the first local authority in Britain to have a unit like this one. It's when I speak to them that things get really interesting. The minute my colleague Lionel from SASBU sees my report, he's on the phone. He's a big, energetic guy with a deep, booming voice. I know as soon as he says hello that he's excited.

'Charmain?' he says. 'I've just read your report.'

Lionel has been investigating antisocial behaviour – drug-dealing and prostitution – at Stonewall House. It's a big SASBU operation, coordinated with local police. They've seen some pretty awful stuff going on, but before they take any action, they want to find out who's really behind it. And one name keeps getting mentioned – a guy called Donald. He's a big fish, often on the move, staying one step ahead of the law. Up to now, no one's known exactly where he is.

'I did hear a rumour,' Lionel tells me, 'that he's operating from somewhere on the estate. Somewhere close. He wants to stay local, you know – to keep an eye on his operations. And I think you just met him.'

Wow. Just by chance, I've stumbled on the people who are running all the criminal business in Stonewall House. Now we have a lead, we're able to investigate and close Donald down pretty quickly. His exploitation of Lewis is stopped. We move Lewis urgently to supported housing where he can get help with his rehabilitation. The Department for Work and Pensions cuts off the carer's allowance – £106 a week – that Donald's been collecting, and the man himself is arrested while he's driving Lewis's car. He is meant to be using it to help Lewis get around, but of course, Lewis isn't there. The council puts a Closure Order on the flat, which has to be done when a place has been used for criminal activity. No one can go in there while the police investigate. But after that, it will be refurbished for someone who needs a home.

It's a very positive outcome and I'm pleased. But on my inner-city patch, keeping up with criminal activity is a constant challenge. It scares me to think how many Lewises might still be out there, cut off from the outside world and waiting for us to rescue them.

• • •

2002

My very first case of cuckooing – back before the word was even used – was a man called Mohamed. He was a vulnerable guy with mental-health issues who'd always kept himself to himself, so when there was suddenly a lot of coming and going at his flat, his neighbours got suspicious and rang me to report it.

When I went round to check, I found four men in Mohamed's front room. He didn't usually have mates round, so that made me suspicious straightaway. All four of them were totally spaced out, sitting in the gloomy living room with the curtains drawn in the middle of the day, and the flat was in a much worse state than the last time I had carried out a check. To be honest, I couldn't see how anyone could live there, with no furniture apart from two disgusting old sofas and a big pile of blankets in the corner. But even though the place was so neglected, a very new-looking flat-screen TV was sitting in the corner. Flat screens weren't so common back then, and they were very expensive. Somehow I doubted that Mohamed would have bought it. They were watching a chat show.

'Right, I'm from the council,' I told them. 'I've come to see Mohamed. Who are you?' They all stared at me.

'Ahhhh... we're his friends,' said one finally.

'So is he in?'

Silence. More staring. No one moved.

'Where's Mohamed?' When nobody could manage an answer, I took a look around without their help. The rest of the flat was in the same disgusting state as the living room. The only sign of life anywhere was a stack of pizza boxes in the empty kitchen. I went back and found the four guys still sitting where I'd left them.

'I need to see Mohamed,' I said. 'Can you tell me where he is?'

Yet another long pause. And then, to my horror, the pile of blankets moved. It wasn't a pile at all – it was a person.

'Jesus!' I exclaimed, and pulled at the top of the pile. Underneath lay Mohamed, stick-thin and wasted, his face ashy grey in the half-light. If he hadn't moved just a second before, I'd have wondered if he was still alive. The four guys on the sofa just went on staring.

'Did you know he was under there?!' I asked them pretty sharply. No answer. The situation was so awful that I couldn't help raising my voice. 'What the frig are you lot doing? He shouldn't be lying on the floor!' I shouted.

But I was wasting my time. All they could do was gape. I looked down at Mohamed again. He was very ill, and whatever was going on in this flat, he was a helpless victim. My first priority was to get him out of there.

• • •

'Thanks so much for coming, Philippe,' I said.

Philippe was one of a team of community police who patrolled the estate. Their names and faces were known to the community, and that made it easier than it is nowadays for tenants to report their concerns to someone they recognised. The local officers were very clued up and always responded fast. When I told Philippe what I'd seen in Mohamed's living room, he just said, 'Right, then, let's go round,' and we did.

'There were four guys in his flat when I was there,' I

warned him on the way. 'Not sure if they're living there or not. They're junkies, so there's somebody in the background supplying them. But Mohamed's lost control of his home and he's completely neglected.'

'Where is he now?' Philippe asked.

'Guy's Hospital, thank goodness. I rang for an ambulance and they took him straight there.'

'How come he wasn't being supervised, Charmain? He's a really vulnerable guy.'

I sighed. 'Well,' I said, 'I rang the Maudsley hospital. Somehow his notes had got closed. He'd been left to Care in the Community, but his mental-health worker hadn't checked on him. So he was on his own. There was no food at all. There was nothing.'

Philippe and I walked along in silence for a minute. Of course, we both knew what Care in the Community can mean in practice – overstretched services, unmanageable caseloads, vital information getting missed, people who desperately need help falling through the net. Philippe was shaking his head. 'At least the CPN's on the way now,' he said.

We went upstairs together. This time we found Mohamed's front door had been left wide open. 'Right, then,' Philippe said to me briskly. 'Let's see if we can't sort this lot out. You wait there.' He gave a very loud knock and marched straight in. From the hallway, I could hear him doing some pretty assertive talking.

'Off you go right now! Unless you can prove that you're the family of the man that lives here, I don't want to see you again. He didn't invite you. If you show your faces back here, I'll bring the wagon round and have you arrested for trespassing.'

I could hear them coughing and shuffling. 'Charmain?' Philippe called out to me. 'We're done here. This lot are off.' As I went into the flat, I saw the four men I'd met earlier, this time on their feet. They still seemed confused, but at least it looked like they were leaving.

'Off you go!' said Philippe again, even more firmly.

One of the men looked a bit less confused than the others. He gave a sharp glance at Philippe. Then he picked up the flat-screen TV and briskly headed for the door. 'Oh no you don't! What d'you think you're doing?' Philippe demanded. 'Is that yours? Did you buy it?'

'Nah, nah, man – I did!' the guy said. 'I bought it, honest! This is mine.'

'Really? I don't think so!' replied Philippe sharply. The would-be TV thief lost his nerve. He plonked it down on the sofa and legged it.

'Trying to steal a TV right in front of me!' said Philippe indignantly. 'That's it – just get out, the lot of you! And don't come back! This flat's not for you!'

It was a real piece of old-fashioned community policing. It worked, and it helped to rescue a vulnerable man from the cuckoos.

• • •

2005

'Mr Sweet, I've told you before! This cylinder of gas in your kitchen – it's dangerous! You can't have that in here!'

Mr Sweet looks sheepish. He's in his eighties now, and he's definitely a vulnerable tenant. But although he suffers from diabetes, arthritis and high blood pressure, he still has his own ideas about his flat, and one of these ideas is that he wants to cook with camping gas. I've no idea how he gets the huge gas canisters up the stairs, but somehow he's managed to rig them up to a portable unit with two cooking rings. I can also see that he's tried to mend the wiring in here again since my last visit. He doesn't understand that he's not qualified to even look at it. I keep explaining the danger that he's causing to other people and himself, but he's obstinate. Now I'm looking at the mass of tangled cables in horror. He either doesn't believe what I'm telling him or he just can't grasp the risks.

Whatever I say, Mr Sweet always argues with me, even though I'm trying to help. I've suggested that he claims his attendance allowance: money that's available to seniors to pay for services like physiotherapy so that they stay healthy and mobile. But he doesn't want to fill out any forms, or have anybody knowing his business. He sees everything official as a threat to his independence.

'Mr Sweet!' I tell him very firmly. 'We had all this removed last time, didn't we? And I told you not to get another canister. I put it in writing. Do you remember that letter?'

He scowls. It offends him deeply when he can't have his home the way he wants it. Once or twice when we've discussed the camping gas, he's been quite rude. I don't think he really means it, and when I imagine myself as an old lady one day, watching my control over my life slipping away, it gives me real compassion for Mr Sweet.

I feel a sharp itch on my arm, and quickly scratch it. Mr Sweet's not living alone in the flat – he has hundreds of tiny companions living here with him. The place is crawling with fleas, to the point where members of the housing team have had the little biters hitching a ride back with them to the office. We had to call in the exterminators and a housing officer ended up in A&E after a flea bite went septic. The Health and Safety at Work Act allows us not to go into places that might damage our health, but somehow I always keep visiting Mr Sweet. There's something about his mixture of pride and vulnerability that really touches me. Then when I get home, I have to strip off all my clothes by my front door and fling them straight in the washing machine.

'Right,' I tell him, pointing to the canister and the piles of tangled wires, 'all this has got to go. You know it's not allowed. It's a fire risk. We have to keep the building safe for all our residents.'

'This is safe,' he mutters angrily. 'Mi fixed it up.'

'But you're not an electrician, Mr Sweet. You don't know how to fix it up. And do you remember how we talked last time about your cleaning?'

Mr Sweet tuts and sighs. He gets angry when he thinks I'm interfering in his home. I'm not sure how long it's been since this place was cleaned, but it wasn't in this millennium. Everything in sight is a dark and sticky brown. The bath has a thick crust all over it, like soil, and I keep my eyes averted from the toilet. I find it hard to believe he doesn't see what a terrible state his flat's got into, but somehow he doesn't seem to notice. It goes far beyond just wearing rose-coloured glasses.

'It's fine! What's wrong with mi home?' he demands.

I share his West Indian background, and I decide that I should use this connection. I think it can help me have a sense of what will and won't seriously offend him.

'Look,' I say, 'just look around you! It's nasty in here! Tell me now, what would your mother think? If you tell me she'd think this place looks good, I'll go away and leave you alone!'

Mr Sweet bites his lip. 'Nah,' he says at last. 'She would ha beat mi, fe true.'

'Well, there we are.'

'But, Charmain! This is the way mi like it!'

I try to keep the situation from getting too tense by making a joke.

'Look,' I say, 'my manager's going to ask me what's happening in this flat. I can't tell her there's a canister of gas in your kitchen. I'll be out of a job!'

'Mi know you council lot!' He raises his voice. 'You want put mi in a care home!'

'I just want to make sure that you're safe, Mr Sweet, and everyone else in the building as well. And this kitchen is dangerous.'

49

'But mi cats!' he points out. 'Mi can't move! Where dem goin' to go?'

What Mr Sweet really needs is sheltered housing – not a care home, but a safe place where he can be independent with assistance when he needs it. But how can I persuade him to accept this? For now, I make arrangements – again – for the canister of gas to be urgently removed and the scary-looking tangle of cables in his kitchen to be inspected. Two days later, I go back to the flat in the late afternoon to check on progress.

I'm extremely surprised to find he isn't alone. There's an attractive young woman in his kitchen. For a moment, I think that she must be a relative, but of course Mr Sweet has no family. That's why he's so isolated and vulnerable.

'This mi friend Raquel,' he tells me.

Raquel says hello, but I immediately have an instinct that she's not pleased I've come round. I look at her curiously. What on earth is she doing hanging out with an elderly man in his grotty, smelly flat? I especially notice that she won't meet my eyes.

'Did you get your petrol, Raquel?' Mr Sweet asks her.

I see a flash of unease in her face before she forces a smile. 'Yeah. Yeah, I did. Here's your card back.' She takes a bank card from her bag and hands it to him.

'Petrol for what?' I ask casually.

Raquel doesn't answer, but Mr Sweet is happy to explain.

'Raquel the daughter of mi friend. When mi got errands,' he tells me, 'she give mi a lift in her car and mi pay fe petrol.'

I'm finding all this a bit suspicious and strange but I don't say anything else to make Raquel aware of my concerns. There's a short, tense silence, then her mobile rings. She grabs it. I swear she looks relieved. 'Sorry!' she says after a moment. 'Gotta go! Nice to meet you!' She quickly disappears out of the door.

'Raquel's a good girl, Charmain,' says Mr Sweet happily. 'She always help mi out.'

'I'm sure she does,' I say to him. 'What kind of help?'

I ask him some more questions, and what he tells me worries me a lot. Raquel drives him around to do his errands. She tells him what she's spending on petrol and he gives her his bank card to cover it. That might be okay. But when her car needed fixing a few weeks back and she had a problem paying for it, she mentioned it to Mr Sweet and he helped her out. A fortnight ago she was short for her rent and she mentioned that as well. Once again, Mr Sweet paid.

'Erm, so you seem to be giving Raquel quite a lot of money,' I point out. I know he's going to get defensive with me, of course, and straightaway he does.

'Mi help her one time with di rent! It's difficult for her! An' she got bills!'

'That was very kind of you,' I say to him. 'I hope Raquel's paid you back.'

'She pay mi when she can,' he says. 'She's a good girl.'

I don't think she's a good girl at all. I'm starting to suspect that she's financially exploiting a vulnerable old man. But I'm going to need proof before I can take action, and I have to try to get it without offending or upsetting him. 'So, she's like your next of kin, then?' I ask Mr Sweet.

'Yes! Dat what she is! So yuh can leave mi to manage mi own business!'

'That's fine,' I say. 'In that case, I just need to update my records. If she's your next of kin, I have to keep her informed. Can I please have her phone number?'

• • •

Next morning, I give Raquel a ring.

'Hi,' I say. 'It's Charmain here, from Southwark Council housing department. We met the other day. Mr Sweet is my tenant.'

'Oh, yeah,' says Raquel. 'Yeah, right. Can I help you?'

'You certainly can. I'd like to find out a bit more about the assistance you've been providing.'

'Sure. Yeah. I help him out.'

'So he tells me. He says you're like family.'

'Yeah,' she says again. 'Yeah, that's right.'

'But that flat of his – it's in a bad way. So I'm wondering why you've never helped him clean it up a bit.'

'He's happy with it, ain't he?' she snaps back.

I leave a moment's silence before I go on speaking. 'And you withdraw his money from the ATM?' I ask her. 'He's given you his PIN number?'

'Yeah.' It's obvious that she doesn't like these questions.

'Do you keep a record? You know – write down what you've taken out?'

'Yeah. 'Course I do.'

'And—'

'Sorry!' she says. 'I got another call!' She hangs up.

I've heard enough now to have reasonable suspicions that Mr Sweet is being financially exploited. I put in an online safeguarding referral for a vulnerable elder. That means he'll have a social worker to check up on him and look after his interests. At the same time, I submit a fast-tracked application for sheltered housing. Whatever he says, he's clearly not able to take care of himself financially or personally. There are people around who are taking advantage of him. *On my patch, that ain't going to happen.*

• • •

At first, however, things don't go so well with Mr Sweet and Social Services. A woman called Frances is appointed as his social worker, but the gas canisters are still in his kitchen, and when Frances sees them, she won't go inside. They're removed but she still won't go in because she's still concerned about the fleas. I get that it's a problem, but three weeks have gone by and Mr Sweet still hasn't had a visit. I'm pretty sure that his financial exploitation is still going on but when I ring Frances to discuss it and try to get something done, she's unhelpful. She's just not proactive enough for me – this is a serious safeguarding issue. In the end I have to put in a complaint in writing to Frances's manager that she's not dealing with this situation urgently enough. I copy her in as I wouldn't go behind her back – but we really need some action.

The second social worker appointed to the case is called Shakera. She shares my sense that this is urgent, and she goes into the flat straightaway. She's of West Indian origin herself, and she's much more direct with Mr Sweet. I hear her joking with him, accusing him of trying to blow up the whole estate with his gas canisters. But while she's making him laugh, she's also building rapport, getting him to trust her and talk to her. She quickly organises a care package. I hope things will be easier now that we have this under-standing between professionals.

Next I help Mr Sweet to fill out a form to claim attend-ance allowance. I want to make sure he understands exactly what we're doing, so I ring him for a catch-up once the form has been submitted. But instead of being prickly and defensive, telling me to mind my own business like he usually does, today he sounds worried and confused.

'What's wrong, Mr Sweet?' I ask him. 'Has something upset you?'

'Since we did dat form, mi got a letter, Charmain.'

'What kind of letter?'

'It tellin' mi council goin' to take mi money!'

'I don't think that's right, Mr Sweet.'

'It is, Charmain! Dat's what it say!'

'Why don't you bring the letter to the housing office for me to see? If it's okay with you, I can read it and explain it to you.'

'Okay,' he says anxiously. 'Mi do dat.' I don't like him

being upset, but I'm pleased that he's allowing me to help him. Perhaps we're making progress in our relationship. When he turns up at the housing office, he's clutching a bundle of letters and bank statements, and we sit together in an interview room and go through them. The problem is very quickly solved.

'Mr Sweet,' I tell him, 'this letter says that the council is going to *give* you money, not take it away from you. These amounts are your attendance allowance – it's for you to use, to help you stay healthy.'

'Oh. Oh right. Dat's nice.' He looks a bit happier.

'And...' I remind him, 'I can see you've got a nice little nest egg here in your bank too.'

'Yes, mi do.'

I'd not actually realised until I saw these bank statements that he had any savings. He doesn't spend very much, but I'm pleased he's more financially secure than I'd thought. 'Nearly three and a half thousand in there for you,' I say. 'Good to have that for a rainy day.'

But when he hears this, he looks startled.

'What yuh say, Charmain?'

'Three and a half thousand pounds, Mr Sweet. Look – it's here on the statement.'

'What yuh mean?'

I hold the statement out towards him, and Mr Sweet peers at the small print.

'No, Charmain!' he says sharply. 'Mi should have seven thousand pounds!'

'Are you sure, Mr Sweet?'

'Yes! Mi sure!'

Suddenly I get a really bad feeling.

'Well,' I say, trying not to worry him too much, 'I can see here that you've made some withdrawals.'

'What withdrawals?' he demands.

I run my finger down the statements. Some of the withdrawals have been small ones – £10 here, £5 there. I'm sure those were made by him – there's an ATM in the road where he lives that still gives out fivers and he uses it quite often because he doesn't like to keep much cash in his flat. But there are also some bigger amounts on the statements. None of these withdrawals have been taken from the local machine – they've been made in Lordship Lane, Denmark Hill, Queen's Road, even up at London Bridge. I can see one for £300. Then £400. Then another £300. It's been going on for months. I point out the figures to him. Then, although I know the answer already, I ask the most important question.

'Did you make these withdrawals, Mr Sweet?'

'No, Charmain!'

'Does anybody else use your bank card?'

Mr Sweet doesn't answer for a long time. But I know he understands now. 'Raquel use mi card,' he says finally, in a low voice. 'But she tell mi what she tek out!'

'Can you remember the last time she used it? How much did she say she took?'

He thinks for a moment. 'It was when she need tyres. She tell mi 100 pounds. Day before mi birthday.'

I find the date on the statement. There's a withdrawal

there. It's for £300. I put the sheet of paper in his hand with my finger alongside the amount. I don't need to say anything else. He sits there looking crushed. I feel intensely sad for him. Finally he tells me, in a very quiet voice, 'Mi trusted her.'

'I know you did. I'm so sorry. Raquel didn't deserve your trust. Remember that what's happened is her fault, not yours.'

• • •

'Humph,' says Mr Sweet when he sees me back again at his front door. Things are a bit better between us since I helped him with the bank statements, but he still doesn't like me interfering.

'Hello,' I say. 'Can I come inside?'

He lets me in, still grumbling. It's a warm summer day and the flat is stiflingly hot. Then I notice a strange metallic smell. Mr Sweet is wearing extremely dirty shorts. I've seen bandages around his legs before, but today the bandages are soaked right through with blood. 'What on earth's happened to your legs, Mr Sweet?' I ask him.

He looks down at them as if he isn't sure. 'Oh, Charmain, dat's nuthin'. Dat's okay. Mi got sores. Mi jus' need a new bandage.'

'It doesn't look okay to me. You're bleeding! Have your carers seen this?'

He doesn't want me to do anything about it, but I have to. I call Shakera and she hurries round at once. When she sees the state his legs are in, she calls an ambulance. His diabetes has got worse and now it's causing ulcers on his legs. Some of them are getting infected. Of course Mr Sweet doesn't want to go to hospital, but everyone agrees that he must. He asks who'll feed his cats. I quickly ask a neighbour if she can help, and she kindly agrees that she'll do it.

• • •

Two days later, I visit him in King's College Hospital. He's sitting up in bed in a hospital gown, looking so clean and tidy that it's hard to recognise him at first. I've been thinking a lot about the best way to talk to him, and I've noticed how directly Shakera always does it. It really seems to work.

'Mr Sweet,' I say to him, 'you know you can't live in that flat any more.'

He looks at me mournfully.

'Mi know it's a bit diff'rent in dere,' he says.

'It's more than different, isn't it? I don't think it's safe.'

'But, Charmain, mi got my cats,' he points out. 'Mi can't go nowhere. Dey won't know where mi gone.'

'Well, I know about your cats. So, I've got good news for you,' I tell him. 'I bid for some sheltered accommodation for you, and it came through.'

He looks so worried. He's very scared of change, and of losing control of his life. And he's proud, too – I can see it. If he accepts help from me, he feels that he won't be a man any more.

'It's not a care home, you know, this new place,' I say. 'It's a one-bedroom flat. You can live how you want. You'll have your own door key. But if you do need help, there are people around.'

Finally he says, 'Mi need to t'ink about dat.'

'Okay, Mr Sweet. You have a think. Have you heard from Raquel?'

'Nah. Mi tried to phone. She not answer.'

I don't tell him this, but I've tried to phone her too. Raquel has changed her mobile number. There's nothing I can do about the money she stole from Mr Sweet because he gave her his bank card and his PIN. But she knows that she's done wrong, and I hope her conscience troubles her for a very long time.

'Your new place is on the ground floor,' I tell him. 'You can take your cats there. You'll be safe.'

Not just safe from gas canisters and dodgy electric cables, I think to myself. *You'll be safe there from people who say you can trust them, but then tell you lies.*

CHAPTER FOUR

THE IMMACULATE HOARDER

2005

I'm at Nutwood House to see Mr Jennings. He's a smart, well-dressed and polite gentleman who lives alone and works in a library. We've been having regular catch-ups in the housing office, but I've not been round to his flat since he took over the tenancy from his late mother. Now, though, I need to make a home visit because the housing team's procedures have changed. From now on, the tenancy checks that we used to carry out in the office are going to be done in people's properties.

I've left two voice messages about this home visit but he hasn't called me back. Up to now, he's always been so good-mannered that I'm quite surprised by this. I hope that he's managing all right. Polite, quiet tenants like Mr Jennings can easily be overlooked while housing officers run around all day dealing with a few troublemakers. After the third phone call, to my relief he rings me and we set up our appointment for the following week.

When I press his bell, it takes Mr Jennings a long time to answer. Then I hear strange muffled thumps from inside the flat. It sounds like something heavy being dragged. There's a scraping sound. I'm becoming quite concerned, but finally he opens the door.

'Good morning,' I say to him. 'Nice to see you. I'm here for your tenancy check.'

'Good morning, Charmain.'

'This won't take very long. I need to take a look around for repairs issues – anything that might be a problem for you.'

'Yes, of course. That's absolutely fine.'

But the minute I step inside, I can see that it isn't fine at all. Something's dreadfully wrong. Mr Jennings has always loved reading and his flat looks a bit like a library, but now it's just books and books and books – as if they've come to life, leaped off the shelves and decided to take over. And it's not just the books. His flat is also rammed from floor to ceiling with newspapers and magazines. They're stacked very neatly but the piles are six feet high and to get the front door open, he's had to push some of these towers aside. That must have been the rustling and scraping noise I heard.

I've come to inspect the flat, but it's almost impossible. The hall's a narrow book-canyon and I have to turn sideways to push my way along. As I edge past the bathroom,

I glance in. The floor's completely covered, and there are even books piled up in the tub. There are dozens and dozens of magazines in there too, half of them still in their plastic postal wrappers. Mr Jennings hasn't even read them. When I try to nudge the bedroom door open, something I can't see is jammed behind it and it only moves four inches.

All I'm thinking is *fire, fire, fire* – and that's before I've got into the kitchen. This is where the fire's going to start. There's hardly an inch of floor free. The counters and the draining board are covered. Even more books and magazines are leaning in stacks against the cooker, right up to the level of the gas rings, and a few of them even higher than that, close to tottering over right next to where Mr Jennings cooks. It's life-and-death dangerous. The kitchen is one spark from becoming an inferno. I feel rising alarm.

'Mr Jennings,' I say, 'this is very worrying. We can't have your flat like this. It's a serious fire risk.'

He looks shocked. He's standing very close to me – he has to – in the only bit of available space. I feel so sorry for him. 'I – I – erm – I don't think it's really such a p-problem,' he says. 'Maybe a – a few too many—'

'Honestly, Mr Jennings, this is an emergency. This place is like a bomb. If it catches fire, it would just go *whoosh*! How would you get out?'

'But it's properly organised!' he tells me. 'It won't get messy! Can you s-see – I keep tw-twentieth-century authors in the living room and older ones in the hall?'

Mr Jennings' is one of the earliest cases of hoarding I've seen. I'll never forget my very first one – a man whose flat

62

was so full of newspapers that the furniture was totally buried and he had to use the filthy stacks as chairs. He refused to let anybody in, but the flat was overrun with cockroaches and mice and the council had to intervene. In the end, his housing officer was forced to climb through the window. It just seemed like a really sad case, a one-off, but it was only the beginning of the hoarding epidemic. As time's gone by, I've seen things like it more and more often – people whose possessions have completely over-whelmed them.

Nowadays hoarding is recognised as a mental-health issue. We have a Hoarding Panel, including a mental-health worker, as part of our safeguarding strategy. The panel notifies the fire brigade of every hoarding case, and housing officers can get advice from panel members. We assess the level of hoarding using official guidelines and report on the actions we've taken to reduce the problem. If a situation reaches 'intolerable', the council intervenes.

But right now, none of this exists. I'm on my own with the problem of Mr Jennings and his library. As housing officers in the 2000s, we were learning about hoarding on the job, and there was much less awareness of mental-health issues. But we quickly realised one thing: we had to respect how our hoarding tenants felt before we could help them to change their behaviour. Just clearing out their stuff didn't work. Instead, we would try to show respect and to say to them, 'These are your things. This is your home. How can we help you?'

As I look around, I'm also noticing that Mr Jennings is

an unusual hoarder. His kitchen is still extremely clean. The cooker top is immaculately polished, the piles of books are tidy and the windows are sparkling. He's made a storage system. He's meticulous in his head, and in one kind of way, I can see he still takes care of his home. But the flat has run completely out of his control.

'I understand that you've organised your flat very carefully, Mr Jennings,' I say to him. 'But you really must clear all this paper out of the kitchen. There has to be space around your cooker.' As I say this, I wonder where on earth he's going to put it all. He starts getting flustered and upset.

'Um – well, all right, Charmain. Of – of course, if you – if you think I should. I can – um – I'll try to do that.'

'I know you have a storage system here, so I'm sure you can work something out. I have another appointment soon, but I'll come back tomorrow to give you a hand.' My diary is packed with visits, but I'll have to find the time somehow. On his own, I can see he's going to struggle.

• • •

Next day I bring a roll of bin bags and help Mr Jennings with the kitchen for nearly an hour. I manage to persuade him that the magazines still in their plastic covers can be thrown away: if he didn't read them when they arrived, he's not going to read them now. The bin bags are heavy and it's difficult to drag them along the narrow channel in the hall and out of the front door. We pile them up outside and when I leave, I lug them down to my car. It takes three journeys. I'm hot and tired when I've finished, but at least his kitchen is safer than it was.

'Mr Jennings, you need to do some work every day on this,' I tell him. 'A bit at a time will make it easier. I'm going to leave you these bin bags.' He nods at me uncertainly. 'And I'll come back as soon as I can and see how you're doing.'

He nods again.

'It's really important that you do this. It's not safe the way it is.'

He stares anxiously after me as I'm leaving. When he closes the door, I stand there quietly and wait. After a few seconds, I can hear the sound of piles of books being pushed back into place.

After this, I don't hear from Mr Jennings for weeks. He doesn't take my phone calls or respond to my emails. He's avoiding me. I'm sure that he feels threatened and upset by the way I've intervened in his home. I really don't want to upset him and I go round to his flat several times and peer through the letter box to see if the piles in the hallway are getting any smaller. Sadly, they're not. I ring the bell but if he's in, he doesn't answer.

When he does answer the phone at last, I arrange another visit. The flat is more or less back to square one, with the spaces that we'd started to clear in the kitchen already filled up again. It's very discouraging – and scary. I flag the hoarding problem in his file at the office and discuss what's happening with my line manager. We know that Mr Jennings is an intelligent, functioning person who doesn't like interference. We therefore decide that we must monitor the fire risk in the kitchen, but we can't force him to accept us taking over his home.

We also wonder how this hoarding problem got started. I remember speaking to him when his mother died and he took over her tenancy. He seemed so alone, and I wonder now if he should have had some kind of grief counselling. The way he's closing himself off in this flat, blocking the world out with books, makes me think he might have depression. He doesn't want anyone to see his pain or his grief, so instead he's enveloping himself with books. In some strange way, I think all these piles of paper are giving him comfort.

As we're discussing his case, my manager and I both feel – as we often do as housing officers – that we're in the middle of a minefield of personalities, trying to understand people, to take the right steps. It's hard sometimes to know how we can help. I'll just have to manage this situation as well as I can.

• • •

I'm really pleased when I see Mr Sweet's new flat on the ground floor of his Howden Road unit. He's not the only person who automatically thinks that 'sheltered' means a care home, and it can take quite a lot of time to convince people otherwise. Usually we get there in the end. Howden Road is a two-storey modern building with around sixty residents, mostly single people plus a few couples, all of them fifty-five and over, who live in self-contained units with their own bathrooms and kitchens. It's got a large social room, facilities to do laundry and guest flats for visitors. The housing officers who work there are on site during office hours and there's an alarm system the rest of the time.

Mr Sweet's flat has just been decorated and it's peaceful and quiet. There are nursing staff available round the clock. It even has a door leading out into a little walled garden, which is perfect for his cats. I want him to take a look at it, but he's in and out of hospital with his infected leg ulcers. He can't keep them clean on his own. Eventually the hospital agrees that he can visit the flat in an ambulance, but he'll have to be taken back there afterwards. On the day of his visit, I make sure that I arrive before he does, hoping that the viewing will go well.

But the moment he turns up in a wheelchair, attached to a drip, I can see from the expression on his face that we're going to have a problem. He doesn't like it. Although I'm pretty crestfallen, I force myself to stay upbeat.

'So what do you think, Mr Sweet?'

He looks down at the floor and mutters something.

'What was that?' I ask him.

'Mi said – it too small.'

'I don't think so. There's room here for you and your cats. The cats can go out in the garden, and you can sit out there too when the weather's nice.'

'Humph!' says Mr Sweet. 'It don't look right.'

'What do you mean – it don't look right?'

'It too bright in here. It hurtin' mi eyes.'

I look around and try to see the place the same way that he does. The fresh white paint is sparkling-clean. The sink is shiny-new. It's drastically different from the sticky, dingy browns that he's been used to. 'I know, Mr Sweet. It must be strange for you. You'll take a bit of time to get used to it,' I tell him.

'Anyway, how mi t'ings fit in?'

While he's been in hospital, I've done a quick inspection of his flat. Most of his possessions are a threat to his health. A lot of them are rotting. There's woodworm-riddled furniture, piles of moth-eaten clothes, and heaps of brown stuff that could be anything. If we try to move them, I think they'll fall to bits.

'Mr Sweet, I don't think your things can come with you,' I say gently. 'But don't worry. We can get you a new kettle, and some mugs, and saucepans, and—'

'Mi not like it here,' repeats Mr Sweet stubbornly. 'It don't look right.'

The paramedic catches my eye. His expression is sympathetic.

'I know this is a shock for you, Mr Sweet,' I say.

'Mi want mi t'ings!'

'But your things were all brown!' I have to tell him. 'They were rotting away! We can't bring them here.'

Then, to my surprise, he gives me a wry smile.

'You lot are lickle bullies, ain't you?' he says. But the way that he says it makes me think that he knows I'm here to help.

'We just try to look after our tenants, Mr Sweet.'

'Humph.' There's a thoughtful pause. 'Maybe dem t'ings was gettin' old,' he says finally.

'They were *very* old,' I agree. 'So, are you going to accept your new home?'

'Dunno.'

'Mr Sweet, I'm asking you again. Will you accept?'

'Charmain, mi think it's no choice, is it?'

But he smiles at me now, and I smile back. I think we just might be getting somewhere at last.

. . .

It's hard to make safety checks on Mr Jennings' flat because he keeps cancelling the appointments I make, doing it all through voice messages so I can't suggest another date. I try to ring him regularly and when we do speak, I chat with him a bit. I think that our rapport is very slowly improving. He's just guarded, and he never likes to talk about himself. I keep on trying to make him smile.

'Mr Jennings!' I joke. 'You cancelled me again! I'm upset now! You know I have to come round and see you.'

'Oh yes, Charmain. I'm sorry about that.'

'So when can I come? Does Thursday work?'

'No,' he says, 'not Thursday. I have to get my treatment on Thursday.'

'What treatment, Mr Jennings?'

'My hospital treatment. I've got cancer.'

This news is so sudden that it really shakes me up. He

sounds so calm and matter-of-fact about it. 'Oh, Mr Jennings! I'm sorry to hear that. When did you find out that you were ill?'

'A few weeks ago.'

'So, all this time we've been talking and leaving messages about your flat, you've had your diagnosis? Oh my goodness. I wish you'd told me.'

'Why would I tell you, Charmain?'

'Because I could help you, Mr Jennings. I'd like to do that.'

'What can you do?'

'Well, I can help you get support. With your property, with things you might need doing.'

Eventually he agrees to an in-person visit the following week. But two days later, he leaves a voice message cancelling it. His message says that the date of his treatment – I think he's having chemotherapy – has been changed. The same thing happens again the next time I try to see him. I'm not sure I believe what he's saying about his appointments because I know that chemo appointments are usually regular, but how can I argue with such a seriously unwell man? He does pick up the phone to me one afternoon, but I think he's answered by accident because the minute he hears my voice, he says, 'Sorry – I'm at the hospital!' and hangs up. He's avoiding me.

Eventually I manage to set up a visit. I ring the bell and hear him slowly pushing the piles of books out of the way. It's taking him far longer than it used to. There's the sound of books falling to the ground. He's still trying to block the world out. When he gets the door open at last, I try not to let the shock show in my face. He's lost a lot of weight, and he was a small man to start with. He's still dressed smartly, but the collar of his shirt isn't touching his neck any more. The rest of his clothes hang in folds. I can see the cancer taking hold of him.

I try a bit of gentle teasing about the piles of books as I squeeze my way along the hall. His kitchen's not too bad now, so that's an improvement. But his health is growing worse and I'm starting to worry about something else. What would happen if he was taken ill? How would the paramedics reach him in an emergency? If he needed a stretcher, how would they carry him out?

'Mr Jennings,' I say to him, 'you're really not so well. What do you think would happen if an ambulance had to come here?'

'What do you mean, Charmain?'

'Well... if the paramedics came, I don't think they could get inside the door, could they?'

'That's all right. I'd move my things when they arrived.'

I hesitate, wondering how directly I should deal with this. If I frighten him too much, I'm afraid he'll push me away even more. 'Hmmm,' I say carefully. 'You see, I don't think you could do that. When I got here today, it was difficult for you to move the books and open the door, wasn't it?'

'It was fine.' He won't look at me directly. He stares down at the floor. I'm sure he knows that his behaviour isn't normal, but he's gripped by something that he can't

71

control. Whatever this problem is, it's taken him away from reality.

'I don't think you can move them now, so if you were really ill, Mr Jennings, it would be even harder for you,' I say.

'I'm sure I could manage, Charmain.'

I can't push him any harder. Mr Jennings has rights, and his rights are important. Southwark Council can't dictate to our tenants about how they are choosing to live, so I'll have to find another way to persuade him. But as I'm making my way back to the front door, I accidentally push one of the stacks over and it triggers an avalanche. Several more piles come crashing down, and suddenly I'm hip-deep in books and magazines. It's pretty scary, and it's also exactly what I've been worrying about. If Mr Jennings was here on his own and something like this happened, it would knock him off his feet. I'm not sure he'd be able to get up again. I manage to shove the books aside and make my escape. As he shuts the door behind me, I can hear him slowly and painfully starting to build his book-barricade once again.

Each time I get back to the office from a visit, I have to make a note in my file. The notes are a crucial record of all my actions, and if anything happens – if the very worst thing of all occurs and Mr Jennings dies in his property – I'll need them to write a report. Right now, that report would have to say that my tenant has been living in dangerous conditions with hoarded materials blocking the doors and stopping paramedics from reaching him. His death would be a tragedy and then I imagine the enquiries, the headlines in the papers, the scandal all about how Southwark Council doesn't care. It would look as though I'd done nothing to help him. But what can I do? Those massive mountains of books are appearing in my nightmares. I'm at my wits' end.

. . .

'Hello? Is that Miss Bynoe from the housing department?'

'Yes, it is,' I say. I'm sitting at my desk in Meeting House Lane. I don't recognise the anxious voice on the phone. 'How can I help you?'

'My name's Terry Benn. I'm a friend of Stanley Jennings.'

'Oh, hello, Mr Benn. Is everything okay?' I'm sure before he speaks that something's wrong because the voice sounds really stressed.

'I hope it's okay to call you like this,' he goes on. 'I found your business card in Stan's kitchen. Stan's in the hospital. I thought you ought to know.'

'Oh goodness,' I say. 'Thanks so much for ringing. Can you tell me what happened?'

'He phoned me yesterday. He doesn't often call. He sounded bad.'

'I'm quite surprised he rang you, to be honest,' I reply. 'He doesn't often ask for help.'

'Yeah, I know. He doesn't like people knowing his business,' answers Terry. 'Or about his health stuff either.

Anyway, when he rang he got me that worried that I called 999 and gave them his address. Then I went straight over – I've got his spare key, you see.'

'That was ever so kind of you,' I say.

'The paramedics got there before me but they couldn't get inside. When I arrived, they were trying to break down the door. So we used the key, but even when it wasn't locked there was a load of stuff behind it and it still wouldn't open. They were getting really worried.'

Oh no, I think. *Oh, no*. I'm gripping the phone very tightly in my hand. I feel sick. It's the very situation I've been trying to prevent.

'How long did it take them to get in?' I ask.

'Well, in the end they got a broom. They pushed the door open a few inches and used it to sort of shove the books further in. Then one of the guys could squeeze through and get to Stan. Stan was in a bad way in there. He couldn't move.'

Oh my God. I can hardly bear to listen.

'Did you know about all those books, Miss Bynoe?' Terry asks me.

'Yes,' I say, 'I did. I tried to explain to him so many times how it was dangerous. I knew this could happen.'

'Ahhh,' he says, 'well, then. You tried. I mean, that's Stan, right? He's stubborn. He likes what he likes.'

I know Terry's right about this, but it doesn't really help. I still feel awful. 'Thanks so much,' I tell him, 'for everything you did. I'll visit Mr Jennings and see how he is.'

I must sound really stricken, because then Terry says to me, 'Miss Bynoe, don't beat yourself up about it.'

I do, though. I go over and over what's happened and wonder and search in my memory for something – anything – I could have said or done differently to protect Mr Jennings. Surely I could have found a way. And yet, I couldn't order him to do as I wanted. I didn't have the right to take his liberty away from him. I stay in touch with him and offer all the help that I can. A few weeks later, he dies peacefully in hospital. And I have to make my peace too, and accept that I did all I could do for him with the powers I have.

Even today, with the Hoarding Panel in place to help us, housing officers can't just go wading in. We've taught ourselves the best ways to approach someone who's hoarding: that first of all, they might not want to see the problem. Even when they know realistically that there's just too much stuff, they can't let go. So I try to help my hoarders get into the present, where they can understand that something has to change. That's often the hardest part, and I hear lots of explanation and excuses. I try to keep it light and use humour, so that it feels less threatening. I'm responsible for keeping my residents safe, but these are their possessions and they all have the right to live their lives the best way they know how.

When things go badly wrong, the public tends to judge us ('The council should have done more!' people always say), but our tenants have autonomy and dignity. It's wrong to take either of those from them. For those who aren't on the front line, living it with our residents, the decisions housing officers have to make might sound easy. In real life, they're not easy at all.

• • •

'So how exactly am I going to change my life, Charmain?' Pleasant asks me shyly.

She's started visiting the housing office in Meeting House Lane from time to time to give me updates. It's lovely to see her so relaxed, checking the time because she needs to pick up Isaac from school, planning to stop in the park on their way home so that he can play. There's no more pressure to anxiously rush back to start fixing Samuel's dinner, worrying in case it's late or not to his liking and he loses his temper again.

Not that Pleasant hasn't had some problems in the past few months. Her husband is still awaiting trial, on remand at first, but then out of prison on bail. The first day he'd been released, he broke the conditions of his bail by trying to get his cousin to contact her. I'm not at all surprised: guys with big control issues don't stop their controlling behaviour just like that. If they're blocked from doing it directly, they want to carry on another way, and most often what this means is they'll go through someone else. Luckily, though, Pleasant mentioned what was happening to me at one of our meetings. I called the police from my office and Samuel was arrested again.

But things are looking up now. Pleasant's lucky that she

can still see in both eyes after the damage he did to her in that final beating. Her tenancy is in her name at last. But the most hopeful thing of all is that she believes in a new life for herself – and that's what I think will make the difference.

It can be difficult to help survivors of domestic violence. For many of them, there's a terrible kind of familiarity about their situation. However horrific it might be, it becomes all they know. There's not one sudden starting point in most cases: the abuse begins gradually and the pattern of behaviour gets slowly worse over time. Violence creeps up on its victims emotionally and physically, getting more and more serious and gradually wearing them down. Changing starts to feel too hard. Eventually the abused partner just can't imagine a way out. But Pleasant can imagine being free. Each time we meet, I see the strength of her will to make a new life for herself and her children.

'You've already taken the first step,' I say to her encouragingly. 'You should feel good about that. You're sitting in front of me, we're talking. You're moving.'

'What I really want,' she tells me, 'is a good job – a career – where I can earn some money of my own.'

'Okay,' I say, 'so what do you think you'd like to do?'

'There is something.' She hesitates, then gives a nervous little laugh.

'Go on, tell me,' I say. 'What?'

'I always wanted to – to be a nurse. When I was a girl back in Ghana, that was my dream.'

'Well, that sounds great,' I say.

'But, I have children. Do you think – would I be able to get childcare while I did it?'

'Yes!' I tell her. 'Yes. You definitely would.'

'Right,' Pleasant nods. But there's still something worrying her.

'Pleasant?' I say. 'What's bothering you?'

'Well.' She stops again. She looks so embarrassed.

'Spit it out!' I grin.

'But you will think I am very stupid, Charmain.'

'I definitely won't think that at all! Just tell me!'

'For the training, there would be a lot of studying. And I – it's difficult – I –' She hesitates, then it comes out in a rush. 'I can't read English very well. Or write.'

Looking back, I should have realised sooner. I think about our chats, and about the way she quickly skimmed through the legal documents in Samuel's briefcase. She's curious and smart and she was terribly worried about her situation, but even when I showed her the most important legal papers, she never once tried to read them herself.

'Okay,' I say, 'so first things first. We can help you sort this. You're a really intelligent person, that's obvious. There are adult learning centres you can go to. You can sign up for classes and learn English.'

I don't give Pleasant too much information for now. I don't want to overwhelm her. All I want her to take from today's chat is confidence to plan her future. And as she's leaving, I can see that I've succeeded. She walks out of Meeting House Lane with a big old smile. As I watch her go, the building's automatic doors swing wide open in front of her. It's a beautiful image, as though a curtain's rising and she's stepping out onto a stage. I feel really uplifted by the sight. What will take place on that stage is the most wonderful, exciting performance – the rest of Pleasant's life.

CHAPTER FIVE

GOOD MORNING, YOUR HONOUR

2006

It's a sunny Friday morning in June and I'm sitting on the No. 37 bus. I've got a busy day at the office ahead of me, catching up with paperwork and making phone calls, but still, I'm in a pretty happy place. I can already smell the weekend. My Motorola phone starts vibrating in the bottom of my bag. I reach inside and flip it open to answer. Back in those days the screen doesn't show me who's calling.

'Hello?'

'Charmain?' It's Laurie, my manager. I pick up on the tension in her voice straightaway. *Uh-oh. This can't be good.*

'Charmain,' she says, 'Uh – have you left home yet?'

''Course I have. It's nearly 9 o'clock. I'll be there in a few minutes.'

'Change of plan. I'm afraid I have to send you to court.'

Oh, frig. My lovely sunny Friday just went straight down

the pan. 'No, you don't have to, Laurie!' I answer jokily. I'm still trying to keep it light. But she really isn't kidding.

'Yes, I do,' she says. 'Something's come up. I really need you to go.'

My heart plummets.

'Why me? Surely someone else can do it?'

'No, they can't. I've checked the diary. Everybody else has got appointments. You're the only one who's clear.'

I glance down at my clothes. This morning I got ready for a day at my desk catching up with paperwork. It's going to be warm so I'm wearing a white vest with spaghetti straps, black leggings and a white lacy cardigan. The cardigan is really more like mesh. It's a *very* informal outfit. 'Laurie,' I tell her firmly, 'I'm not dressed for court.'

'It doesn't matter.'

'Trust me, it will matter when you see me! I really don't look right.'

'Well, we don't have a choice.'

'Can I at least go home and change?'

''Fraid not. I've got a cab on the way. When you get here, I'll give you the file and then you need to leave.'

I stare at the other lucky commuters still in their Friday-morning mood. Then for the rest of the journey, I sit holding my head in my hands. I make it to the office and when Laurie sees my outfit, she can't help but smile. 'See, I wasn't kidding!' I tell her. 'You're sending me to court in my leggings.'

She hands me the file for the case.

'It'll be fine,' she says confidently.

'It won't be fine. What if I get Judge Stern?'

'You won't.'

What if I do?

'Well, if you do, you do.'

Thanks, Laurie, I think to myself. *That really helps.*

'At least it's Friday,' my cab driver says to me cheerfully as we head for Lambeth County Court, where all the south London housing cases are heard. I glower at the back of his head. He doesn't understand the trauma I'm going through. How could he?

• • •

As the cab moves through the traffic, I quickly read the file on this morning's emergency. A tenant who's scheduled for eviction has requested a stay. That means a short delay in the proceedings, so he can put more information in front of the judge and – he hopes – be allowed more time to pay his arrears. But he's had three stays already, and Southwark Council wants to stop him from getting another.

Sometimes our tenants take for granted that the council won't evict them. We certainly don't want to do it. Eviction is our very last resort, and before things get that bad, we'll always help as much as we can. I find some of our arrears cases heartbreaking, particularly when the tenant is elderly and ill or confused. I remember a distraught widow whose husband had paid the rent and dealt with all their finances, but then she was left alone and had no idea at all what to do or who to pay. I've had cases where the person who pays rent has abandoned their partner or spouse. Faced with a sudden shock like that, people can panic and do nothing, then, a few months down the line, they're close to being homeless. Of course, the council has sympathy and compassion in cases like those. We signpost tenants towards charities that can assist them, and give them advice about benefits.

But we can only help our residents when they talk to us. Sometimes, we don't hear a word. To just stop paying rent and hope that nothing will happen is the worst thing that anyone can do. Revenues from rent pay for all the council's vital services. Without them, we can't do repairs and upkeep on our estates and properties, so there are times when we just have to take action.

This morning, as I look through the file, I don't have much sympathy with this guy. His case has reached the end of the road and he's really not helped himself at all. He's not paid anything for months, and the council already has a Possession Order on his property. But each time an eviction day is set, he applies for a stay. He comes along to court and makes all sorts of promises to deal with his arrears, and then he disappears and doesn't keep to the arrangement. He's done it three times already.

I think of Southwark's tenants who badly need more space: families with kids, young people who are coming out of care, a disabled resident who's desperate to move to a ground-floor flat. All of them are paying their rent and bills on time and doing everything the system asks them to do. It's people like this guy who are stopping them from getting what they need. So today the council is requesting no more stays. If we can evict him, his flat can be offered to someone else on the waiting list for a home.

When I reach court, of course everyone else is suited and booted. I look completely out of place. It's not just my leggings – although they're pretty bad. It's also how low my neckline is. I wrap my cardigan tightly around me, but it doesn't really cover up much skin. I feel as though I'm wearing a bikini. I don't know yet which judge will be dealing with the case, but there are some seriously worrying possibilities. On the noticeboard downstairs in the foyer is a list of the four court-rooms and each judge's chambers. It shows the names and details of the cases that will take place in each one.

Not Stern. Please, let it not be Stern. My stomach gives a lurch as I go over to look at the list.

• • •

Court appearances are a regular part of my job as a housing officer, but they're still pretty scary. I seriously believe that everything in court is designed to be as intimidating as possible. The atmosphere is really, really formal. Everyone's dressed up. All legal procedures must of course be followed exactly. So when you're asked a load of detailed questions and everyone is watching you, you must make sure that you're using precisely the right words in precisely the right way. It makes for an awful lot of pressure. And the more you try not to respond to all this like a nervous kid, the more you feel like one.

Most terrifying of all are the judges. Even the ones who are kind and sympathetic feel a little bit like aliens to me. They come from a world so far away from the council estates of Southwark that they might as well be from Jupiter.

I clutch my lacy cardigan together at the front and cross the foyer to take a look at the day's list. When I see Judge Stern's name next to my case, I honestly think that I might lose the plot. Judge Stern is the bane of every south-London housing officer's life. This guy spreads fear. He doesn't like local authorities and he doesn't try to hide it. He doesn't like anyone who isn't on the ball. I've seen him reduce a big tough professional to a shaking wreck after her phone rang in his hearing. Fair enough, she should have turned it off, but then she *did* turn it off and the phone rang again for no reason. There must have been something wrong with it. That poor woman felt the full-on fury of Judge Stern. By the time he'd finished, she was sweating, practically in tears. Apologising frantically, she took the battery out. We all felt for her. We knew it could have happened to any one of us.

Another of my colleagues had an even worse time when he appeared in chambers without a tie. 'How dare you,' said Judge Stern in a voice carved out of sheer ice, 'how *dare* you appear in my court in improper attire?'

'Uh – uh –' the housing officer stuttered.

'Please ensure that you are suitably dressed when you enter my court again.' After that, a lot of people started keeping a spare tie in their desk.

Not everyone's like Stern and you do get soft-hearted

judges sometimes. One or two will sympathise so much with tenants that they won't ever evict them, no matter how much evidence there is that they could have paid their rent. It's maddening for a housing officer when someone who you know drives a Beamer, wears expensive clothes, spends their money on having a good time but just never gets round to paying the rent goes on a shopping trip to Oxfam and turns up in court in a sad-looking second-hand outfit. *See, times are hard*, they tell the judge. And the judge buys their story and lets the tenant off. The first time it happened, I just stared. I knew perfectly well that the guy had a wardrobe full of bling. But I could only mention legally admissible facts before the court, and that wasn't one of them.

Nobody would dare try a stunt like that one with Judge Stern. I think he might be a relative of Scrooge. His voice is cold. So are his eyes behind his little half-moon glasses. If you're not properly prepared or – even worse – if you actually make a mistake in court, he won't spare you. He doesn't suffer fools, and no one yanks his chain. I always make sure that my papers are on point when I'm in court, but even when you've got it all covered, you still don't want to appear in front of him.

Right now, I just want to run away. I can't believe this is happening. *Why did I agree to come? I'm dressed like a hoochie mama. Now I'm up before Judge Dread. Could today get any worse?*

Actually, it could get worse – and two minutes later, it does. The next thing I discover is that our brief – Southwark

Council's solicitor – hasn't turned up. I'm the only person here. This case is so last-minute that nobody expected it to happen. I can still appear before the judge and do all the talking for Southwark Council on my own. It's just that I'll have to do it dressed in my leggings and my vest.

Court hearings start at half past ten. Before that, your brief normally goes through the facts with you – the details of the tenant, their address, how big their debt is, what their rent is, any mitigating factors that might explain why they didn't pay. Today I'm on my own, so I read through my file extra carefully, drumming the case into my head.

I know the Lambeth County Court ushers pretty well. For work they dress in black suits and ties, and right now, every single one of them is staring at my outfit. And grinning. I catch a comment about not knowing that today is 'dress-down day'. My favourite usher, a guy called Troy, is looking at me worriedly.

'Charmain?' he says. 'Is everything okay?'

'Yeah, sure. I'm okay.'

'You sure you're not the defendant today?'

I have to smile at that.

'Cheeky! 'Course I'm not!'

'So – um – why the unusual outfit?'

'I've got a last-minute case. I had to come straight here.'

'You're not going into chambers like that?'

'Don't have much choice, do I?'

'Who you got?'

'I got Stern.'

Pretty unhelpfully in my opinion, Troy bursts out

laughing. 'Oh my, Charmain. He is *not* going to like you!'

'Cheers, mate. Thanks for the confidence-booster!' Troy laughs some more. I glare back.

All I can do is wait. I sit down on a chair in the corridor. I fiddle with my clothes, which doesn't help, and struggle to collect my thoughts. A very long few minutes go by.

'Southwark Council versus Robinson!' calls the usher.

I grab my files and hold them up to protect my extremely exposed front. Then I take a big deep breath and head on in.

• • •

Judge Stern's chambers are high-ceilinged and forbidding. The walls are lined with legal tomes in heavy leather covers. He's seated at his desk in a massive leather chair, dressed in a collar and tie. His half-moon glasses are resting on his nose. When he catches sight of me, I think I see him hesitate just for a second. His eyes flick up and down, taking in my outfit. I wait for his wrath to descend. But his chilly expression doesn't change.

'Good morning, sir,' I say. He gives me a slight nod. I take my seat in front of him. The usher's standing just beside the door. There's a pause while the judge waits to see if anyone else is coming in. No one does.

'Is the defendant here?' enquires Judge Stern.

'No, sir,' says the usher.

'Have you heard from the defendant?'

'No, sir.'

'Has there been any communication from the defendant?'

'No, sir.'

'Is there any representation here for the defendant?'

'No, sir.'

Another pause. It's pretty unusual for a tenant to request a stay of eviction then not bother to show up. Judge Stern's eyes rake over the documents in front of him. Then they rake over me. I clutch my papers close to keep my chest covered up.

'Miss Bynoe?' I try not to jump when his chilly voice says my name. 'Have *you* heard anything from the defendant?'

'No, sir.'

I realise that I might need to look inside the file for information. Just in case, I try to lower it onto the table. But as soon as I move, it feels as though I'm doing a strip-tease – there's way too much on show. I'll have to keep the papers where they are.

'We've made efforts to contact him,' I explain. 'But he's not answered the phone. We've heard nothing about his attendance today or about any difficulties with payment.'

'Hmmmm.' I can feel Judge Stern's stare. My palms are sweating. I'm waiting to be told that my clothes are a disgrace and that I should get out of his chambers.

'What exactly has this tenant paid?' the judge inquires.

'Fifty pounds, sir, after the last stay was granted. Nothing since then.'

'And when was this payment?' Judge Stern enquires.

'February 15th, sir. Over four months ago.'

'When was he last in contact?'

'That was it, sir. He's not responded since.'

'Hmmmm. Is there anything else?'

'Yes, sir.' Judge Dread raises an eyebrow. 'Southwark Council requests that no more stays of eviction should be allowed in this case.'

What I'd really like to add at this point is: 'Judge – the man ain't doin' jack.'

'Hmmmm. Are you looking to have costs attached to this?'

When the council has made every effort that it can to contact someone but they haven't responded, we add the costs of the work we've had to do to their debt. 'Yes, sir,' I say.

Judge Stern picks up his fountain pen and signs the form on top of the pile in front him – the order for eviction. I'll receive my copy later. Then he reads out the decision.

'The order of the court is that the stay of eviction will not be upheld.'

That's it. We did it.

'An additional order has been placed that no further stays can be attached to this case,' he goes on. 'Eviction is agreed for the earliest possible date.'

'Thank you, sir,' I say.

And we're done. I can't believe I got away with this. I practically jump to my feet. Just a few seconds longer and I'll be outside in the corridor.

'Miss Bynoe?' says Judge Stern, in an extra-icy tone. I

freeze like a runner at the starting line, halfway across the room.

'Errrr… yes, sir?'

He looks at me over his half-moon glasses. His laser eyes are locked right onto mine. 'Miss Bynoe, have a wonderful weekend.'

Just for a second, he breaks into a grin. I've never seen anything like it. And suddenly I realise that he knows how I've been feeling all along. *He thinks this situation is funny. Judge Stern has been having a laugh.*

'Uh – uh – thank you, sir!'

Still clutching my papers underneath my chin, I practically run for the door.

• • •

'Charmain?' Brian, the Southwark Council bailiff, calls my name from inside the flat. I'm standing in the hallway outside. 'Our lady-friend's moved out. The place is empty. But there's something you really need to see!'

We're in Nutwood House, and we're doing an eviction. It's never something I enjoy, but the case is straightforward. This tenant turned her flat into a very lively brothel, and, not surprisingly, complaints came pouring in from her neighbours. I've been through the whole legal process: first the Notice Seeking Possession, which gave her twenty-eight days to close her business and leave, and then the court referral, where I presented my evidence. Finally the Possession Order has been granted. If a tenant's still inside when the bailiff arrives, they have to leave at once. If they refuse – and this has happened – the council needs to obtain a second Possession Order. That order allows a police officer to physically remove them while the housing department changes the locks.

'What's going on in there, Brian?' I ask him.

He appears in the doorway. He's pinching his nose very tightly.

'Well,' he tells me, 'before she left, she decorated.'

'Decorated?'

'Yep. It's a symphony in brown.'

'In brown?'

'Oh, yes. Deepest shit brown. Part of the new range from Dulux.'

We're both grinning now. A sense of humour seems the only way to deal with the situation. 'Do I really want to see this, Brian?' I ask him.

'Oh, yes. Yes, you do.'

The minute I step inside the flat, the stench hits me and I bury my nose in my sleeve. Our former tenant has smeared faeces all around the walls of her living room. She's also expressed how she feels about Southwark Council's housing department, scrawled in big letters and using a stick dipped in shit. 'PIGS,' it says. 'FUCK YOU.' My heart goes out to our 'clean team', our troop of cleaners – they're the ones who'll have to sort this mess out.

'Well, she certainly got her point across, Brian,' is all I can say.

• • •

2005

Mr Banze has rent arrears – a very large amount. The problem has been going on for years. But each time we get to court, the case doesn't go the council's way. That's because Mr Banze has what he considers a legitimate reason for being unable to pay his rent on time – or indeed to pay it at all. It's a particularly complicated story, and in other circumstances it might even be considered a convincing one. He used to be a soldier in the Congolese army, and he claims that he's entitled to a pension. When this pension finally comes through, or so he says, it will clear all his arrears and put him on a sound financial footing. But his efforts to extract his money from the tangle of Congolese bureaucracy aren't going well at all.

Each time he goes up before the judge, Mr Banze represents himself. He brings folders packed with paperwork – when they're stacked up on the table, his documents are three inches high. At each appearance, he starts explaining at great length the problems he faces with the authorities in Kinshasa. But by the time he's finished talking, no one understands the situation any better. However, these remarkable performances have won him three stays of eviction.

Except that I don't believe a word of it. Mr Banze has a good job – he's a pharmacist. There's no reason why a professional man can't pay the rent on a council flat. None of his explanations make sense and it frustrates the whole housing team each time a judge seems to accept them. I've also noticed that sometimes Mr Banze will pay money into his council tax account instead of his rent account, then tell us that he did this by mistake and ask us to pay the money back. It's annoying, and I also think he's doing this deliberately to cause as much confusion in his financial records as he can and make it difficult for us to keep track of his accounts.

I've been round to his flat to do a tenancy check on more than one occasion. The place is neat and tidy, but Mr Banze always seems to be out at work. This happens even after we've arranged a specific appointment time – and that's always something that presses a housing officer's alarm bells. I don't think he's living there. I think he's illegally sub-letting – which means he's renting out the flat to someone else without seeking permission from its legal owner, Southwark Council. If that's the case, the council will seek to have him evicted and repossess its property.

In 2005, we only have a small band of officers to investigate and assist us in gaining information on persons of interest like Mr Banze. These days the enquiries are much more sophisticated, but even back in those early days, our officers were pretty ingenious. I ask them to see what they can find. Is this guy registered at another address? Does he own a property somewhere? They do their job, and an email from Investigations lands in my inbox just before Mr Banze's latest hearing – yet another attempt by the council to get him evicted. When I read what's in the email, I punch the air.

'Yes!' I shout – so loudly that the office falls silent.

'What's the good news, Charmain?' asks my manager, Jackie.

'Guess what? Banze owns a house!' I tell her.

'Ooooh,' Jackie says. 'He is *not* going to like us knowing that! What have they found?'

'A four-bed place in Ealing, plus proof that it's his principal home. That is really going to sting the man!'

Now that we can present this evidence to the court, there's an excellent chance that – finally – Mr Banze will find himself no longer a tenant of Southwark Council. Then his flat can be re-let to someone on a low income who really needs it.

Two days later, the case will be heard in a judge's chambers. When I arrive, I discover that it's Stern who's presiding. Although this makes me nervous as always, I also think it might just go our way. *Judge Stern ain't going to listen to bullshit like Banze's, I'm pretty sure of that.* I take my seat in chambers, along with Southwark Council's brief. On the table opposite us, I watch Mr Banze getting ready to make his case sound as complicated as he can. Today he's brought along a huge pile of pink slips – *nope, no idea at all what those could be* – and what looks like a stack of overseas bank statements, plus other paperwork with logos I can't read properly. *Ah, well. You gotta give the man marks for trying. Here we go…*

Our brief presents the facts: the tenant has not honoured the last order made at the last stay hearing, he's paid very little rent and he's not cleared his shortfall even though he's still employed. Mr Banze clears his throat, getting ready to reply.

'Sir,' he begins, 'if you will permit, as you know, this problem is concerning the payment of my army pension. So I would like to explain the latest developments. I have recently had contact with—'

But Judge Stern won't permit anything of the sort. He cuts in, using his chilliest tone. 'Mr Banze. This pension issue certainly needs to be resolved.'

Mr Banze looks most surprised at the interruption. 'Ah – yes, sir, yes – indeed it does – and if I may – uh – I have here the latest correspondence from Kin—'

Judge Stern's normally expressionless face is now wearing a slight frown. 'But I don't understand the relevance of these documents to your case, Mr Banze. You have a job in London. Whatever your pension arrangements may be, I see no reason why you shouldn't pay your rent from your salary.'

'But, sir—' Mr Banze is starting to look worried. He's not used to being spoken to like this.

'I see no justification whatsoever for non-payment,' the judge goes on. 'Indeed, I cannot imagine what such a reason might be.'

'If you will permit me to explain, your Hon—' says Mr Banze, sounding very stressed by now.

'You have not complied with the rulings of the court,' Judge Stern continues. 'Your rent arrears are –'

He turns his laser eyes on me. 'Two and a half thousand pounds, sir,' I say promptly.

'Indeed. A considerable amount. This issue has been discussed at previous hearings and these apparent – ah

– difficulties with your pension should have been resolved by now. But notwithstanding, the local authority requires its rental to be paid in a timely fashion.'

Bingo. It sounds like the judge is on our side. Mr Banze is getting flustered and sweaty.

'But I have – I have made payments, sir!' he insists. 'And there have been errors on the account! Serious errors! Southwark Council is—'

'Miss Bynoe,' says Judge Stern, 'is there anything to add here?'

This is the moment I've been waiting for. 'Yes, sir,' I say promptly. 'We have recently learned that Mr Banze owns a four-bedroom property with a mortgage in Crown Lane, Ealing.'

Judge Stern's expression seldom changes. But now his eyebrows go right up. He turns his gaze on Mr Banze, whose face looks to me like a clay statue melting. Everything drops very slowly – his mouth, his eyes, his chin… and then he looks straight at me and all I can do is smile. At least, until I notice that Judge Stern is watching me. I quickly pinch my lips together to keep my face straight.

'No, no, no, Your Honour!' cries Mr Banze. 'I can explain, if you will let me!' But the judge is remorseless.

'Stay of eviction is revoked,' Stern announces. 'No further stays will be permitted. Eviction will take place on the next available date.'

Mr Banze looks too stunned to reply.

'Thank you, sir,' I say.

But he isn't finished yet. He's frantically flipping through his papers, trying to come up with something else. 'Sir!' he cries. 'There has been a mistake! I must draw your attention to the latest correspondence regarding—'

'Mr Banze,' Judge Stern tells him, 'the order has been made.'

'But this is not right! I am not able to pay the rent because—'

The court usher steps up behind Mr Banze.

'Sir, you need to leave now,' she tells him.

We're done here. I gather my documents together. Alongside me, our brief does the same. There's still only one work mobile in our office, and today it's in my pocket so that I can report the outcome of the hearing to the team. The second I'm outside the chambers, I dial the number.

'We got him!' I tell Jackie.

'Go straight to the bailiffs and get that date!' she replies.

As I head along the corridor, I hear Jackie pass on the good news and the cheers from my colleagues. The whole team is delighted: this guy has been taking the mickey out of us and out of Southwark Council for far too long. Finally, we've managed to stop him. Now someone else, someone who really needs it, can have a home.

Mr Banze is evicted, but back in 2005, what he's been doing isn't yet a criminal offence. The law's been changed since then, and sub-letting can now be punished by a prison sentence. I think that's absolutely right, and I'm proud of how much better our monitoring system works these days. Checks on new tenants are rigorous and we've worked hard to uncover cases of historic fraud. Our investigators have found cases of people with two or three council tenancies, all of them sub-let, who also owned property in other parts of London.

In one case I dealt with, a couple pretended they'd split up and the partner who moved out applied to the council for another flat, which they sub-let for a large amount of money. They were of course still happily together, and their sub-letting money was covering the rent on their original home. In another case, a sub-letting tenant realised that we'd cottoned on to what he was doing. He rushed back home to change the locks while his sub-lessees were out, not caring at all that this would make them instantly homeless. But his callous actions came too late: we'd already gathered all the proof we needed.

Council housing is there for those who don't have the money or status to buy their own homes, and sub-letting it is a nasty, greedy fraud. None of these swindlers should ever have been council tenants in the first place.

• • •

2006

'Why is there a Yale lock on the outside of your bathroom, Miss Barrington?' I ask my resident.

It's my second visit to Miss Barrington's house, and this time Southwark Council's assistant contracts officer, Ronald, has come with me. I can tell that Miss Barrington's getting a bit nervous. And so she should be. I already know exactly what she's doing. But she doesn't quite believe that a housing officer from Southwark Council is going to be smart enough to catch her out.

'Are you a mother yourself, Miss Bynoe?' she enquires. She gives me a wide, warm smile as if we're just two fellow mums, and both of us are certain to see things the same way. 'I'm sure you understand. You know how things are when you're bringing up a family. These locks are security for my children.'

'Security? Putting locks on every door in the house?'

'Yes. Yes, that's right. I'm sure you know what a mess children make. The locks keep them out of the – ah – tidy areas.'

Of course, this makes no sense at all. But I decide that I'll let it go for now. 'Anyway, I need you to open these doors, Miss Barrington.'

'Now?'

'Yes. Now.'

'It's not a particularly good time, I'm afraid.'

'Otherwise,' I tell her very firmly, 'we will have to come back with assistance and carry out forced entry.'

'I see.' She's trying not to look annoyed, but she's failing.

'Miss Barrington,' I say to her, 'you were well aware that we would carry out this inspection today. When I came round last week to do a check, there were two men here in your home who told me that you were out at work. That's why I left my card with them and arranged to come back.'

I can see her gathering her thoughts. She still thinks she can play me.

'Ah, yes,' she tells me smoothly. She's got her excuses all ready. 'The two men you met here last week – ah – I happened to have my cousin staying with me. He had only just arrived. And I'm afraid he brought a friend along with him.'

Ronald and I exchange glances. He gives me a huge eye-roll.

'Right,' I say. 'Your cousin and his friend.'

'The day after your visit,' Miss Barrington tells me, 'I had to ask them both to leave.'

'They'd only just arrived? Gotta say, they both seemed pretty settled in to me,' I tell her.

'Well, quite!' She tosses her head, trying to laugh it off. 'They'd made a terrible mess of the place, both of them. It looked like they'd been living here a fortnight. So thoughtless of them. I was extremely annoyed.'

'When they showed me round,' I say to her, 'I found the whole place pretty strange. I couldn't see anything belonging to your children. No toys, no clothes, no games, no school things. I can see a few things now...' I glance around the living room as I'm speaking, 'but last week, there was nothing at all.'

'Well. Yes. There's a reason for that. My children spend half the week at their father's.'

'Your kids don't keep anything here at all?' Ronald asks her.

'No. Not really. No, they don't.'

'Right,' he says wearily. 'The kids live here half the week, but they don't keep any stuff here. Gotcha. Now can we take a look around?'

As far as I'm concerned, Miss Barrington's already in court. It's obvious what's really going on and the whole time she's been speaking, I'm planning for the process of evicting her. Finally, reluctantly, she opens the doors one by one so that Ronald and I can carry out our inspection. The upstairs bedrooms are all set up like little bedsits, dingy and musty-smelling, as though whoever lives here doesn't wash their clothes all that often. In the first one, there's a pile of bright pink and purple My Little Pony toys in a corner and a scrappy poster of a boy band hanging on the wall. They're the only items in the place that might belong to a child. It couldn't be more obvious that this is not a family home.

'Are these things your daughter's?' I ask Miss Barrington.

'Yes.'

Ronald is strolling round the room.

'There's mould on this window,' he points out. 'Don't you tell her to open it?'

'Oh, you know what it's like when they're that age!' she replies breezily. 'You can't tell them anything!'

'How old is she?'

'She's eight.'

We continue our inspection in silence. 'And this one is your son's room?' I ask her in the bedroom next door.

'Yes.'

'These shoes,' I say, 'they're his?' The shoes are very large indeed. 'These shoes belong to a thirteen-year-old?'

'Yes. He's a big kid. He's got big feet.'

'And the aftershave?'

'He's been trying it out. He likes the smell.'

'And the porn?'

'The *what*?' Miss Barrington's face turns as purple as the My Little Ponies. Ronald has turned his back and is gazing out of the window.

'The porn under the bed. It's sticking out – look!' All three of us look. 'You let your thirteen-year-old son keep porn in his room, do you, Miss Barrington?'

She can't come up with an answer to that. Next we go to inspect the locked bathroom. Alongside the bath there's a rolled-up sleeping bag. By now Ronald and I have both had enough of her ridiculous excuses.

'Are you trying to tell me that this is the way you have your bathroom?' I ask her.

'Yes.'

'Miss Barrington, downstairs in your kitchen there are clearly different cupboards being used by different people. You don't live in this house, and neither do your children. I've seen enough to know that you are sub-letting these bedrooms. And there's a third person here too, isn't there? The one who pays you to sleep in your bathroom.'

Finally she can't think of anything to say. We've got her, and she's going to be evicted.

• • •

I've been on my feet for hours in the cold and I'm starving. As I'm walking through the Friary estate, all I can think about is getting back to the office, and food. Then I hear someone shouting, 'Charmain! Charmain!' At the door of her ground-floor flat, I see Mrs Kamara waving her hands at me like she's flagging down a car. Well, there goes lunch for another hour… As I head towards her, she's welcoming me with a big smile. I know she's got some problems but she always smiles, no matter what.

'Oh, Charmain, I'm so glad I saw you! We really need help. Can you come inside for a minute?' She beckons and I make my way along the narrow hallway. The family's coats are all hanging here on hooks and we have to push our way past them. Mrs Kamara lives with her husband and their four children in a two-bedroom flat. I follow her into the kitchen. To be fair, it's a blessing to get inside out of the cold, but she's cooking in here and that just amplifies my hunger.

'Hello, Mrs K, so what can I do?'

She looks nervous, but I can see she's determined to make her point.

'Well,' she says, 'you know you don't hear a thing from me about this normally – but look. The flat's so small. It's getting too much. The children – they are outgrowing this place.'

I know she's right. I'm already aware of just how cramped they must be feeling.

'George is the one I'm most worried about,' she goes on anxiously.

'How old is he now?' I ask her.

'Fourteen. He's growing up so fast.' She shakes her head in disbelief. 'Where does the time go?'

'Tell me about it,' I reply.

'Very soon he will be a young man. But we can't give him space of his own. He keeps his stuff in boxes in his sisters' room and when he wants to get something, they have to let him in. Then they have arguments about it. I'm sure you can imagine.'

I certainly can. I know just how stressful it must be. Mr Kamara is a bus driver and his wife is a cleaner: both of them work very long hours with gruelling early-morning starts. Their home is classified as overcrowded: their three girls share a bedroom but George, who's the eldest, has to sleep on the living-room sofa. I've put in a statutory over-crowding referral to Housing Options, making them a Band 2 priority. This is the official process I have to follow to move the family to a larger, more suitable home.

'I don't blame the children for fighting,' she goes on. 'They've all outgrown the place. A few weeks from now, Lucee will be a teenager too. She needs privacy, but the girls can't get away from each other.'

I can see how upset Mrs Kamara is feeling. It's certainly not the first time we've had this conversation. She and her husband work hard and follow the rules, but the system's not delivering for them. *Or for thousands like them*, I think to myself.

'I'm praying for an answer, Charmain,' she says to me. 'Every day I ask God for a better home for my children. For them to have a better quality of life.' She looks totally downcast, close to crying.

'I understand how difficult this is, Mrs Kamara,' I reply.

Everybody on the waiting list is in housing need and everybody wants a date – something definite, something to hang on to. Tenants ask me again and again how long it will be. Ten years earlier, as a Band 2 priority, I'd have expected the Kamaras to have to wait six months. But nowadays – how long is a piece of string? I can't tell them the time they'll be sitting on the list. This could take years.

I can see that she's feeling overwhelmed today. She's a caring, sensitive mother – perhaps it's the thought of her two teenagers having such a limited space to grow up. I need to give her hope because without it, she's struggling. I decide to show her a light at the end of the tunnel.

'There's somewhere for you, you know, Mrs Kamara,' I say. 'Somewhere that's meant to be yours. I'm certain about that. It's just that it isn't ready yet.'

She meets my eyes and manages a smile.

'I'm sure that you're right, Charmain,' she says bravely. 'I know that my prayers will be answered.'

Weeks and weeks go by. The weeks turn into months. I spot Mrs Kamara regularly when I'm visiting the Friary estate and she always smiles and waves. Lucee must be past her thirteenth birthday by now, and George will be turning fifteen. Then one day as I'm following the path between the houses on my way to a visit, I suddenly see Mrs Kamara running towards me.

'Charmain!' she shouts. 'Charmain!'

'Hello! How are—'

She rushes up to me, panting and beaming a huge smile.

'Charmain! We've got a place! It's a new-build – brand

new! At Surrey Quays! It's beautiful! And it has five bedrooms – five! The kids will have space to do their homework!'

She laughs with such delight that it's infectious. It makes me laugh too. I'm so, so pleased for her.

'That's marvellous news, Mrs Kamara!'

'God has answered my prayers, Charmain!'

'You see,' I tell her, 'your place wasn't ready yet. And now it is.'

'You were right! All this time, they were building it! And now – it's there!'

Next day, a big bunch of flowers and a card arrive for me at Meeting House Lane, saying thank you from all the Kamaras. It's so kind of them, but really I've done nothing. The only power I've had is to try to give them hope while the process grinds on. And there are so many others still caught in it, others who deserve a better quality of life every bit as much.

The national shortage of housing is acute. In London back in 2018, the mayor set a target of 11,000 properties to be built in four years, but it was never going to happen. In any case – 11,000 properties? That's just a drop in the ocean. Southwark has approximately 18,000 people on its waiting list for housing – and we are just one borough. We can't build what we need – we don't have money and we don't have permission. But still I don't think that the public really gets it and, as always, local councils take the blame for the crisis. All we can do is to make sure that every single council home is occupied by someone who has the right to live there.

• • •

The young man in the doorway looks confused. His name is Novak, his English isn't great, and at first he's not sure why I want to inspect the flat where he's renting a room. Only when I show him my Southwark Council badge and manage to convince him that I work for the government does he finally let me in.

I'm here as the result of a tip-off, after the neighbours realised that there are far too many people coming and going from the flat. It's a three-bedroom place, but Novak can't tell me exactly how many people live here. 'It changes,' he explains. 'All the time – it changes.'

I discover that all the flat's three bedrooms have bunks in, and two are fully occupied right now. Novak tells me that the sleepers have just come off a night shift. Alongside each bunk is a pile of locked suitcases, and the bathroom windowsill is jam-packed with razors and toiletries. I can hardly take two steps in the living room because more beds have been shoved in. There are dirty working boots lined up everywhere – and definitely far more boots than beds.

I can see what's going on: these guys are bunk-sharing. They're paying to use the beds in shifts, with one renting the daytime hours and another renting the night. I don't have a camera on my phone yet and I need to gather evidence, so I walk around the flat counting shoes and making notes, trying to work out how many occupants there actually are. It's heart-breaking to see that there are people in London who are desperate enough to live like this.

'So, this Mr Dulka,' I say to Novak. 'The man who told you that he owns the place. You've told me he comes round each week to collect your rent. When does he come?'

Novak looks puzzled and defensive. To him, Mr Dulka is his landlord, and this is a legitimate arrangement. He doesn't understand that he's done anything wrong. 'Er, he come Fridays,' Novak tells me.

'In the mornings?'

'Yes. The morning.'

Okay, then. I quickly put a note in my diary. The next time Mr Dulka shows up here, Ronald and I are going to be waiting for him.

• • •

When Mr Dulka appears the following Friday morning, we serve him with notice to quit the flat. We've got plenty of evidence that he – the named tenant – is not in occupation. But of course, Mr Dulka doesn't see it that way. He goes through the roof, ranting on and on as though he has some legitimate grievance. 'These people are my lodgers! You are saying I can't have lodgers?'

'You can certainly have lodgers if you tell us. And if you tell us who they are. And if you are resident in the property. But we knew nothing about this. And these people aren't really your lodgers, are they?'

'Yes, they are!'

Ronald gives a deep and irritated sigh. He doesn't have the patience for listening to nonsense like this. Quite frankly, neither do I. 'Anyway, you don't actually live here, Mr Dulka, do you?' I go on.

His face is turning scarlet. 'Who do you think you are?' he yells at me. 'You don't own this flat! This is government housing!'

He's certainly not the first resident who's tried to give me lessons in housing law. 'You are a tenant, Mr Dulka,' I say. 'Southwark Council is your landlord. And you have broken the terms of your tenancy by sub-letting.'

When he finally realises he can't argue any more, he starts abusing me. 'You can't do this!' he bawls. 'You're making me homeless, you fucking bitch!' That's pretty much the end of our conversation.

There's something else I'd like to ask Mr Dulka, but I don't. These people in his flat, these young guys – they come from Eastern Europe. So does he. Why, I wonder, is he willing to exploit his own people? What kind of person does that? £400 a month he's been charging each one, and there were twelve of them. Twelve people in a cramped and grotty bedshare far from home, all of them believing that London is just a terribly expensive city where it's hard to find accommodation and that their landlord is doing them a favour. Some favour. Mr Dulka's own rent to Southwark Council was just £80 a week. He's robbing all his tenants blind. That's what a shitty business sub-letting really is.

CHAPTER SIX

DEATH AND LIFE IN RYE LANE

2009

Anytime a housing officer dares to take a holiday, we know we're going to pay for it afterwards. I'm heading back to work after my sunny staycation, braced for the pile-up of emails in my inbox that I know will be waiting for me. Still, it was worth it. My daughter Indya and I have had a great time. It's been a chance to switch off from work for once, to have a rest and properly relax. But now it's back to life, back to reality. And it's Monday morning too – always an extra-demanding day as the team catches up with everything that's happened over the weekend.

'Charmain,' says my manager, Lanre, the moment he sees me, 'can we have a quick word?'

'Sure. What's going on?'

'We've had a death, I'm afraid. One of yours, in Waghorn Court. Tenant by the name of Joyce Collins.'

I'm really shocked to hear this. I've known the Collinses

for years. They're a retired couple who don't go out much. They don't have grown-up children, or any other relatives as far as I'm aware. They live in their own little world, but they're happy together. Bernard must be devastated by her loss.

'Oh my God,' I say. 'That's awful. How's Bernard doing now?'

'Not very well. This is really upsetting, I'm afraid. What happened was, she'd died two weeks ago. Maybe a bit longer. He found her body but he didn't report it.'

As housing officers, we're used to distressing situations. There often isn't time to take on the emotion of a case – if you did, you'd be overwhelmed pretty quickly. That's what happens now: as I listen to Lanre's account, I can feel my professional detachment cutting through my shock. I need to deal with the facts, and work out what should happen next.

'The neighbours called the police in the end because of the smell,' Lanre goes on. 'I mean, you can imagine. They went round but they couldn't get in. So they called us and Claudia headed over there straightaway with the chippy.'

Claudia's the housing officer who was covering during my holiday. I imagine all the banging and commotion as the police tried and failed to force entry. This was an emergency – as far as they knew, the tenants in the flat might both be dead or dying. But the multi-secure doors on those flats are rock-solid and can't be kicked in. They'd have to get the carpenter to take the locks off.

'Then when they got inside, they found her in the bath,'

Lanre goes on. 'She'd been dead at least two weeks, maybe more. We're waiting for the exact details from the post-mortem.'

I have to feel glad I didn't witness this horrendous event. If I hadn't been away, I would have been the housing officer in attendance. I think of the police at the scene and my colleague Claudia having to deal with the incident, and how traumatic it must have been for them all.

'Her death was natural causes?' I ask Lanre.

'Yes, it was.'

'And where was Bernard?'

'Just sitting on the sofa. I think he was in shock.'

'He'd stayed in the flat all that time?'

'Yeah. They reckon he'd found her quite soon after she died. But then he sort of froze. I don't think he'd eaten since. They called an ambulance and took him to hospital.'

I have a sudden memory of Bernard and Joyce happily celebrating their golden wedding anniversary a few years ago. *My God, this is so awful.* 'Perhaps he couldn't believe she was dead, so he really *didn't* believe it,' I say.

'Yeah,' said Lanre. 'It must have been something like that. It's just so sad.'

'He's a lovely man,' I say. 'They were such a nice couple.'

Later on that morning, I sit at my desk and read Claudia's report in detail. A team from the coroner's office attended the flat, took photos and gathered evidence before Joyce's body was removed. Then the housing department arranged for the flat to be cleaned up. Social Services have been visiting Bernard in hospital. They've offered him counselling and a move to sheltered housing if he'd like that. But all he keeps saying is that he wants to go home.

I pick up something else in Claudia's report. All the time that Joyce was lying dead, Bernard hadn't gone into the bathroom. He'd peed in plastic bottles and lined them all up neatly on the windowsill. At first those bottles of pee just seem like a sad little detail in the story. I don't realise how serious this problem's going to grow.

• • •

The Southwark clean team goes into Mr Sweet's old flat in full PPE. They'll scrape off the layers of dark-brown grot and deal with the mice and the roaches and the other urban wildlife that's been calling the place home. And somehow, when they've finished, the place will be like new, clean and shiny, ready for its next occupant.

While all this is going on, just over a mile away, Mr Sweet is starting his new life and settling into his sheltered accommodation. At least, I hope he is. I decide to pay him a visit. Even though he's not my responsibility any more, I feel a real connection. However difficult he was as a tenant, I've always liked him and I want to make sure that he's going to be okay. As I look around his new sheltered flat in Howden Road, I feel pretty happy. No more fleas or dangerous gas canisters or neglected, bleeding leg ulcers. He'll be well looked-after here, with weekly visits from the district nurse. The staff will make sure he takes his medicines when he should. It's going to be so good for his health and wellbeing. The whole thing is such a relief.

When I arrive, he's sitting in a chair by the window. He looks almost out of place in this bright, attractive room. *Wow*, I think, *so if it's weird for me to see him here, what must it be like for him? Gonna have to be patient with this one.*

'Good evening, Mr Sweet,' I say to him. 'So, how are you getting on?'

He doesn't answer.

'It's a bit different in here, eh?' I joke. He still doesn't speak. He just stares down at his knees. Finally he mumbles, 'Not sure mi like dis, Charmain.'

'Not sure you like it, Mr Sweet! Why is that?'

'Dey keep on coming in.'

'Who does?'

'Dem people. Dem nurses. Social people. All in mi business.'

'I know,' I say. 'It's not like what you're used to.'

'Mi not like dis, Charmain.'

'I bet your cats like it,' I say. Outside the window, I can see one of them strolling down the garden.

'Maybe so,' Mr Sweet mutters.

'Will you do something for me?' I crouch down beside his chair so I can look him in the eye. 'Will you give it a bit longer? Just to get used to it. Wait 'til it seems less strange, and then decide if you like it or not.'

'Humph!' It's exactly the same grumpy reaction I used to get when I was telling him that he wasn't allowed gas canisters in his kitchen.

'Will you do that for me?'

Finally he says, 'Okay, den. Mi do dat.'

'Okay, then.'

He's dazed right now, I think. In a few weeks' time, though, when he's settled in, I'm sure there's a good chance it will seem different. He might still be suspicious of the help he's receiving, but he'll get used to being more comfortable.

'I'll come back to see you, Mr Sweet,' I promise him. 'And we can talk about it then.'

• • •

Back in the noughties, every housing officer managed around 1,000 properties. It meant that responsibility for the safety and security of up to 5,000 people rested with each one of us. As I gather my belongings together to head out for a visit, Sylvie, one of our area housing assistants, comes over to my desk. She's rolling her eyes.

'Charms! Oh my God! It's all happening today. There's water pouring down at Chadwick. You need to get over there.'

I head to the whiteboard on the wall where the grid for this week records everybody's visits with a marker pen. As each week goes on, the board sprouts more and more crossings out and hasty alterations. I quickly add mine, then hurry off to Chadwick House.

By the time I get there, Sylvie has also alerted other members of our team. She's still trying to reach the tenants of the second-floor flat, where the flood has started. A police car is just drawing up at the kerb and I can see Ronald, our assistant contracts officer, hurrying towards the stairs. He needs to get inside, but no one's answering the door. This is going to be a forced entry. The carpenter and plumber are both on their way.

Chadwick is a long red-brick block of flats, usually a quiet sort of place. The door of each flat opens out onto a walkway running the full length of the building. There are round brick spaces in the walls at the end of each balcony, like portholes on an ocean liner, and today the place does feel a bit like the sea, with sheets of water streaming down the walls at the end of the building. Absolutely everything is soaked. The residents affected by the flood are going to need temporary accommodation.

Ronald, the chippie, the plumber and I hurry up the stairs with a policeman close behind. Tenants are standing anxiously on the walkways, escaping from the flood. Some have started carrying their possessions outside in a desperate attempt to keep them dry. The chippie quickly unpicks the lock. As it swings open, we're totally taken by surprise.

'Oh my *God*!'

'This is insane!'

It's such an extraordinary sight that our first reaction is to laugh. I've seen plenty of attempts to grow weed, but nothing quite like this. In every room, there are rows and rows of tables filling every single foot of the space, and sitting on top of them are hundreds – I'd say thousands

– of very healthy-looking cannabis plants. It's like a jungle on trestles, all in swampy half-light from the thick black bin liners taped across the windows. Hanging overhead is a spider's web of black electric cables and what must be bright lights when they're working, and wound around all that is a sprinkler system made from garden hoses. There are even little gadgets that look to me like thermostats attached. Everything smells leafy and musty and damp and the floor is two inches deep in water.

As we quickly rip the bin liners down to let in light, everywhere we look, we see more leaves. This isn't just somebody's ganja garden – it's *industrial* weed. I throw open every window I can reach while the plumber splashes his way through the foliage, looking for the stopcock to shut off the water.

'Somebody knew what they were doing here, you know, Charmain,' he calls to me from the kitchen. 'These sprinklers have been properly plumbed in.'

'Wow,' is all I can say.

'Pretty smart set-up,' observes one of the policemen with a grin. I can tell he's seen this kind of thing before. 'It all stays nice and warm and well-watered. The only thing you have to do is pop in now and then for a check-up!'

'Yeah,' I say, 'it was efficient, all right. Right up 'til the day it sprang a leak and flooded the whole building.'

Now the police can take over. As housing officers, our job is to sort out temporary accommodation for the tenants who've been flooded from their homes. It's going to take weeks to dry out their properties, and we're going to need humidifiers and special vacuum cleaners that suck up all this water. With flooding as serious as this, we'll also have to check the place for structural damage.

I look at my watch. I have visits to do and I'm running late already. In this job, the pressure just never seems to stop.

• • •

'Would you like a transfer to another flat, Bernard?' I ask him. 'Because we can arrange that for you.'

It's two months since Bernard Collins lost his wife and we're sitting in his living room. He's got a support package now: his flat is being cleaned and he has carers to do his shopping and make him simple meals. A social worker visits him every fortnight to check up on his welfare. But mostly he just sits on the sofa. He doesn't seem interested in anything and it's difficult to get him to talk. The carers' notes say that he'll swallow a few mouthfuls of whatever food they prepare for him, but he never finishes a meal. He's lost weight and he badly needs a haircut. I'm increasingly concerned about his welfare, but what's worrying me most are the bottles of urine.

There are more of them now than there were on my last visit. They've spread onto the bookshelves as well. The carers are pouring the contents away when he's not looking and rinsing out the bottles, but they're quickly refilled. If anyone gets rid of them, Bernard buys more. The living room is starting to smell.

'I think it would be easier for you to live somewhere else,' I go on. 'You had such an upsetting experience here, didn't you?'

No reply.

'Maybe just have a think about moving? We could arrange somewhere smaller – somewhere that's easier for you to take care of.'

But Bernard shakes his head adamantly. 'Oh no,' he says. 'No, no. I can't leave Joyce.'

He looks across the room. The urn containing her ashes is sitting on the sideboard. Face to face with his loss, professional detachment doesn't work any more. I find I'm close to tears. 'She could go with you, Bernard,' I say to him gently.

'No, no. She doesn't want to leave. She likes this flat, you see. She really loves the view.'

'Well, maybe you could wait a while, then when you've had a chance to think—'

He shakes his head. He won't go. Although I'm getting worried about him, I still have to honour his wishes. I also think that I should respect his reality, his truth. He does understand that Joyce is no longer with him, but he also very much believes that she is. I've noticed that he'll never say the words 'She's dead'. Perhaps if he said them, he'd have to join the real world – and he really doesn't want to. It's certainly not my job to force him there. My job is to ensure that he lives in a safe and adequate environment.

'Okay,' I say. 'You and your wife want to stay here – that's fine. But why have you got all of those?'

I point at the row of plastic bottles on the windowsill, and Bernard glances up. The late-afternoon sun is shining outside. It gleams behind the bottles, lighting them up. I wonder what else I should say, and then I decide that I should go with my gut. If I tell him to stop hoarding his pee, or give him a lecture about hygiene, he's not going to talk to me at all. I need to be gentle and respectful and I have an idea how I can do it.

'Actually, those bottles are kind of pretty,' I say to him. 'I only just noticed it. They're all different colours, aren't they? All those shades of yellow!'

It's heart-breaking to be having a conversation with this poor man about the colours of his piss in a bottle. But Bernard nods. He looks almost proud of what I've said. For the first time, he gives me a small smile. I think I'm getting through. The only way to persuade him of anything, or to communicate at all, is to engage with what's real and important to him.

He knows he shouldn't be peeing in bottles, but he's still not able to go into the bathroom, and he certainly won't move out of the flat. All I can do is concentrate on building trust with him, a relationship. That way, when he hears my voice, at least he'll let me in. 'I'm going to keep coming back here until I see you, Bernard,' I tell him. 'You can't get rid of me, you know!' He gives me another little smile, but doesn't answer.

So I go on dropping by at random times. I notice that it's taking him longer and longer to come to the door. Twice he doesn't answer at all, and I call Social Services both times. They confirm that his carers, who have keys to the flat, have been in that morning and that Bernard is okay. I also speak regularly to his social worker. He has the capacity to make his own decisions, she tells me. If he was ill with dementia and his judgement was affected, she could intervene – but he won't leave his flat because all his memories of his wife are there. He's allowed to make that choice. All he really wants is to be with Joyce again.

But nobody can get him to eat. His weight keeps on dropping. I can see his condition deteriorating. Each time I visit, I notice the uneaten sandwiches that his carers have made for him curled up and dried on his plate. 'What's your favourite sandwich?' I ask him. 'Tell the carer what you like, then she'll make it for you. How about ham and tomato?'

'Joyce likes ham and tomato,' he replies. What can I say? It's heart-breaking.

'How about I make you a cup of tea?'

• • •

Bernard Collins lives a further two years. Occasionally I feel that we're making some progress together, but then he retreats back into silence. The carers go on pouring away the bottles of pee and washing them out as often as they can. But the stacks of empties are always refilled. He neglects himself and only eats when he's supervised. Without the social care team to keep an eye on him, he'd be in a really bad way.

Then one winter morning, his carer arrives and notices that he isn't breathing properly. She calls an ambulance and he's taken to hospital. He dies of heart failure a few days later. I'm glad it didn't happen while he was alone in the flat, that we managed to look after him to the end. But he's wanted to go all this time and even though I've tried, I couldn't give him any reason to change that decision. No one could make things better, and it's just not possible sometimes to mend a broken heart. I believe that's what he really died from.

It happens just before Christmas, and a few days after that we have our office party. We turn one of our meeting rooms into Santa's grotto and all the team's kids are invited. There's mulled wine and mince pies, and as I look around, I feel a sense of community so strong that it's almost like family. We've been through so much together – after all, how many other workplaces have Peckham police station on speed dial, to make sure the emergency call-outs get made as quickly as possible?

I feel so proud of this team – proud of all of us. Housing officers are the backbone of the local community. We're not perfect, but we're the system that helps vulnerable people in dreadful situations. I raise my glass of mulled wine, and drink a quiet toast to Bernard and Joyce Collins.

CHAPTER SEVEN

JUDGEMENT CALLS

2007

Whenever Pleasant comes into the office, I'm delighted to
see her. This morning, I notice straightaway how well and
happy she's looking. 'How are you doing?' I ask her. 'And
how are the kids?'

'They're great, thank you. Ama's walking now, and
Isaac's doing really well in school.'

'That's fantastic. And how's the flat?'

Pleasant gives a little smile. 'Very different,' she says.
'I've been decorating.'

'Wow. With two kids to look after – I'm impressed!'

'It was hard work. But now, it looks the way I want it
to. I changed the colours, you know. Got new curtains. It
– it feels really different now.'

I know from the way she says this that she doesn't just
mean her flat feels different. She means that everything
does. 'I bet the kids love it too?'

She laughs. 'Oh yes. Isaac chose the paint for his bed-room. And he likes Spider-man, so now there's Spider-man all over the place.'

'That's so great. I'm really pleased for you.'

She gives a little nod of satisfaction. I don't ask her what's happening with Samuel. He's not relevant to her life any more. The shadow of his cruelty is passing and it's wonderful to see her so confident. 'So,' I say, 'I did some research about English courses. I've got you some brochures.'

'Thank you so much, Charmain.'

'Listen,' I tell her, 'it's my pleasure. I really enjoyed doing it. These –' I flip through the pages and show her '– are local to here. They'll give you the language skills you need for nursing.'

As she picks them up and flips through the pages, a shadow of doubt crosses her face. 'Charmain,' she says hesitantly. 'When I go and see them, um, how shall…?'

'I tell you what,' I say, 'why don't we run through what you need to say? I'll practise it with you.'

'Okay.' Her expression brightens.

'And don't worry!' I add. 'You'll be their best student. They're lucky to have you.'

She gives me her shy, determined smile. 'I'm feeling quite excited,' she says. And I feel excited for her. I love finding solutions to tenants' problems. It's wonderful to watch a person like Pleasant taking control of her life and making a home and a future for herself and her family. This is why I do this work, and have for twenty years.

When somebody's quality of life gets better – that's my job satisfaction. A day like today, when I can see that all my effort is worthwhile, that I've really made a difference – no matter how small – does a lot to make up for all the tough days when I can't get anyone to listen and I feel like I'm going round in circles. It gives me the strength to move on to the next problem, and then to the problem after that.

• • •

Mr Payne is a pain. He's a vexatious complainant. We have bulging box files of his letters in our office. He grumbles that there aren't enough dustbins in the park and that dogs pee on the grass and that local kids play football. And he certainly knows how to escalate a problem. If a housing officer doesn't fix his issue immediately, long screeds go flying in the direction of Southwark's neighbourhood managers and councillors. He even writes to his local MP.

The council's just introduced a new rule: no one can have laminated flooring above ground-floor level. Some tenants grumble about this, but carpets muffle sound and hard floors don't, so laminated floors always lead to noise complaints. But Mr Payne's upstairs neighbours have had carpets for years, so when he makes an angry phone call to tell us that they're walking around at 10 o'clock at night, there's not much a housing officer can do. He doesn't like hearing children laughing at 9 p.m. on a Friday either, but it's hardly a domestic disturbance. Nevertheless, we have to be professional each time we receive a complaint from

Mr Payne. His problems are trivial, but he doesn't think so. We take what he's saying seriously, scrutinise what's happened, resolve it if we can and give him reasons if we can't. Every resident has the right to be listened to, even if there's not much we can do.

• • •

It's my counter-duty day in our Meeting House Lane office and I've just finished taking in a housing application when I look up and see my colleague Elizabeth speeding down the ramp towards the entrance. Elizabeth's not known for doing any type of running – she's a well-dressed and gentle soul, very empathetic towards tenants. But she's panting as she sprints into reception and looking anxiously over her shoulder. As she gets nearer to the desk, she shouts out, 'Charmain! Let me in, please!'

There's no time for asking questions. I quickly come out from behind the desk to open the staff entrance. She rushes in past me and leans against the wall. She looks seriously scared.

'Elizabeth! What's going on?'

'Oh my God!' she puffs. 'Oh my God! It's that bloody man again! Mr Smith. He's outside.'

'Are you okay?' I ask her.

'Yeah.' She's recovering her breath now, but she's still shaky. 'I parked my car and there he was,' she tells me. 'He started giving me the usual shit.'

Mr Smith is a tenant in his seventies who suffers with

cerebral palsy and lives in sheltered accommodation. He also has a drinking problem, although he won't admit it. A couple of years ago, when Elizabeth was his housing officer, he made a complaint about some action that she'd taken. The issue was minor and it wasn't upheld, but for Mr Smith this small incident was the beginning of a furious campaign of revenge against her. Ever since then, I don't think there's been much else in his life except his vendetta. If he spots Elizabeth in Peckham, he follows her. He waits for her outside the office, then the moment he sees her, he starts to yell four-letter insults and threats of violence. Elizabeth's a tough professional and she shrugged it off at first – it's nothing she hasn't heard before – but now she's getting worried. She has no idea what he might do next.

'And don't tell me he's seventy-eight and disabled, Charmain,' she says firmly. 'I know that. He's a little old man. But I'm telling you – he's a dangerous little old man!'

I wasn't going to say it. I can see that he's really scaring her. She heads off to the kitchen for a cup of tea to help her calm down, and I go back to the counter as I'm the only housing officer on duty. I get there just in time to see a thin figure swaying down the ramp towards the entrance. Here comes Mr Smith. He shuffles closer to the counter and stares directly at me. When he's near enough, he opens his mouth and a barrage of horrible abuse, all directed at Elizabeth, starts to roll out of his mouth. I can smell the booze.

'Good afternoon, Mr Smith,' I say when he stops to take a breath. 'Can you go into Interview Room One, please, and we can discuss your issues?'

We use Room One for our more challenging tenants. It has a window made of reinforced glass dividing the interviewer from the interviewee – that way, if things get difficult, the housing officer is protected. Back in the 2000s, it's as near to security as we get. Mr Smith does as I've asked him, but the second I appear on my side of the screen, he starts yelling again. His cerebral palsy can make him hard to understand, and when he shouts he spits quite a lot. I'm glad I decided to use Room 1.

'So, Mr Smith,' I say, 'what exactly is the problem?'

'It's that Elizabeth!' he roars at me. 'Nasty woman! Nasty bitch! When I get hold of her—'

I don't catch everything, but there are plenty of four-letter words in there. I give him half a minute before I cut in. 'Mr Smith! I haven't got time to listen to you insulting my colleagues. What is it that you need?'

But he's on a roll by now, and he just keeps on shouting. It's all so unpleasant I don't fully take it in. I don't feel personally angry, just a professional detachment. As his spit showers towards me, the main thought in my mind is: *Gonna have to disinfect that screen…* But then he comes out with something else.

'…it's typical of all you fucking people!' he yells. He's jabbing his finger towards me.

Whoa. Stop right there. I show zero tolerance of racist abuse in any situation.

'Who are you talking about, Mr Smith?' I ask him. 'Who are "you people", exactly?'

'You lot!' he shouts again. 'That bitch Elizabeth! And you! All you fucking lot!'

Okay. I'm gonna tackle this head-on.

'So let's be clear,' I say to him. 'Do you mean "you people" housing officers, or do you mean us as Black people?'

He's not expecting me to challenge him directly about what he's said. Surprise shuts him up. He just looks at me.

'I need you to be very careful what you say next, Mr Smith,' I say. 'Who are you referring to?'

He knows he's gone too far. I can see him trying to think of what to say. Then he mumbles, 'Ahh, I meant you people housing officers.'

You didn't mean that at all. I know exactly what you meant. But now he's changing tack.

'Anyway... you know what?' he goes on. 'I love Black women! Really – I love 'em!'

Good grief, that's a new one, I think to myself. But at least now we're having a conversation. It gives me a chance to take control, and that's what I need to do. 'Mr Smith,' I say, 'you're drunk. I cannot have a conversation with you when you're drunk. I suggest that you go home. I also suggest that you refrain from your abuse of Elizabeth. Do you hear me? She is no longer your housing officer and if you continue like this, we will involve the police.'

He starts giving me the eye. He's even smiling. 'Did you hear what I said? I said I *like* Black women! Especially plump ones, nice and round.' He makes gestures with his hands to show me exactly what it is that he likes.

'Well, that leaves me out,' I say flatly. 'Now get back home. I am warning you, if you ever come back here in this state, or if you chase Elizabeth anywhere in Peckham, action will be taken against you. Do you hear me?'

When I speak directly to him like this, he understands that he's overstepped the line. He calms down. He's not shouting any more. He gets up slowly, nearly falling over the chair as he tries to manoeuvre his way out of the room.

'I like you,' he tells me again. 'I like you *very much*!'

'Yeah, whatever, Mr Smith. Now go home and get some coffee in your system.'

As he leaves, I walk back out into the reception area. Mr Smith turns round to wave and beam at me as the main doors open. There are two customer care officers back on duty by now, and they both stare in amazement.

'Right, then,' says Shirley. 'When that man appears again, we're calling you. We ain't dealing with him again – that's it.'

'But what the bloody hell did you do to him?' Sylvie laughs.

I shake my head. 'Honestly,' I say, 'I'd just had enough. You got to talk to him like he's a naughty child.'

After he's left, I clean the spit off the screen. Not a nice job, but it's the middle of the day and someone else will need the room pretty soon. Housing officers have to turn our hands to anything.

• • •

I know exactly how Elizabeth feels when Mr Smith is scaring her like that. It's not so long since I had serious trouble of my own with a resident.

Gertrude was only in her twenties, but she suffered from mental-health issues and was a very demanding tenant. She made constant complaints about the condition of her property and visited the neighbourhood office weekly with a long list of demands. There were problems with the windows, the doors, the floorboards, the damp… and eventually I received a letter from a solicitor Gertrude had employed to take up all these issues of disrepair. Back then, in the late 1990s, matters like these were dealt with by each individual housing officer, not by the disrepair division, so the issue was on me. I was less experienced and had less on-the-job knowledge, although I was learning very quickly, but the biggest difference between those days and now was the practical powers I had then to take action and get things done. Southwark's lawyers instructed me to organise a survey of the property and of course, now that the tenant had a solicitor, all communications would have to go through them.

Gertrude had appeared to understand this, until the day she turned up at the office, aggressively demanding to see the surveyor's report. When we tried to explain that it had gone to her solicitor just like she'd wanted, she stood in the waiting room yelling that I was keeping her from seeing it. She was shown into a waiting room. I went in there and tried to explain, but it didn't go so well.

'You fucking bitch! You're withholding information that

belongs to me!' she screamed. It was obviously pointless to go on. I told her that our meeting was terminated and that if she needed to know anything else, she should just go to her solicitor. More screaming. I wasn't accepting it, so I left.

Then my line manager arrived. Isaiah had heard all the noise and seen the argument in the interview room kicking off on CCTV. As he tried to ask me what had happened, our conversation was drowned out by Gertrude bellowing to a crowded waiting room that I was a prostitute. This certainly wasn't the first time I'd been abused while I was doing my job, so I just tried to let it all go past me. But Gertrude locked her eyes with mine across the room. She raised her finger and drew it threateningly across her throat.

'I hate that fucking bitch!' she yelled. 'I'm going to slice her!' She pointed straight at me. 'You're a fucking dead bitch! You'd better watch your back in Peckham!'

Isaiah was always very calm and in control. No matter how challenging a situation was, I don't think I'd ever seen him riled. Suddenly, that changed. His eyes, his body, everything – I just saw pure anger flooding through him. 'Get out!' he said coldly. 'Just get out! I will not have anyone threaten my staff! You are barred from this office and all further communication with you will be via our legal department.'

He spoke with such authority that everyone went quiet. Even Gertrude was looking pretty shocked. She tried to say something but Isaiah had reached the limits of his patience. Sometimes you have to draw a line. Right there, that's just what Isaiah did.

'Charmain,' he said calmly, 'thanks for dealing with this. I think we're done here.'

• • •

Mr Windsor comes into the neighbourhood office to complain. His housing benefit has been reduced, he tells us, and it's causing his rent to go into arrears. He needs to speak to the benefits officer, William, but William is busy so I step in to try to sort it out. But the moment I step into the interview room, I start to feel uncomfortable. I look at Mr Windsor. He's smartly dressed, in his early sixties, a large man with bushy grey hair. I can understand a tenant being angry or upset, but there's something about the way he speaks to me that puts my teeth on edge.

'What the hell is going on with my benefits, then?' he demands.

I'm holding his rent print-out, plus as much detail about his case as I've been able to gather together. 'Well,' I say to him, 'I can see what's happened here. Your housing benefit dropped off for about eight weeks. You were supposed to re-apply. This is a copy of a letter that we sent to you at the time. But we didn't hear back, so your payments were stopped. Can you tell me why you didn't respond?'

'Because I was inside,' he snaps back.

'Right.' I make a note of what he's said. 'How long were you away for?'

'Six weeks. I was arrested for having sex with a minor.'

I wasn't going to ask him what he'd done. I don't need to know and, as a housing officer, it's my job to treat all my tenants in a professional manner. But as the mother of a small child, I freeze. 'I didn't ask why you were sentenced, Mr Windsor,' I say. 'I'm only here to assist you in reinstating your benefits.'

'You know I'm still affected by the state of that prison?' he loudly informs me. 'Bloody awful food! Freezing cold! It's ruined my health. Completely ruined it! We keep dogs in better conditions than people in this country!'

You trouble a child, you get six weeks. That's what I'm thinking as I listen to all this. *You'd get a longer sentence if you burgled a house.*

'And you see, I wasn't guilty!' Mr Windsor's still shouting. 'The boy told me he was sixteen! Not thirteen! Not a minor at all! He lied! How is that my fault?'

Every fibre of my body recoils from him. His tone of voice, his body language, his refusal to take any kind of responsibility, his lack of shame. All he cares about is getting me to see things the same way that he does. *I can't be in this room with you*, I think. *I want out of here.*

I take a deep breath and explain to him what will happen next: he needs to go on paying his service charges while his re-application is confirmed. When that's been done, the backdate will be attached to his rent account. I make another appointment for next week, when he'll need to show us his ID.

'So is that it, then?' he demands. The sneer across his

face clearly says that someone as important as he is expects much better service.

'That's it, Mr Windsor. Everything's a process. There's nothing else we can do right now.'

As I escape from the interview room, I run into my manager, Frances. She gives me a quick glance, then asks, 'Are you okay, Charmain?'

'Yeah, I'm okay. I just found out about Mr Windsor's child sex conviction.'

'Right.' She shakes her head.

'Look,' I tell her. 'I'm sorry, but I can't deal with that man. I'll do his paperwork, but not face to face. There's...' I'm not sure how to go on because I've not thought it through before I started speaking. I just know that this is something I can't deal with. Frances stops me with a firm hand on my arm.

'It's okay,' she says. 'I get it. I'll do the interview next time.'

I appreciated Frances's action very much. But if there's a paedophile in front of me now, I know that I have more detachment. If a younger colleague has a problem, I've stepped in just like she did. Experience has given me the ability to focus only on what the tenant needs and deal with the issue they're presenting – the rent, the payments, the property. I don't think about what I know, or about what they've done. It's the only way I can be effective in that moment. This doesn't mean I ever forget. But I'm always a professional who does the job I have to do.

• • •

About a month later, I visit a lady in her seventies who's having a problem with her sink. Mrs Jones is a proper Bermondsey girl – that's how she describes herself to me – and that means old school, no nonsense, takes no prisoners. We've always got on well. She's also Mr Windsor's next-door neighbour.

'Thanks so much for sorting this, Charmain,' she says to me as we stand in her immaculately tidy kitchen. 'I've got the grandkids coming round on Sunday. I'm doing a big roast dinner.'

Her two sons and their families still live in Bermondsey. They're a close family. The boys look after their mum and are very protective of her. 'Sounds wonderful,' I say. 'How old are the kids now?'

'Kyle's comin' up to twelve, Harrison's nine and Darcy's just past her sixth birthday. Those are Gary's three. And me other son Alan's wife's expectin' now as well. They been tryin' a long time, so they're made up.'

'Another one?' I say. 'Awww, Mrs J – that's such good news! You'll be a nana four times over!'

She beams in delight. 'They love comin' down,' she says proudly. 'They play out on the grass. That nice Mr Windsor – you know, the next-door neighbour – he sometimes plays football with 'em.'

I hadn't realised this. It isn't welcome news. 'Oh, yes,' I say carefully. 'I know him.'

'He gave 'em drinks in that 'ot weather,' Mrs Jones continues. 'Said they could knock on his door anytime they was thirsty. Kyle said they was chattin' for ages.'

However sick I feel about what I'm hearing, I know that my response must be professional. I don't want to scare Mrs Jones. I also can't share my knowledge about Mr Windsor's criminal history with another tenant. 'So... do the kids play out a lot when they visit you?' I ask.

'Oh yes. It's very safe,' she smiles. 'Not too much traffic round here.'

How do I tell her that the danger isn't cars?

'I hope you keep an eye on them, Mrs Jones,' I say. 'You can't be too careful, you know.'

'Oh yeah. When it's warm I get me chair and sunbathe and watch. Gary and Al keep goin' on about skin cancer, but I do love a tan.'

She bursts out laughing, and I laugh along too. Inside, though, I don't like where my thoughts are going. *Could Mr Windsor be grooming Kyle? How can I warn her about him?* Then there's Gary and Alan, her sons, the two Bermondsey boys – I know they're decent guys but if they have any suspicions about their mum's next-door neighbour, they won't react well. Let's just say that the situation could get out of hand. I couldn't guarantee Mr Windsor's safety. And I can't put him at risk, whatever crimes he's committed. I have a duty of care to him too. I run my hand across my forehead. I feel a deep furrow there and realise how much I'm frowning.

'You know what?' I say. 'If it was me, I'm not sure about letting the kids knock on anyone's door. I know I couldn't do that with my daughter, no matter who they were.'

'Oh dear. I did think about that, Charmain,' she says anxiously. 'You 'ave to be so careful.'

'Yep,' I said. 'Quite right. If it was me, I'd say as long as you're around, the kids can talk to people, but not if you're not there. I just don't trust anyone.'

'You're so right. That's what I think too!' Mrs Jones replies.

'It's sad,' I say, 'but even if someone seems nice, well...'

'My Gary,' she tells me, 'he'd agree with you. Very protective, Gary is. If anyone tried to hurt one of 'is kids, he'd murder 'em.'

'I know he would,' I answer.

I've done as much as I can. I hope that it's enough. But every tenant has to be protected, one way and another – even Mr Windsor, who arrogantly told me that the boy he abused had been lying. Even if it causes me intense conflict sometimes, a duty of care to all my tenants is a part of the job.

• • •

2008

We need to have an urgent conversation about Rudy Green's rent arrears. He's arrived in an interview room at Meeting House Lane, and I have all the paperwork ready in front of me. But I realise pretty quickly that Rudy's not listening. He's slumped in his seat. He can barely keep his head up. His body is shaking so hard that his knees keep on banging against the table. He's gripping a cloth bag against his chest so tightly that his knuckles have turned white. Unfortunately, I know what the matter is.

'Rudy?' I say to him. He lifts his head and struggles to focus his eyes on me. 'You didn't have a hit today, did you?'

'Nah, nah, I'll be all right though,' he mutters. Then he slumps even lower in his chair. The awful shaking just won't stop. Every time I've seen him, I've signposted Rudy towards support for his heroin addiction. It's the only kind of help I can give him. And right now, as his housing officer, I have to sort out his rent arrears because unless he pays them off, he's facing homelessness. If he ends up sleeping on the streets, he could die. It's not about the money – it's about saving his life. That's how vital it is. But there's no point trying to talk to him about rent until he's had his hit. Without the drugs, he can't function, and we're going to get nowhere.

'Rudy,' I tell him, 'you should go and get your fix. If I talk to you now about arrears, you won't hear a word I say, will you?'

He looks surprised, but then he nods and tries to smile. 'S-sorry, sorry, yeah, yeah. You're right, thanks,' he mutters. Little frothy bubbles are forming in the corners of his mouth as he's speaking.

'Okay, then,' I say to him. 'So you go and do that. We'll make another appointment and we'll talk then.'

'Yeah, I will, I will. I'm s-sorry. Right.' He stumbles to his feet and makes his way towards the door. He's still clutching the cloth bag to his chest as though it's got the Crown Jewels inside it. As he's leaving, he half-turns back towards me.

'Th-thanks. Yeah.' And he shuffles out of sight. I feel a wave of pity. He's a really sweet guy. I wonder how he got into such a bloody awful mess.

He doesn't call me back to make another appointment. But two days later when I'm out on the Cloister estate, I decide I've got time to go and see him. Hopefully I'll find him in a clearer state of mind and we can set a date for him to come by the office. Our discussions have to take place in Meeting House Lane because his flat is too flea-infested for housing officers to enter, for their own safety. I ring on his door, expecting to hear his three dogs come running and panting up the hallway. Today, though, there's not a single sound.

I ring again, and I hear shuffling footsteps. The door slowly opens. It's not Rudy. A pale young woman I've never seen before peers out at me. Her eyes are bulging and staring and I realise she's in a state of panic. 'I'm Charmain from Southwark Council,' I say to her. 'What's happening here? Can I speak to Rudy?'

'Yeah. Um. Yeah.' All she can do is point behind her.

As I peer into the hallway, I see Rudy lying on the floor. There's a needle jutting out of his arm, and a thin line of blood running down towards his wrist. The arm is pitifully thin. His dogs are crouched around him, ears down flat. Not a single tail is wagging. They're obviously scared. They've picked up in the way animals do that something is terribly wrong.

My God, I think, *this is unreal. It's like a movie set. I don't want to be here.*

'Oh shit,' the young woman mumbles. 'Oh shit. I think he's OD'd. Or maybe a bad hit. I dunno. I dunno. Oh shit. What do I do?'

Right. Okay. I take a deep breath. *We need to get some help quickly here.*

'Have you called an ambulance?' I ask her.

'Uh-uh – no.'

I know that there's no landline in the flat. And I don't have a mobile on me – this is happening before they became such a vital part of a housing officer's arsenal. Suddenly, Rudy starts convulsing.

'Right, what's your name?' I ask the woman.

'Paula.'

'Paula, go next door. Ask to use their phone. Call 999 and get an ambulance. I'll keep an eye on him.'

I'm hoping that giving clear instructions will help her pull herself together. She nods and stumbles along the corridor. I stand there alone. There's nothing I can do for Rudy: I'm not a doctor and I know the risks of touching needles – things like hepatitis, AIDS. I watch his rapid, shallow breathing. *Hold on*, I think. *Hold on.*

Paula's back behind me now. 'Did you call 999?' I ask her.

'Uh, yeah. They're on their way. Uh –' she points nervously at the syringe '– shall we – do you think we should take that out?'

'I don't think we should touch anything,' I tell her firmly. 'The paramedics are coming.'

The wait for the ambulance feels endless. I fill the silence with my thoughts. Did I make the right decision about Rudy's fix of heroin? I go over and over the judgement call I made. What else could I have done? Was there another way to help him? One of the dogs keeps whining softly, distressed to see his master so sick. I wish that Rudy could learn how to love himself as much as they love him. Nothing will change until he does.

At last I see the blue light flashing through the window at the end of the corridor. The medics are outside.

· · ·

2000

I'm staring at my tenant's name in the *News of the World*. *It's true*, I think. *This story's really true.*

Mr Nemo first phoned me three weeks ago. Actually, he phoned me four times. He was complaining that his toilet was blocked and he was pretty persistent. I followed up the problem with the neighbourhood office, and that's when it got tricky. Instead of getting the information I was asking for, I kept not hearing back from my colleagues. For a day or so, I felt a bit paranoid. It was like there was something that nobody was telling me. Then I had a call from the neighbourhood office manager.

'Charmain? You've been dealing with Mr Nemo's complaint, so I think you need to know about his history.'

'What history?'

'The guy's a convicted paedophile.'

'Riiiiiight,' I say. 'I see.'

'So there are some issues with this, okay? First of all, there's his location.'

I'd realised this the moment I found out about the tenant's criminal record. 'Yeah,' I reply. 'He's living on Eastfields Road. How'd he get put there?' His building is opposite a nursery and just along the road from two schools. I can hardly think of a location less suitable for a convicted paedophile, even if he's living under supervision.

'I know, Charmain. I know. They were trying to make sure he was close to the police station. He has to report there every day. But, yeah. It wasn't joined-up thinking, really, was it?'

'Nah,' I answer. 'It wasn't.' These are the days before multi-agency connections and digital information-sharing. Mistakes like this can happen sometimes.

'Anyway,' the manager goes on, 'it's all been flagged up now and he's going to be moved to somewhere more suitable. But there's another issue.'

'Oh God,' I say. 'What's that?'

'You know the toilet leak he had? Well, when the plumber went round, he saw a load of kids' videos in the guy's flat. Disney stuff, you know. He has no idea of the history, obviously, and it's lucky he even mentioned they were there. He just thought that his daughter loves *The Little Mermaid* and it was weird that a man in his fifties had it.'

Right. So there's only one reason why a paedophile would have children's videos in his flat, I think to myself.

'You understand what I'm saying, don't you?' the manager asks me.

'Of course I do,' I say.

'Okay. Well, it's gets worse. The guy's got himself two puppies.'

'Right. And kids love those,' I mutter.

The neighbourhood office manager's voice is tense as he explains. 'This is his offending MO. It's what he's done before. He got access to his victims in the past by befriending their parents. You know, making himself like their favourite uncle. He got mum and dad to trust him, then he offered to help with their childcare. *Don't you worry, I'll entertain the kids while you work late.* You can imagine how it goes.'

I feel sick. I don't have to imagine. I know. My daughter's young and I'm juggling work and home all the time. I understand exactly what it's like to run full tilt to nursery at the end of the day and still only make it just in time to pick up your child. I know how much parents need help. What I'm hearing makes me want to throw up.

'Videos. Puppies. He's planning to offend again, isn't he?' I ask.

There's a pause. Then a simple answer: 'Yes. What else can it be?'

• • •

This all happened a few days ago. And now there's a double-page spread in the *News of the World*. The tabloid has been naming and shaming convicted paedophiles living in the community after they've served their prison sentences. *If you're a parent*, blares the headline, *you must read this!* Their campaign is pretty controversial. And here's my tenant's name right at the top.

I've never met this man. To me, he's just a voice on the phone, complaining angrily about a blocked toilet. I scan the pictures until I find him. He's distinctive-looking – a really heavy guy. He has mobility issues and he uses two sticks to get around. I stare at his photo. *It's weird how vulnerable he looks*, I'm thinking to myself, *like he's down on his luck, a person you'd be sorry for. Someone you would smile at and help. He doesn't look one bit like the dangerous predator he is.*

I remind myself that action is already being taken. This tenant is being moved to a location where he won't be such a risk to local children. I know my colleagues will take care of this quickly. The police are monitoring him and the situation is under control. But I stare at the image until I've locked it in my head. I'm not going to forget that face.

• • •

I spot Mr Nemo as I walk across the park a few weeks later. It's 3.30 on a February afternoon, that busy time just after the schools turn out, when children in uniform are everywhere, making their way home. The sky is grey and low and there's a strong wind blowing. I double-take when I see him. He's leaning on two sticks, with a heavy scarf wrapped around his neck. *I know you. Where have I seen you before?*

He's standing by the fence that runs around the children's play area, talking to two boys. *Wait. I know where I've seen you. You were in the News of the World.* The boys he's talking to look about ten, both in their school clothes. Old enough to walk to school alone, naughty enough to stop off at the playground when I bet their mothers told them to come straight home. The big guy's got two dogs on leads. They're not much more than puppies. The dogs are mad excited, lashing their tails and jumping up at the boys, who are patting them and laughing.

Suddenly I realise exactly what I'm seeing. A massive alarm bell goes off in my head and my mother's instincts come to the fore. I can't just walk past and leave these kids here talking to this man. It's a judgement call, made in a moment. I change direction, leave the path and walk across towards them. As the boys see me approaching, they slope off. I probably remind them of a teacher. I go up to my tenant and speak very quietly. We've never met; he doesn't recognise me. I come straight to the point.

'I know who you are,' I say to him, 'and you shouldn't be here. If I see you in the park again, the police are going to know about it.'

He freezes. The puppies are still jumping round my feet. I've no idea how this man will respond to what I've said, and I can feel my stomach clenching. His face turns white, but he doesn't try to argue. 'C'mon! C'mon!' he mutters to the dogs. He pulls them with him and heads towards the exit, away from the kids in the playground.

CHAPTER EIGHT

ARE YOU A PSYCHIATRIST, CHARMAIN?

2007

'It was a burst pipe, Wesley,' I say to the tenant. 'It's all back to normal now.'

'My personal waterfall!' says Wesley. He's trying to smile but he looks exhausted – not surprising, as he suffers from sickle cell anaemia. As if his life's not difficult enough with such a serious illness, a fortnight ago he woke up to find water pouring through the ceiling.

I smile back at him. 'Yeah, it was quite something,' I say.

'Thanks for sorting this, Charmain.'

'No worries. You shouldn't have any further problems.' But I'm crossing my fingers as I say it. There's no point in worrying Wesley, but the minute I'd arrived at the Ascot Street flats on the day of the flood and saw the damage, I'd known it was no normal domestic disaster. In the flat upstairs, the cold-water tap was gushing out full blast. The waste pipe under the sink had been unscrewed, the U-bend under the hand basin had a hole drilled in it and under the sink, the cold-water pipe had been unscrewed as well. The brand-new boiler had been taken to bits, its wiring completely dismantled and the coverings removed. The result was a biblical-style flood. Every single thing in Wesley's kitchen had been destroyed. The Southwark Council chippie, the ACO and I just stared in disbelief. No insurance company on earth was going to accept that all this was accidental. We all knew straightaway that it had to be Ethan.

I've had an uneasy feeling about this tenant for a while. Perhaps it's my housing officer's sixth sense. Ethan's very ill, with a diagnosis of paranoid schizophrenia, and although he doesn't act with malice – not exactly – he's frightened and anxious all the time and believes that other people are trying to control him, even hurt him. That makes him a danger to others and himself. Another big part of his problem is that nobody on his mental-health support team is making sure that he's taking his medication. But it's the same old story there, as I've seen in so many other cases – too many patients and not enough staff to look after them. Care in the Community is working its magic yet again.

There's no point leaving Ethan alone until the next crisis happens. We have to think about prevention, so I contact the mental health team. Ethan's outreach worker is called Adu, and I ask Adu and Ethan to come along to the Neighbourhood Housing Office to discuss the situation further. I also arrange for Isaiah, my housing services manager, to be present at this meeting as well. I want everyone to know, including Ethan himself, just how seriously Southwark Council takes this matter.

When Isaiah asks Ethan about what happened on the day of the flood, Ethan insists that he'd gone out for a walk and that everything was normal when he left. But when Isaiah describes the mess we found, Ethan eventually admits that he might have touched the pipes.

'Why, Ethan?'

'I was frustrated, weren't I?'

'Did you know what would happen? That there would be a flood?'

'I thought water might leak out. But not like that. Not as bad as that.'

'Are you happy in your flat?' Isaiah asks him. 'You said you're frustrated – can you tell us what's frustrating you?'

Ethan explains that Wesley downstairs has been watching him. He tells us that he sees Wesley's face on the screen when he turns on his telly and that Wesley is sending him messages during the programmes. Sometimes he's using Ethan's body to play on his PlayStation. To Ethan, this is all completely real.

'So all these things that are going on, they must scare you?' Isaiah asks him.

'Yeah. Yeah, they do.'

Isaiah asks Ethan to leave the room so that he can talk to Adu, and Ethan goes outside without complaining. Adu tells us that a blood test on Ethan shows he's not been taking his medication and his schizophrenia is therefore uncontrolled. *No shit – we'd worked that out already.* But then Adu gives us really worrying new information. Quite often, he says, Ethan isn't sleeping in his flat. Every night, he goes up to the Maudsley, the local psychiatric hospital, and asks them to admit him. He tells them he feels safe there. When they won't take him in, he tries the local police station. As I'm hearing all of this, I start to have a problem.

'Adu,' I say, 'you need to tell me things like that. I'm trying to support him but I haven't got a clue what's going on. And now he's done something that's actually endangered people. And you're telling us he's still not taking his medicine – so what's to stop it happening again?'

But Adu sees it differently. He reckons that once Ethan's back on his medication, things will stabilise. 'He's not a threat, Charmain,' he assures me. 'Things went off the rails with the damage and the flood, sure, but that's not going to happen again. Definitely not.'

I don't share Adu's confidence at all. 'I think he needs to be in supported accommodation,' I insist. 'I'd like to apply on his behalf. Can we set up a meeting about that with the doctors at the Maudsley?'

Adu gives a sigh that's rather loud. I can see he's getting annoyed. I plough on anyway.

'We need to do something,' I say firmly, 'because Ethan's going to do this again. This or something like it. Something even more serious. I don't think he can manage on his own.'

'Are you a psychiatrist, Charmain?' Adu asks irritably.

It's clear from his expression that he doesn't think a housing officer should have an opinion here. It's true that sometimes we aren't looked at as professional members of a care team. This attitude always makes me bristle, but it certainly doesn't make me back down. Housing is an emergency service, so why don't we get treated like one? Anyway, I'm not prepared to be hauled up in front of Southwark Council's director when a catastrophe happens to a tenant – and it will, if this situation goes on.

Isaiah has noticed the tension rising in the room. 'Right, folks,' he says. Like the diplomat he is, experienced at chairing tricky meetings, he suggests a way forward. 'What we need is a CPN assessment.'

We agree that a community psychiatric nurse will meet Adu, Ethan, Isaiah and me at Ethan's flat. The CPN will assess Ethan's mental state and decide if he should stay there. But now Adu feels overruled, and he's not happy. He doesn't say out loud to me, 'How dare you?', but as he leaves the meeting room, it's written all over his face.

The CPN assessment is arranged and its findings don't come as a big surprise. The CPN decides that Ethan can't remain in his flat and should be admitted to the Maudsley. I'm relieved when I hear this as I'm sure he needs much closer supervision from his doctors. I wonder what Adu's response will be. We also have a duty to keep Wesley informed about what's happening in the flat upstairs. I give him as much reassurance as I can.

'Ethan's in hospital now, Wes. At least he'll be properly looked after. You'll be cool.'

'That's good, then,' Wes says. 'There's a problem with that guy. He's right off-key, man.'

I'm glad Ethan's in hospital too – it's the only place he really feels safe. But I still have a feeling of unease. 'And if he does come round here, Wes,' I say, 'the water's been turned off now. He can't cause another flood.'

• • •

'Charmain? It's Wes. You need to come down here, man. I got a serious problem.'

It's lunchtime, about a month later.

'What's happening?'

'I just came home. I'd been down to the shops. I can smell gas. It's really strong. I started up the stairs to see if Ethan was there, and his door's been broken down.'

'Wes, ring Transco right away. Somebody from Southwark will be there very quickly.' Wes knows that Transco is the area's gas supplier, and I'm certain he'll take care of it at once.

'I'll do it right now. Charmain, I think it has to be Ethan. The guy's not in hospital, you know. I saw him this morning round the corner.'

I jump in my car and head for Wesley's flat. I can smell the gas as I turn the corner, and it gets stronger and stronger as I head down Ascot Street. There's a primary school right there. I go into Wes's building but the smell is so bad that I have to step outside again to breathe. Just the same as with the flood, this gas leak is so serious that it doesn't feel quite normal. But at least Transco's here now, and they quickly turn off the supply. I go into Ethan's flat to take a look, but there's not much to see and I leave the engineers to investigate. To be on the safe side, the fire brigade evacuates the whole of Ascot Street for three hours.

• • •

'Unfortunately, Mr Jay,' I say, 'this was deliberate damage caused by Ethan. He drilled two holes in the main gas pipe.'

Mr Jay is the manager of the mental-health support team. He's Adu's boss, and he's come down to Ethan's flat to see the damage. To be fair to him, he does look uncomfortable about what's happened. He's not got much to say as I'm showing him around. 'I see,' he keeps replying with a frown. 'I see. I see.'

'It took three hours before the gas supplier gave the all-clear for local residents to return to their homes,' I go on.

'I see.'

'Ethan's admitted that he caused the damage. His neighbour also saw him that morning very close to the building. We thought he was being kept in hospital for observation, but I understand he'd been given a day pass to leave.'

I look at Mr Jay enquiringly. He clears his throat.

'Ah, yes,' he says. 'Yes. Apparently that is the case.'

'When we contacted the Maudsley late that afternoon,

they told us Ethan had been out, but he was back now and he was sleeping so nobody could talk to him.'

'I see.'

There's a rather awkward pause. 'Mr Jay, the last time I spoke to Adu, I did make him aware that Ethan might do something like this.'

Mr Jay frowns again. I'm not getting pleasure being right here, but my gut instincts warned me and nobody would listen. Perhaps if Adu had taken me seriously, and not just disregarded the housing officer's opinion... 'I have to tell you,' I go on, 'that at our last meeting, Adu was quite dismissive of what I had to say.'

Mr Jay clears his throat.

'I think,' he says carefully, 'that everyone should listen to their professional colleagues.'

I can't get him to offer more than that, but it's something. The last thing we discuss is a security grille on Ethan's front door. I tell him that it needs to be installed ASAP. Under no circumstances can Ethan get access to the place ever again. Mr Jay nods agreement. He doesn't say a word.

The Maudsley hospital boardroom is painted dazzling white. On this sparkling late-April day, the sun's reflection bounces off the walls and almost makes me squint as I'm shown to a seat at one end of the table. A consultant psychiatrist is going to chair a big case conference, requested by Southwark's housing office, to review what has happened in Ethan's case. It's the first time I've encountered such senior members of the hospital's medical staff. To be honest, I'm peeing myself a bit.

'Can't you talk for me?' I'd asked my manager Jackie, five minutes before the meeting, as we waited in the gleaming corridor outside. I was having a serious last-minute wobble. 'I don't think I can do it!'

But Jackie wasn't having it. 'Of *course* you can do it, Charmain. You know all about this case and you can talk about it to anyone. Just go in there and do your job. Tell 'em what you need to tell 'em.' Right, then. In we go.

Face to face with all these big-shot medical powerbrokers, I feel like a kid, as though this huge expanse of gleaming wooden table only fits adults. It's like I've started shrinking down so small and childlike that it's a surprise when my feet still reach the floor.

The consultant calls the meeting to order, and everyone around the table introduces themselves. There are nine of us: psychiatrists, social workers, psychiatric nurses, and the mental-health worker, Adu. Back then, this meeting is the first opportunity we've had to share all the case information. Nowadays everything is digital, and details flow between the agencies much faster.

The consultant turns to me first of all, and asks me for an update. I take a nervous breath. Once I get started, though, I'm fine – I do know my stuff and once you're talking, it's easier. I set out the whole chain of events. I don't miss anything out – even the awkward part about how I felt dismissed by Adu when I expressed my concerns after the flood.

Adu immediately cuts in. 'Chair,' he says sharply, 'if I can just—'

The consultant raises his hand to stop him speaking.

'I think Charmain needs to brief us all first, before we start having discussions,' he says firmly. Adu slumps back in his seat and the consultant nods at me to go on.

'I have my notes here,' I tell them. 'I've recorded all the meetings I attended and exactly what was said. I was sure that Ethan was distressed and that he might do more damage. But I didn't know at that time that he felt so unsafe that he was going to the Maudsley each night to try to get admitted.'

The consultant's voice stays very calm, but an angry line of red climbs up his neck and then across his face. *Wow*, I think, *you're mad about this. It's really lit your fire.* I can't help glancing across at Adu. He's staring down at the table-top with his lips pressed together. It's not comfortable getting him into trouble, but it doesn't really grieve me. He's a professional, but so am I, and he hasn't treated me like one, so this is all on him. It isn't personal. The people I care about are my residents, everyone who lives on Ascot Street. And I care about Ethan too; blame for this disaster can't be laid at his door. It rests with the team that is supposed to watch over him.

I'm getting to the end of my report now and it's quite a relief. But before I finish speaking, I want to impress on them the damage that Ethan did and the risk he posed to other residents. I've made a plan about how I'm going to do it. 'When he drilled through the water pipes and flooded the flats,' I say, 'he knew what he was doing. He used tools. It must have taken him some time. This was a pattern of behaviour, and it was accelerating. So I believe it was foreseeable that he'd do something like it again. And what he actually did in the end, was this.'

I have a section of mains gas pipe in my bag. It's two feet long and made of copper. When Transco was removing the meter and the pipework, they showed me where Ethan had drilled two holes. This was evidence, I realised, so I asked if I could keep it. Now I lay the pipe on the polished boardroom table. Total silence. Everybody's looking a bit stunned. I spot a few glances being exchanged. Then I take their questions.

'What else did Ethan do to the pipes?'

'What was the effect in the local area?'

'How long was the street evacuated for?'

The members of the case conference pass the gas pipe around from hand to hand, examining the holes. The only one who doesn't touch it is Adu. It's pretty clear to everyone by now that he's played down Ethan's behaviour, and that this was a serious misjudgement. I have sympathy with Adu too; the problems of overstretched resources are constant and difficult for everyone. He must have a very heavy caseload. But when systems are strained to breaking point, it's always the poorest and most vulnerable who suffer.

Next there's a high-level medical discussion. I detach myself from this. I've given my evidence and now the responsibility is theirs. Ethan needs to be sectioned, they decide. No more day passes from hospital. They say it's clear that he also needs to move to supported housing. Ethan himself has been saying this for the past year. So once he's taking his medication and can function again, Southwark Council will terminate his tenancy of the flat and make these arrangements. That's good news for Ethan; he'll be happier when he isn't left alone.

As the meeting is concluding, the consultant psychiatrist turns to me. 'Charmain, I'd like to thank you for bringing this matter to the attention of this case conference. You've taken great care in trying to highlight a serious situation and ensure the safety of your tenant and also public safety.'

I really appreciate him saying that, and I smile my thanks. It's such a good feeling to have my judgement call validated, and to be acknowledged as an equal member of this professional team. I can feel the gigantic wooden table shrinking down – or maybe I'm the one who's growing now, getting back up to adult size.

• • •

I recognise Arvid straightaway. He's sitting on the pavement in Lordship Lane. Unfortunately, I'm used to seeing him there – everybody on our team is. He's quite a local character, a regular beggar, a nice-looking young guy with his hair in a ponytail. He's clearly from an educated background and always polite when people speak to him. So what kind of problems could have led to an intelligent, well-spoken young man sleeping on the street? I just don't know. I've certainly advised him more than once that he could get a place in a hostel, and given him the phone numbers he needs. But he never does anything about it.

There's something different about Arvid today, something even more worrying than usual. He's dressed in a thin blue hospital gown with nothing on top of it, and on this crisp, cold winter's day, he must be frozen. He also looks extremely unwell. His cheeks are sunken and his skin is almost yellow. There are streaks of blood along his arm, and a medical cannula in the back of his hand – one of those plastic contraptions that nurses attach to patients on a drip.

I crouch down on the pavement next to him. He's not wearing shoes and the soles of his feet are black and filthy. He's not got any trousers on either. It's awful to see him like this. *This isn't the time to be officialdom*, I think to myself. *I'll get more from him with kindness right now than from playing the big boss.*

'Hey, Arvid,' I say. 'How are you doing?'

He looks up at me quite calmly, but doesn't reply. I've spoken to a lot of people with poor mental health at different times, and Arvid never strikes me that way. That's not a medical judgement – it's simply based on what I've seen. He seems quite calm and reasonable, but he's just not quite on the same page as everybody else.

'Looks like you've been in hospital,' I go on. 'Were you in King's?' King's is the big teaching hospital just up the road.

Arvid gives me a nod.

161

'It doesn't look to me like they discharged you,' I continue. 'I think you need to go back.'

'I couldn't stay in there,' says Arvid.

I glance up and down Lordship Lane. *If Arvid's discharged himself from King's in this vulnerable state, they'll have the cars out looking for him. Somebody will spot him pretty soon.*

'You couldn't stay in hospital?' I ask him.

'No.'

'But if they put you on a ward, it must mean you need medical attention.'

Arvid shakes his head mildly, but he seems quite determined to stay put. What's worrying me most is the cannula in his hand.

'Were you on a drip in hospital, Arvid?' I ask him.

'I unplugged myself.'

'Look, you really can't be out here,' I tell him. 'I'm going to have to call the police.'

Two seconds after I say this, a police car draws up. I step back straightaway because these officers don't know me. This area is Dulwich, a different local team from Peckham. It's the Peckham officers I know well: we regularly speed-dial them from our front desk when things are kicking off.

'Oh fuck,' says Arvid quietly as two policemen get out of the car. He doesn't try to move. He sounds resigned.

'Hello, young man. Would you be Arvid?' one of them asks him.

'You know I am,' he says reasonably, 'or you wouldn't have stopped the car.'

'Right-oh. I think we need to take you back to King's.'

'All right, then,' Arvid says. 'Do your worst.'

He tries to get to his feet, but he's so weak and shaky that the police have to take both his arms to help him up. As he stands, I see a long tube dangling off him – he really has just pulled his drip out. His hospital gown blows open at the back and he's wearing nothing else. It's a pathetic, awful sight. The police lead him gently to the car to take him back to King's.

• • •

I don't see Arvid for another three months. Then one day, he's back, sitting on the ground in his regular position, just outside the Co-op in Lordship Lane. It's spring now and the weather is much warmer. I go over to see him and we chat.

He looks much better – almost back to normal. That pinched, yellow look around his face has disappeared. Whatever illness he's had, he must be better. But the way he appeared on that dreadful icy day has stayed with me. I want to see a change in Arvid's situation, and I'm wondering how I can encourage him to make one.

'It's good you're feeling better,' I say to him, 'but not so good to see you back out here. You don't want to be sitting on the pavement for the rest of your life, do you?'

He looks at me thoughtfully and doesn't reply. *Maybe*, I think, *this is exactly what he wants. To be out under the sky. To sit here and watch the world go past. And while I don't understand that, I try to look at everyone exactly as they are. As a housing officer, it's what I always try to do. If I'm going to help him or anyone, I have to see the world through their eyes, because assumptions about people can be dangerous. Assumptions are the mother of all the worst fuck-ups and misjudgements that I have ever seen.*

'You're too young to have this kind of life, Arvid,' I say to him.

I give him the number for the rough sleepers team, and try my best to persuade him to call it. But after that, I never see him again. He used to be a regular, and now he's gone. I'd like to think he took my advice, got some support and moved on. I hope what I said to him might have made a difference. But life is messy and sometimes there just isn't a neat and tidy ending. People can't be forced to make changes, even if those changes would be good for them. I made the best judgement I could and I tried to help, but did I? I'll never really know.

CHAPTER NINE

NO SPACE LEFT IN MY HEAD

2008

'For fuck's sake, what's your problem?! I told ya! I need my own flat!'

I'm in the kitchen of one of our properties, face to face with Michael, who's applying for a flat. He's a powerfully built man, and a foot taller than I am. He's losing his temper. Things are close to getting violent. I'm all on my own. No one even knows I'm here.

'You seen my forms!' he's yelling. *'You know I need a flat!'*

I'm sure he's going to punch me. There's nobody around who can help. I've got that shaky fight-or-flight feeling. Then he slams his fist into the door and the crash wakes me up.

I lie there in the dark. My heart's pounding. I've not thought about the incident in years, but now it keeps on playing in my mind. It was a close call. I was lucky. Risk has always been a part of my job and I have always accepted that risk, so how come this nightmare's suddenly on repeat? And sometimes the memory of the day in Michael's ki⊥⁻ ˡ comes back when I'm awake too. Out of the blue, his face keeps jumping up in front of me, staring eyes and angry, screaming mouth.

It was okay in the end, I remind myself. *His sister came along. Nothing bad happened. That's life and you just have to move on. Dwelling on what-ifs won't get the work done.* I remember hearing the rattle of keys in the front door. I didn't even think; I just yelled really loudly, 'We're in here!' There were footsteps in the hall and Michael's sister pushed the kitchen door open. She was dressed in the uniform of a carers' company and she looked really worried. She'd heard her brother shouting and immediately realised that something was wrong.

'What's goin' on?' she asked.

Michael mumbled defensively, 'I'm havin' a meeting with the housing officer!'

His sister looked at me. 'I'm so sorry about this,' she said. Then she turned to him. 'Michael! You think this is going to help your situation? Shoutin' at her like that? Why should she do anythin' for you now? Just go and sit down through there while I talk to her.'

I was feeling very shaken, but I went into professional mode. For the next few minutes, she showed me around her home. The maisonette was lovely, but the living room was clearly being used by Michael – his clothes were up on hangers all around the picture rail. He hadn't drawn the curtains and there was an overflowing ashtray. I could see that his sister was really embarrassed by the mess.

'I asked you to draw the curtains, Mike,' she said to

him. Then she looked at me. 'This is what I've got to live with, man. In my front room.'

She explained that although she'd been happy to help her brother out, he'd overstayed his welcome. He couldn't keep himself in order and it was having a bad effect on her children. She kept on apologising for how the place was looking. Life in the maisonette was tense, she said, with not enough space and more and more arguments. It was starting to get them both down. I told her how the council application system worked and what I needed her brother to do. I reassured her that we'd get him registered. Once we could get that done, there would hopefully be some progress.

It wasn't until I'd thanked her and we'd said goodbye that I got a chance to think. As I caught up with what had just happened, I started to feel shaky. Michael's sister had finished work early and decided to head straight for home… but if she hadn't, no one else would have come to the flat in time. Back in those days, I always made sure that my location was written on the whiteboard at the office every time I went out. All the team did, because it gave us some protection. But not really enough. How much time would it have taken before somebody had asked, 'Where did Charmain go? She's been ages.' Impossible to know – but it would have been too long.

The incident was just another close call. But it could all have been so different. Michael could have hurt me. And now I just can't shake off that thought. Even though my racing heart slows down, it's hours until I can fall back to sleep.

Most nights I'm waking up like this, and it's beginning to catch up with me. I'm starting each day exhausted, dragging myself out of bed, ragged round the edges and far too quick to snap when little things go wrong. To-do lists go racing through my head. Have I flagged up this problem, seen that tenant, rung this person back, sent that email, set up those vital meetings? It's always been like this; my work is constant and demanding. But now there's something else happening – a new, frenetic edge. I can never find the off switch.

I've been promoted and I'm busier than ever. As an income team leader, I'm managing ten other income officers as well as doing my own work. Every income team leader except one is a person of colour. Frontline workers very often are: somehow, we're the ones who deal with all the problems face to face. So I notice this but think no more about it. In the new role, I'm responsible for trying to reduce Southwark Council's mounting rent arrears, and I know I'm doing a good job. My area, Peckham, jumps up the league table of neighbourhood areas from No. 8 to No. 1 for successfully tackling overdue payments – and stays there. But the workload is massive and the pressure never lets up.

Then Southwark Council announces a big reorganisation. It decides to get rid of all its income team leaders as part of this restructure, and alter how its rents are collected. Jobs will therefore be 'deleted' – that's the term that's used. It's an awful, demoralising, dehumanising word. What it means is that 700 people who work very hard suddenly have their lives thrown into uncertainty and stress.

Our workplace feels different from the moment the redundancies first get mentioned. Everybody's scared that they're going to be deleted. The timeline that's been set for the restructure is short and these enormous decisions seem too rushed. As the branch health and safety officer for the trade union Unison, I feel as though the meetings regarding the changes are never-ending. My union duties are unpaid, yet I spend all day every day sitting round tables listening and trying to give support as managers break bad news. The toughest meeting of all takes place weekly – it's called the Departmental Liaison Committee, and as each DLC comes around, I find I'm getting more hyped every time. I go into these meetings wondering: *So what's going to shock us today?*

The council is creating new jobs too, as part of the restructure, but unless their responsibilities are a 90-per-cent match with a previous position, the person who lost that job can't be transferred into the new one. If the match is less than that, that employee is put into the redeployment pool and if they can't be redeployed, they're made redundant. If they're offered a new role but they don't want to accept it – perhaps it's lower-paid or it's clearly a demotion – then that means redundancy again. But we spot that the wordings of some roles have been adjusted to prevent the 90-per-cent match being made, even though the jobs are still the same. Our meetings with management get fraught as we argue about why certain words have been altered.

What's the reason for this change? And for this one? We trawl through old job descriptions: how is this new role really different from that? Then we're criticised for nit-picking, but we don't like what's going on. After all, if a job can be downgraded, its pay can be reduced. Whose interest is that in?

The whole situation is managers versus staff. It feels relentless and our sense of teamwork starts to break down. Meanwhile, no concern is being shown by senior leaders about the emotional impact of all this. I keep on going, keep on doing, running on adrenaline, finding the energy somehow. There are good people who need me to be there for them. But the anxiety everywhere is catching, and as so many strong feelings swirl around, life in the office becomes exhausting. My motivation steadily sinks.

After a while, I notice that I've started just existing, not thinking deeply about what I'm doing any more. I don't feel anything except tired. I answer questions automatically when my rent officers ask me, and speak to residents as though I'm reading from a script. I mostly want to sleep, and that's it. I could go into the staff rest-room anytime, flop down, and I know I'd nod straight off. One day, one of my officers asks about a tenant who spoke to me last week: she wants an update on his situation. I had the conversation, but I can't remember anything he said. I tell her that I need to check my records and get back to her later. She's fine with it. 'Sure, Charmain, thanks,' she says, and off she goes.

I'm not sure it is fine, though. It's never happened before.

For a very long time, every single thing that I've been told, every problem, every new bit of tenant information, has zipped off to be stored inside my head. Even when there's masses going on, I've always had a good grasp of the details. Now I can feel my grasp has slipped. I sit quite still, just thinking to myself, *Oh, so there's no space left in my head. My brain ran out of room and from now on anything I'm told will just float across the surface then trickle away.* I realise that I should probably be worried about this but because I can't feel much, I'm not too sure I even care. I don't have time to wonder what it means, so I just forget about it.

The following week, as yet another of the heated meetings that have been arranged for the income team leaders' group is breaking up, I overhear something that floors me. It's a comment from the interim deputy head of one of the council's departments to a colleague. I don't catch the beginning, but it definitely ends: '…*too many of them are managers*.' These words are spoken softly and I only pick them up because I'm walking right by. Alongside me, another income team leader has heard them too. The meeting room is emptying around us and as we walk away, we look at each other.

'Charmain,' my colleague says, 'did you hear that?'

I just nod. We both know what it means. I feel so shocked. This organisation thinks that there are too many Black people in management.

• • •

'Charmain? Charmain? Can you hear me? I said, are you okay?'

I look up. 'Oh! Sorry, Lanre. Yeah, I'm okay.'

I'm sitting at my desk, staring at my computer, watching the reflection of my face in the screen. Right across it there's a screensaver – a wild, bendy shape that keeps on twisting and flipping then swooping back on itself. Its movement is hypnotic. My manager, Lanre, is just behind me and I realise he's been speaking all this time but I haven't heard anything he's said.

'Are you sure, Charmain? I've been standing here for a few minutes.'

'Sorry,' I say again. 'Yeah, I'm okay. I'm fine.' I'm normally so focused, zooming on from one thing to the next. Today, though, I'm just sitting here staring at the screensaver. When anyone approaches me, I deal with their issue but as soon as they've finished, I fade out and go back to my staring. It's a bit like meditation, except that when you meditate, you try to clear your mind. Right now, though, I'm not trying. My mind is staying empty because I can't get any thought to stick.

Lanre just smiles. He's going to take what I've said at face value. 'So how's everything going, then?' he asks me. I can't think of how to answer, so I just tell the truth.

'You know when you haven't got any room left in your head?' I say.

'Ah. Right. Okay, then,' he replies. He seems a bit uncomfortable with that, and leaves me there still gazing at my PC. I've stared so long by now that I can't make out my reflection any more. All I can see is that wild whirling shape in a big empty screen. The minute 5 p.m. arrives, I pick up my bag and turn off my computer. Without saying goodbye to anyone, I walk out of the building.

Next morning my eyes open but I can hardly move. 'Tired' is not the word for how I feel. I call my colleague Debbie and tell her I'm not coming in today. 'I don't feel well,' I say. 'I think I'm coming down with something.' It's not like me to take time off work, and she sounds worried.

'Look after yourself, Charmain, okay?'

'I will.' And then I sleep for two days.

When I still don't feel better, I decide to see the doctor. I can't put a handle on what's wrong, but perhaps I need to rest, so I'll have to get signed off for the week. All I know is that exhaustion has hit me like a cosh, and my will to keep on pushing through it has collapsed.

• • •

'So, Charmain,' Dr Panton is asking me, 'how are you feeling today?'

Getting to the surgery is normally a stroll along my road and round the corner. Today it must have taken me twenty minutes. 'Well,' I say, 'I'm tired. I've been at home for three days. I was asleep and then yesterday I watched telly. I've no idea what I saw, though.'

'Hmmm,' Dr Panton looks at me thoughtfully. 'You don't remember?'

'No. I can't take in new information,' I tell her. 'It's like I have no storage space. It's weird.'

'Hmmm,' she says again. 'Sounds like you did right to take a break. How are you dealing with your daughter?'

'Oh, you know, just the basics,' I confess. 'I get through the things I have to do.' As I say this, I feel awful. Indya deserves so much better. Dr Panton is typing on her keyboard.

'Can you tell me more about what's happening?' she asks me. There's a silence. Ten seconds. Twenty. The question seems completely overwhelming. It'll take me so many words to answer that I don't know where to begin. When I don't start speaking, she looks round.

'At work, perhaps?' she asks again. 'Are things okay there?'

'Work?' I say. 'Are things okay at work?' I repeat this a few more times as though I'm trying to imprint the question on my brain. Then I try to speak, but now there's water on my face. Once it starts, the torrent of tears just won't stop. This is not like normal weeping. I can't even raise a single sob. *I'm crying*, I think to myself. *Wow, I'm really crying. Jesus, how embarrassing.* I start to apologise and wipe away the tears, but the more I try to wipe, the more I cry. Dr Panton puts her hand on mine and tells me to stop worrying. Her voice is gentle.

'This isn't like me,' I insist. 'It really isn't. I don't do this.' Then I cry some more. By the time I finally manage to stop, I've no idea how long we've been sitting there.

'Charmain,' she tells me, 'you're suffering from stress.

I'm going to sign you off work for two weeks to begin with.'

My stomach gives a lurch. What about all the things on my to-do list? But then I feel a big wave of relief. The pressure won't be there any more. So often I assess the needs of others; maybe right now, *I* have needs that have to be attended to. 'Okay,' I say. 'Okay.'

She gives me the sickness certificate and mentions starting counselling, but not until I've rested. Just deal with the present, she tells me, don't go worrying too far into the future. We'll be taking this one step at a time. 'Okay. But I can't be off work too long,' I tell her. 'There's so much going on.'

'You're not fit to be in work right now. We all have our limits. There comes a time when none of us can take it any more. To be honest, you're close to having a break-down.'

'Okay,' I say again.

'It's not okay. You don't need to keep saying that. You don't have to be okay all the time, Charmain.'

• • •

When I was a little girl, Bonfire Night was wonderful. We lived on a council estate in Sydenham, south London, and each year the parents put on a small firework display for the local kids – nothing major, but enough to get us really excited. I loved the hissing and shrieking as the rockets shot up into the sky, the crackle of the sparklers in our

175

hands when we were big and brave enough to hold them. And best of all, I remember the feeling of belonging. This is how I grew up knowing that council housing doesn't have to be a bleak or depressing place to live. My community was friendly and people looked out for one another. It was somewhere I'm proud to come from.

But we were a Black family, and life was more complicated for us. My parents came to England from St Vincent in the West Indies. 'No Blacks, no Irish, no dogs' – those were the signs that some landlords hung in London in the early sixties. It was hard for people of colour to get housing. Well-qualified Black professionals found it embarrassing to go to the Labour Exchange and take whatever work they could. They found they were stuck in low-paid jobs, forced to do long hours to make ends meet.

My family lived in one room in New Cross until I was seven, but lots of people I knew lived just like we did. Some people thought New Cross was a rough place – a ghetto – but as kids, we weren't aware of any of that. My parents' generation weren't complainers and they didn't share their feelings with their children. They got on with it. My mother made our home a lovely place, however small it was. As a trained seamstress, she made sure her daughters were always well dressed, and we never felt poor or deprived in any way. Thanks to the example she gave us, we didn't feel ground down by poverty or hardship.

But even with her friends to support her, I think life was hard for my mum in cramped, chilly London. Back in

St Vincent, her father ran a successful business, but now she went on foot to Deptford Baths to bathe us because at home it cost two shillings in the meter for hot water. Before she put us in the tubs, she'd scour them with Dettol, and always lay a bath mat on the floor.

As the eldest, I was taken to the launderette to wash our clothes while my dad stayed at home with my little sisters. Mum would always buy me a packet of crisps with a tiny sachet of salt in it, and I sat happily crunching on them in the steamy warmth listening to the throbbing of our tumbling clothes in the machines and the voices of our neighbours chatting. It was my special time with my mum and I loved it. But I wonder now what that was like for her, and how her dream of life in England must have jarred with the long hours on her feet, with the low-paid work, with so much effort and so little respect. But whatever my mum was going through, she guarded her feelings and stored them out of sight. A lot was being kept from me, and I think this might be the reason that my memories of that time are so often in monochrome. It's hard to recall any colours in the streets.

My happiest memories are of Margaret, my very first best friend. We always walked back from school together, both of us with our hair in ponytails tied with a ribbon. Our mothers would take bets on who'd lose their ribbon first. I loved those walks home through the streets of New Cross, giggling with her while our mothers were chatting behind us.

Then in 1967 we left New Cross and moved into a council

house in Sydenham – and life was transformed. On moving day, my sisters and I chased each other round and round our new home, tearing up and down the stairs giggling and squealing and singing, enchanted by the echoes in the empty house. This whole estate had just been built, and I was just in awe of the place. Huge spaces! Communal gardens for everyone to share! So many rooms! A toilet downstairs! And, unbelievably, another toilet upstairs in the bathroom!

It was Mum who'd done the legwork. She filled out the forms, trekked back and forth to the council, made sure that our application was in order. She was the one who elevated our family out of one room. But the house would still be counted as my dad's: only the man's name appeared on the tenancy. That's just the way it was – unfair and sexist, with the father automatically regarded as the head of the family.

'Who do we share this bathroom with, Mum?' I asked her on that very first day.

'Nobody!' she said, and I could hear all her pride and relief that her foot-pounding to and from the town hall had paid off. 'Nobody at all. This is ours!'

'So I don't have to have a bath with my sister now!'

'Well, I don't know about that, Charmain,' Mum answered. But she was smiling as she said it.

We'd left a mixture of backgrounds behind in New Cross, where no one even thought – at least no child did – about skin colour. But in Sydenham, it wasn't quite so simple. We were the last ones to move in, and the only Black family.

We arrived during the summer holidays and I started my new school in September. I didn't notice at first that all the other children were white, except for Billy, who was mixed race. But then a boy called Simon started saying nasty things to me.

'Does your family live in a mud hut?' he asked me on my second day of school. A couple of the other children giggled and he liked that. It was the start of a load of other questions I couldn't answer and didn't understand at all. Why would this boy ask me about Africa? I didn't even know where that was. I was born in Greenwich.

'Are you from the golliwog tribe?' 'Do you wear a grass skirt?' 'Are you a jungle bunny?' I was really confused, but I saw that even mixed-race Billy was laughing so I tried to laugh too. Then a girl called Carol, who I didn't like quite as much as Margaret but who was definitely turning out to be a really good friend, pulled me into a corner.

'Charmain!' she whispered. 'You need to stop laughing! It's not funny. He isn't being nice. He's making jokes about you being Black.'

It was my first moment of understanding that somebody saw me as different. That I face prejudice. I looked around my school with new eyes and saw that almost every other child was white. There were so few kids there who looked like me. Suddenly I wanted to go back to my old school, to New Cross, to my friends who were nice to me. I wanted to walk home with Margaret again, talking and laughing about our day. What began as an exciting adventure was turning into torment. I wondered if I could wash my black skin off to make Simon stop saying all these things to me. I even tried to do it, but my mum found me crying in the bathroom and asked me what was wrong. I could tell she knew already.

'Charmain!' I still remember the fury in her voice. 'Now you listen to me! You be proud that you are Black! There's nothing wrong with you. Nobody but nobody is better than you and you are not better than anybody else.'

'But, Mum, I want Simon to stop! How do I make him stop?'

There was no doubt at all in her voice as she answered. 'Next time this nasty boy says anything to you, you get something very hard and you hit him on the head. That's the only way.'

'Okay, Mum.'

Now a West Indian mother is scarier than the police – you never go against her, not ever! – but I must have looked unsure because she added: 'And if you don't, Charmain, I will deal with you.' She was telling me I didn't have a choice.

Simon sat behind me to my left in the classroom. When he'd said the nasty things, the other children had heard him and our teacher, Miss Miller, had heard him too, but she'd never tried to stop him. So the next time he said them, while Miss Miller was writing on the blackboard with her back to the class, I got up from my chair with my mum's words in my head, marched up to the front, picked up the heavy wooden board rubber, marched right back and hit Simon with all the force I had. The board rubber made a really loud crack on the top of his head, and of course he started bawling. I wasn't scared by what I'd done. I just went back and sat down.

'Charmain!' Our teacher looked astonished. 'What do you think you're doing?'

'My mum said that if anybody was being nasty to me, I must get something hard and hit them.'

Miss Miller made me stand up and slapped me on the leg. She didn't say a single word to Simon. It wasn't just my leg that was stinging; this was my first real example of injustice. Mum was furious when I told her that night, and the next day she came along to school with me to talk to Miss Howard, our headmistress. I sat in a chair outside her office feeling secretly pleased. *Miss Howard, you are going to get what I get when I'm naughty...*

'My daughter will carry on hitting this boy as long as he goes on calling her names, as it's clear you're not doing anything about it,' my mum told her firmly. 'No one has the right to do that to her! And another warning: if any teacher hits my child again, I will be back here to see you about it.' Whatever the headmistress said, Mum didn't give an inch.

I had to hit Simon one more time, and then he stopped. The school must have spoken to his parents. But the teacher had heard him all those times before and she hadn't intervened. He didn't stop what he was doing until I showed I wouldn't take it. It all came down to me, and I never forgot that. It built up a fight in me – a fight that's still there.

My childhood innocence was changed by the prejudice of adults. It was changed by Simon's parents, who taught him how to use the words he did. It was changed by Miss Miller, who somehow thought those words didn't matter. It was changed by Billy's parents, who allowed him to laugh along with the insults and try to get acceptance any way he could. I'm lucky that my mum wouldn't teach me to do that.

To this day, I still stand up for the underdog. I really don't like bullies. If they come for you, I will fight your cause. I'll fight the cause of my residents, my friends, my co-workers, the members of my union. I'll write letters, send emails, go to meetings, speak up even when it's awkward and the people in the big chairs in the boardroom would rather that I didn't. To fight for the people who haven't got a voice is the deepest instinct I have. It's the root of my passion for my work. My goal is to make each estate I manage the best that it can be. I want to create a peaceful and dignified environment for everyone who lives there.

• • •

In the end, I'm on sick leave for four months. There's one day, two months in, when I go back because I've been invited to a meeting with HR. They're offering me support, but the minute I get into my car to drive to the office, my headache starts. By the time I get there, the pain is blinding me. It clears away the moment I leave. It's definitely a sign that I'm not ready to return. Eight weeks after that, I'm back in Dr Panton's office.

'I'm okay,' I say to her. 'I can think now. I feel like I can breathe. Actually, I'm getting a bit bored.'

'Hmmm,' she says. 'I'd still suggest you give it two more weeks.'

But I've already decided that this is going to be my last doctor's appointment. I rang the office in Meeting House Lane a few days ago and suddenly I'm wanting to catch up with everything, to get back into it, to know what's going on. The big restructure is complete now, my colleagues tell me. And there's another piece of news: Southwark Council has taken the eleven of us who were income team leaders and put us all back into housing officer roles.

I'm so disappointed they have done this, and I still feel that way – I always will. I wanted to get on in my job, to be promoted, to become the best that I can be. But it's never quite happened in the way that I would like. I wonder if it's because I'm a union rep? Does management see me as a troublemaker? But then I think about my tenants, my estates, all those people and their problems that need sorting out. They're the ones who matter, and I can't wait to get stuck in. That's the moment when I really know I'm better.

'I've got to go back *some*time!' I tell Dr Panton.

I can see she's still reluctant, but this is my decision.

'All right, then. You're cleared to start on Monday. But my recommendation is a phased return. Get back to full-time gradually. And if you feel the way you did before, even for a moment, you need to come straight back to see me.'

'Cheers,' I say. 'I will do. I promise. Anyway, they've told me I'm getting a quiet patch to ease me back in. Nothing ever happens there, apparently.'

'Well, that's good, then,' says Dr Panton. 'A quieter patch sounds ideal. Which one is it?'

'Worcester Grove,' I tell her.

The form that ends my sick leave is lying on her desk. She smiles at me and picks up her pen. If she'd known what was waiting for me on the Worcester Grove estate, I don't think she'd have signed it.

CHAPTER TEN

ROLEXES AND SHIT FLATS

2008

Dear Resident

I am writing to introduce myself: I am the new housing officer responsible for the Worcester Grove Estate. I would be grateful if we could meet in order for me to introduce myself officially to you and to discuss any issues you may have.

Please can you contact me at Peckham Area Office to arrange a convenient time for this to take place.

Thanking you in anticipation.

Yours sincerely

Ms Charmain Bynoe

Housing Officer

The estate cleaners drop my letter through the door of every flat in Worcester Grove on the first Friday that I'm back in the office. I know there are bound to be some issues on my new patch, but at this point I'm expecting a fairly quiet life. When I get back to my desk on Monday morning, I find out just how wrong I am about that. There's a pile of phone messages in my in-tray and a load of calls coming in through the main switchboard. I pick up the first message and dial the number. *Well, here goes.* A woman's voice answers.

'Good morning,' I say. 'This Ms Bynoe from Southwark Council returning your call. How can I help you?' Half an hour later, I lean back in my chair. *Nah, so this is the walk in the park, is it?* I've had five conversations with residents and I've heard the same story every time.

It's about Sharpness Court on Worcester Grove – the place that's meant to be empty? Well, it's bloody not. I seen a load of squatters in there.

It's getting too much now with the squatters round here, and no one's doing anything about it.

I got to tell you – every morning men are showering outside using the cleaners' standpipe in front of Baskerville Court. There's always a pool of soapy water around and they don't even rinse it away. It's the cleaners I feel sorry for – and this is round the time the kids go to school. It's too regular now – who wants to live with that? It's disgusting.

There's music blaring out of the empty blocks next to Baskerville until all hours – specially on a Saturday night. The police don't even bother to come out, no matter how much we call 'em.

I thought that block alongside the old workshop was supposed to be demolished? But nothing's been done and it's getting stupid now. Everyone's ignoring us. Is there anything you can do?

• • •

It's standard to go out and inspect your new patch, and when I arrive it's a peaceful location – well, it all seems peaceful so far. The sun's out and a couple of residents are walking their dogs. I notice how quickly this area is changing as the Peckham Partnership – that's the council plus a bunch of housing associations and property developers – regenerates the north Peckham estate, pulling down the housing that was built here in the sixties and moving residents into shiny new buildings. It's easy to spot Sharpness Court. Once it was connected to the buildings around it by bridges and walkways, but they've all been torn down and bricked off. Sharpness sits there stranded, like a brown concrete island. It's supposed to be uninhabitable now, with no electricity or water. But that's not what those messages from my tenants have been saying.

I walk around and take a closer look. No one's ever lived on the ground floor of these buildings – that's the way they've been designed, with pillars to support the upper levels. There's a small purple hoarding all around them which I guess is meant to stop anyone getting in. I peer in through one of the ground-level entrances and see daylight falling from a doorway that must once have led into the first-floor hallway. But the stairs have been demolished so that no one can get up there, and rubble's piled up everywhere. I think how many rats must be living underneath those bricks, and I step quickly away.

I spot pretty quickly where someone's hacked the electricity. They've rigged up a whole array of cables leading from Sharpness to Baskerville Court. Some of the cables are even wired to the street lights, which is a complicated piece of electrical engineering. *Wow. People are ingenious. You have to admire their tenacity, I guess, except that what they've done is illegal and also extremely dangerous.*

As I'm looking up at the building in the sunshine, a movement catches my eye. I watch in amazement as a young man strolls along the top-floor landing, then disappears through a doorway into one of the corridors. He looks so casual, completely at ease, just like a paying resident. I shake my head and look around as if I'm trying to find someone to agree with me about this. And how on earth did he get up there in the first place?

I've reached the next entrance by now, and I peer inside again. These stairs have been demolished too, but someone has carefully rebuilt them. Rough steps made out of broken bricks and chunks of cement lead all the way up to the first-floor doorway. It looks rickety and dangerous and there's no way on earth that I'd be climbing up there, but in the dust halfway up I spot the pattern from the sole of a shoe. *So this is the way in.*

No wonder I've been getting all those angry emails and phone messages. I head back to the office to find out what's been going on.

• • •

I start asking questions about Sharpness. I send a lot of emails too, but I don't get many answers. My enquiries keep reaching a dead end. I go on pushing, and eventually I ring the council's legal department. Finally, when I tell them what I'm hearing from my tenants, they agree to a meeting. A couple of days later, I'm sitting round a table with one of Southwark Council's senior lawyers and her legal assistant.

'First of all, Charmain,' the lawyer says to me, 'I think we should fill you in on some background.'

'Yes,' I say. 'I'd like that.' *About time*, is what I'm really thinking. 'I don't understand why this building is still there, for a start. Why wasn't it demolished with the others?'

The lawyer and her assistant exchange a quick glance, which I notice. 'Right,' she says. 'So Sharpness was part of the Stage Four redevelopment of the area. The land has been earmarked for a special school.'

'Look,' I say, 'I'm sorry, but are you really telling me that no one's been aware that it's still there? It's a great big building. You can't miss it. And the issues with it are causing a lot of the problems that I've got in Worcester Grove at the moment.'

She clears her throat. 'I can't give you a precise answer as to why this matter has been left so long,' she says to me. 'Let's just say that it's one that's passed its target date.'

All right, I think, *okay. We can all apportion blame and we live in a culture that does that. Someone's ignored this situation, but playing 'he said, she said' won't help put that right. I'm just a lowly housing officer, but I can use procedures to ensure the block gets looked at now and that those responsible ensure something happens.*

'So I've been doing some digging,' I go on. 'It turns out we applied for a Notice Seeking Possession. Except that it expired two years ago. So, surely, we need to get another one? And this time, enforce it right away. Because, look, I've talked to everyone. I went to the council forum for advice about squatters. I went to SASBU. I've told the Police Operations Group all about it. Now I'm here with you. Where's the action on this? I'm feeling like a one-woman band.'

'You're right, Charmain, you're absolutely right,' the lawyer tells me. 'To start with, can you give us an estimate of numbers in the building? How many squatters do you think are living in there?'

I know she's not expecting what I'm going to say next. But I've sent out a second letter to the residents and had some conversations which have been extremely helpful. 'Well, there's 129 flats in the building,' I tell her, 'and I'd say maybe 300 people.'

'Right. Okay.' She's heard things like this before, and she just nods her head.

'First thing in the morning,' I tell her, 'they use the outside tap to wash. My residents have even seen kids with them. The cleaners' cupboards are getting used as toilets.

But that's not the half of it. There's architects living in that building, I'm telling you! The staircases have all been demolished but they've built themselves a new one.'

'What exactly happened to the old staircases?' the legal assistant asks curiously.

'They were pulled down. The idea was to stop people getting to the upper levels. Didn't work, though, did it?'

'Well,' the lawyer says, 'I see what you mean. The squatters are certainly creative.'

'Oh yes. And they've rigged up electricity in there. I've been round at night and seen the lights on. Music systems for parties, according to the neighbours. So that means there's a serious risk of fire.'

There's another pause.

'And something else you need to know,' I continue, 'is that someone's been advertising the squats in the local newsagents and in *Loot*. You know, the ads magazine.'

'You mean like "Friendly flat share, north Peckham, non-smoker preferred, handy for public transport"?' the lawyer asks.

We all have to smile.

'Yep,' I say. 'Exactly like that. So there must be money changing hands somewhere. I bet not everyone who answers realises it's a squat. Then again, perhaps they do realise, but they fancy living there for some reason.'

'A reason apart from not wanting to pay rent, you mean?' says the lawyer.

'Well, one of my residents, first thing in the morning, she saw this guy having a wash from the standpipe outside.

Then later on she saw him again. He'd got dressed and he was wearing a suit – very smart, she said. Little designer backpack as well. And a watch. She thinks it was a Rolex.'

'Hmmm,' says the lawyer doubtfully. 'Yes, well. Her eyesight must be brilliant to identify a Rolex. Did she ask him to roll up his sleeve?'

'She told me he looked like he's working in the City.'

'But what are you suggesting? Why would he be living in a squat? Saving up for his penthouse, is he?'

The lawyer and her assistant both laugh, and I have to laugh too. But for the last few weeks I've been talking to the residents. Whenever I do, I keep on hearing the same story.

'I talked to witnesses who live right across the road,' I tell them, 'and they swear there's a few of them that go off to work every morning. Same time each day, dressed very smart. I'm not sure what's going on.'

• • •

It's the final countdown to eviction day, and I serve a new Notice Seeking Possession on Sharpness Court and stick the notices up at all the building's entrances. As soon as the notice period expires, the legal department gets a fast-track possession hearing, then an outright possession order. When it comes through and an eviction date's been set, I put copies of the eviction order up everywhere. Everyone who's living in there needs to know. Before Sharpness can be demolished, Pest Control also has to go in to bait and trap the rats. If we don't get rid of them before we pull it down, gangs of homeless rodents will be off hunting for somewhere else in Worcester Grove to live.

On 1 September, I'm on site pretty early. It's a hot late-summer morning with bright sunshine, and I watch as a whole bunch of uniforms arrives: police, staff from Repairs, security guys, pest-control officers, assistant contracts officers, estate cleaners, community wardens and police. All the vans and hi-vis jackets start attracting attention.

I know the site well by now and my role is to help the police: monitoring the progress of the operation, answering questions about entrances and exits and making sure they can access all parts of the building. But although it looks official, the vibe of the day is really about helping these people. Whatever their reasons for living as they are, they're about to be made homeless. This situation can't be allowed to go on and I want it sorted, lock stock and barrel, but afterwards all the squatters are going to need support. I've already put up notices giving them advice, and I bring more leaflets to hand out: details of where to go to look for accommodation, and telephone numbers and addresses that will help them if they're homeless.

At 10.30 a.m., the bailiffs go into the building with police back-up. I watch them as they move through the levels, reaching landing after landing as they make their way up. Then the first displaced occupants appear. They're mostly in their thirties and forties. If there were ever kids and families in Sharpness, they must have cleared out already. We hand them the advice leaflets, which most of them accept. Then they start to slowly drift away.

It's been an early start, and by the end of the morning I'm starving so I quickly head off to get a sandwich. When I get back, I'm just in time to see two guys in a different kind of uniform emerging from the building. They're cleaners who work for Lambeth Council, our neighbouring local authority, and they've obviously been living in the building because they've got a load of stuff with them.

'You seen those two?' one of the security team says to me.

'Yeah.'

I don't know what to say, or what to make of it, really. Guys with jobs must have their reasons for squatting. Sometimes people are just desperate. Nobody chooses to be homeless.

• • •

Twenty minutes later, there's time for a catch-up with Lionel from the Southwark Antisocial Behaviour Unit. He's just been inside. 'You ought to take a look in there,' he tells me. 'Some of those flats don't look too bad.'

'Yeah, whatever,' I say. All I want is for this day to finish so that we can get the place secured. How it looks inside is not my priority.

'Some of the flats have been squatted,' he tells me, 'so they look like you'd expect – very basic, pretty rough. But one or two of the others – nice enough that you'd think about a flat share.' He's grinning and I know he's only joking. 'But seriously, there's proper furniture in some of them. Bedding – you know, cushions and stuff. The lights are working. There's a couple that have got music systems set up – speakers and amplifiers. Decent equipment too.'

I watch another squatter coming out of Sharpness Court. He's carrying what looks to me like a very expensive piece of black leather luggage. I wonder what exactly has been going on. Anyway, the operation's nearly done.

'No kidding,' Lionel says, 'the best ones are better than some student rooms I've been in. But then you'd need the bathroom, wouldn't you? That's when you'd change your mind about living there.'

'Oh God,' I say. 'That must be really bad.'

'It's worse than bad. They've got two flats that's used to relieve themselves. To dispose of their bodily functions.'

'Shit flats?' I say. 'Oh, that is minging.' As I listen, my imagination is working overtime. Just the thought of it makes me rub my nose.

'Yep. Everyone's agreed that it's where you do your business, so when you need to… And it keeps it warm and steamy,' he goes on. 'The rats and mice and cockroaches love it.' His voice is matter-of-fact. I know that he's seen worse.

'Enough!' I tell him. 'I don't want to know any more! Anyway, I've just had my sandwich.'

'It's a funny business, really,' Lionel says. 'It was their own little village. Their parish, separate from the rest of the estate. I've not seen anything quite like it. What do you think it's all about?'

'I just don't know,' I say. 'You acclimatise yourself to where you're living, I guess. Did you see anyone wearing a Rolex?'

'Actually, I think I did. There were a couple I saw leaving. One of them had on what looked like a pretty serious Oyster.'

'A Rolex Oyster? For real?'

'I can't vouch for it being real. You sure you don't want to take a look inside?'

A Rolex Oyster and two shit flats, I'm thinking. *How do I get my head round that?*

'Do I want to come in with you and make friends with all the rats, you mean?' I say to him. 'No thanks very much, but I ain't goin' in there!'

'Better than living on the streets, anyway,' Lionel says to me. 'Warmer than outdoors, right? You take whatever creature comforts you can get. We all do.'

I think he's right. Some of those squatters were taking the living piss for sure. They were just there to save money. But some of them were homeless people. Some could afford to be somewhere else; some definitely couldn't. That's how you have to deal with them – as individuals. Everybody's going to have a story.

In the late afternoon, I sign off that the eviction has been completed. There's quite a few locals still hanging around watching, but then our night-time security arrives: dogs, floodlights, 24-hour guards. Nobody's getting back in, and by the time they've done their set-up, the place looks like the Peckham branch of Alcatraz. It takes another five months until Sharpness Court and the adjoining blocks can be pulled down.

• • •

'So, Lanre, I thought you were giving me a really nice estate,' I say to him. 'You know, one that's quiet? To help me get over my stress?'

Lanre just grins.

'To be fair, Charmain, which estate in Southwark did you think would be like that?' he asks.

'So you lied to me!'

We laugh, but I know he has a point. There's no such thing as a quiet life as a housing officer in Southwark. I think that's the moment when I know that I'm happy to be back at work. It feels so good to be doing my job.

• • •

But that's not quite the end of the story of Sharpness Court. Three weeks later, an email from senior management arrives in all our inboxes.

The email lists every individual involved in the eviction, along with plenty of thanks and appreciation for their work: the bailiffs, the Antisocial Behaviour Unit, Environmental Services, Pest Control, legal services, the community wardens, the police. Right at the very bottom, the email mentions me. *'We'd also like to thank Charmain Bynoe, housing officer for Worcester Grove, for bringing this matter to our attention.'*

I read it slowly. Then I read it again. I feel myself starting to get angry.

Three hundred people squatting in a building that shouldn't even have been there and nobody did shit. Not until I came along.

197

I got this started, I did all the legwork, I did all the banging on doors. I went to all those meetings, I kept demanding action, I carried out detailed investigations. This whole thing would still be going on if it hadn't been for me. And now I'm just an afterthought, tacked on at the end. I think it's outrageous – making me a footnote after all the work I've done!

Being overlooked is something that housing officers are used to. Whenever there's a problem, people come to us and ask us what we're going to do about it. So we organise, we mediate, we follow through, we make it all happen – but once the problem's sorted, it's as though we disappear and someone else takes all the glory. Except if anything's gone wrong, of course; in that case, we're still there to act as the scapegoats.

A few weeks later, at the next Worcester Grove Tenants' and Residents' Association Annual General Meeting, they present me with a certificate in honour of my contribution to the works on the estate. I feel really touched by that – it's good to realise the difference I've made to people's lives. Of course, I say thank you. But the 'Well done everybody' email? To be honest, I don't even want to see it. The only thing I do is press delete.

CHAPTER ELEVEN

WHAT DO I DO IF THERE'S A FIRE?

2009

One of the scariest stories I've ever heard was about a roast chicken.

This story was told to me by Desmond, who's a member of the Southwark Council clean team. Desmond and his colleagues don't get enough respect, in my opinion, for the difficult work that they do. They go into empty properties and make them good again, ready for the next tenant. Sometimes somebody has died, and the body might have lain undiscovered for a while. Or perhaps a flat's been used as a drug den or a brothel. Squatters might have lived there without functioning toilets. The team cleans up locations where serious hoarding has taken place, often with infestations of rats and mice and fleas. And they go in after fires, restoring gutted rooms and banishing the trauma with a good scrub before the voids team takes over the job of re-letting the property to a new tenant.

That's what Desmond was doing when he saw the roast chicken. It was waiting in the oven in a fire-gutted kitchen, ready to be somebody's dinner at the end of an ordinary day. When the residents fled in terror, all that was left was the chicken, suspended in time, a family meal that no one was ever going to eat. For Desmond, this showed just how suddenly disaster can strike. He always remembered. He's seen so many sights over the years that he just has to get on with it, like all the members of our clean teams. They can't allow the horrors to affect them – they just concentrate on getting the job done.

• • •

Friday 3 July 2009 is a humid summer's day in Southwark. We're in a temporary office in Springwell Road because of sewage problems: our old office on Cedar was built on underground garages, and all of a sudden the load became too much for the sewers to handle. A backsurge left us walking on sodden toilet paper and unspeakable lumps and we had to be quickly evacuated. This new place is a little bit small, but we're getting on with things.

The office is buzzing. Phones are ringing, keyboards are tapping and housing officers are dealing with too many issues at once, making jokes to keep ourselves going. It's an ordinary day. I've just come off a call trying to sort out an ongoing repair issue for a tenant when I smell smoke. I look around. No one else seems to have noticed: they all just continue with their conversations.

I get up and start walking around our floor, sniffing like a bloodhound.

'What you doing?' Noreen asks. Several of the others look up at me and laugh.

'Nah,' I say, 'but can't you smell that? It's like something's burning.'

Now there's lots more sniffing. My colleagues are starting to notice what I mean. Everybody's walking around, putting their noses close to electrical sockets and trying to identify where the smell is coming from. My line manager, Bernadette, has smelled it too, and she comes out of her office and joins in the hunt. 'It's got to be a computer, or maybe from the server room,' she suggests. I go downstairs to where the customer care and repairs officers sit and find they're doing exactly the same as we are.

But we can't find any explanation, and after a while, we give up. Maybe there's a bonfire somewhere around. We carry on, and ten minutes later I leave the office to make my way home. It's just before 5 p.m. and I get into my car, drive up Springwell Road and wait to turn right into Commercial Way. Traffic's always heavy round here, but this afternoon the roads are at a standstill. Something's going on. I wind the window down, and straightaway the smell of smoke is really strong. Then I hear sirens.

As I edge around the corner, I can see the top of the Lakanal House block directly ahead of me. It looks like a great big blue and white square. Slightly to the left of the building, close to the top, there's an orange slash of fire.

201

Black smoke billows upwards, dramatically darkening that part of the sky. I can't believe my eyes. While I'm stuck in this traffic jam and can't drive anywhere, I grab my mobile from the passenger seat and quickly dial the office.

'Noreen, you know that smell of smoke? It's from the Lakanal!'

'What? Are you sure?'

'I can see masses of smoke, loads of it, man. I've closed my car windows and I can still smell it.'

'Jesus!' Noreen says. I can hear her relaying what I've said to the office, and the voices in the background, all shocked and concerned. 'Oh my God! I hope everyone's okay!'

The traffic jam moves forward and I have to concentrate on driving.

'Noreen, listen,' I say, 'I'll call you when I get home.'

The second I get in, I switch on the TV. The fire in Southwark is right at the top of the news. Although what I saw looked pretty frightening, it's unclear just how serious it is. The reporters who are talking to camera don't have much real information, but there seems to have been no loss of life. On the screen I see crowds of people, Southwark residents, standing around the cordon near the building, shocked and transfixed.

My phone goes on ringing through the evening. It's colleagues and friends, all of us debating what's happened. We hope that no one's been hurt, but all we can do is wait for news. We feel helpless. Of course, there's going to be an inquiry. Residents will have to be rehoused and that will create a lot of work, but it seems that this incident hasn't been too bad and although we're worried and upset, as the hours go by we start to feel relieved. I don't understand until later that in these conversations, we're really just clinging to hope. We want to believe that nothing terrible has happened, that everyone's okay. So that's what we keep saying to each other. We can't acknowledge other, more frightening possibilities.

The next day this changes with the horrifying news that three women and three young children have died in the fire at Lakanal. A faulty TV on the floor underneath them started it, and the blaze spread very fast through the building. As their flat filled with smoke, they called emergency services and were repeatedly told to remain where they were. But the smoke grew worse and worse and the women started to panic. Eventually they all went into the bathroom and tried to block the cracks around the doors with wet towels. That's where they died. The youngest victim was a little girl just twenty days old. I'm absolutely stunned. I sit in my living room and cry for those people and for that little soul who had just come into the world.

Why weren't they told to leave the building at once? It seems insane to tell them to stay, but there's a reason: high-rise blocks like Lakanal were built to high fire-safety standards, with each flat able to contain a blaze. So official advice to all tenants was known as 'defend in place': unless it's your own flat on fire, you close your doors and windows and stay put. The smoke and flames won't spread and you'll be safe until the fire brigade arrives.

At the time the flats were built, that may have been true.

But that was in the sixties. Since then, upgrades have been made. Re-wirings and alterations have taken place. It's hard to believe it, but it seems that no one kept track of the difference this work made. So after a few decades had gone by, were blocks like the Lakanal fire-secure? Was there anywhere safe to go? The stay-put advice to residents hadn't been changed, and that's how six innocents died – because they trusted the advice they were given. Why would they question it?

. . .

Four months after Lakanal, in November 2009, on a construction site in Springwell Road, Peckham, just a couple of hundred yards from our temporary housing office, a fire breaks out at 4 o'clock in the morning. Sparks stream across the road on the night wind, starting fires in the trees and in cars parked in the street. Pretty quickly two blocks of council flats nearby, Meadowbrook House and Ash Court, are burning.

The response couldn't be more different to the one earlier in the year. No one stays in place. Instead, the residents immediately raise the alarm, racing along the landings, banging on each other's doors and shouting to their neighbours to get out. The lessons of Lakanal have been learned by the people in those blocks. They know it's down to them to take action for survival.

My phone rings at around 6 a.m. next morning. As I sleepily reach out to answer, I hear Denise, my manager, shouting for me to wake up. 'Turn on the TV quickly! Go to Sky News!' In my haze, I just do as she tells me. On the screen, I see an aerial view of the dark streets of Peckham. It must be being shot from a helicopter. In the centre there's a bright golden light. For a moment, half asleep, I can't work out what it is.

'It's Springwell Road,' Denise tells me. 'It's on fire.'

'Jesus Christ.' Shock jolts me wide awake. The story is already round the world – Denise herself found out about it ten minutes earlier when a relative in the States rang her because he'd recognised the area where she worked on the TV news. We quickly move past our panic and I get myself together, arranging to meet her in Springwell Road in half an hour. I put the phone down – and two seconds later it rings again. This is how the day is going to go.

Forty minutes later, I've made it to the scene. The streets around the blaze have all been cordoned off. We can't see much, just odd shoots of flame and lots of smoke. I stand there with other colleagues who are also just arriving, staring past the police cars and fire engines. We can't speak, but I know that inside we're all just praying: *Please don't let anyone be hurt.*

'You know our office is right opposite?' I whisper to Denise. 'I wonder if it's burnt down.' We look at each other and raise our eyebrows in unison.

'Yeah, well,' she says, 'better our office than someone's home or their life.'

The winter sun is rising by now, but the cordon stops us from seeing how much damage the fire has caused. As the smoke drifts above us, I find myself thinking of wartime, of the bombs that fell on this city seventy years ago. Maybe next morning it looked something like this. Then our area manager appears and we're told to go to the Baskerville Centre, where all the residents have been evacuated. As we arrive, the Southwark emergency-response-team members have already started putting systems into place. Our top priority is a headcount: is anybody missing? No, thank God. This time, everyone got out. We're just so relieved. Our own office is still behind the police cordon, so a few of us are sent to work in offices nearby and a new base is set up in Cator Street.

It's the start of many sixteen-hour days for our team. First we'll need to sort out emergency accommodation. Some of our residents can go to families or friends, but others need our help finding somewhere to sleep. Then there are the practical problems: how to get people money for food and other basics when their bank cards and cheque books and cash have either been destroyed or are still inside their homes, out of reach. We set up monitoring systems and issue financial support to those who need it.

We have plenty of help, though. It always inspires me to see what the community can do, and the people of Southwark step up. The training centre in Cator Street is our emergency HQ and it's piled high with donations before lunchtime. People keep on coming in all day, and the next day, and the day after that, bringing food, clothes, toiletries, mountains of nappies, toys for children. Local kids bring in their own toys to give to kids from

Meadowbrook who've lost all of theirs. Some of the people who are giving to others don't have much themselves, but they still go shopping in Peckham Primark and arrive with bulging paper bags. We set up groups to arrange distribution, and the forcibly decanted residents of Meadowbrook and Ash Court come regularly to the centre and search for what they need. I'll never forget the help from people outside the borough, either. One couple in London on holiday from the USA comes along to Cator Street with clothes and food that they've bought for our residents. When you see this type of action, it gives you faith in the human race.

There are four of us from the housing team on site, and two more from Housing Options in charge of finding temporary accommodation. I'm totally focused on arranging tenant transfers, so busy that I barely have time to look up from my table. We have staff from the benefits office with us too, to help people with their money, and someone from Social Services. There's also a counsellor for anyone who finds they are struggling. People can seem okay to begin with, and they're trying hard to keep it together while they look after others. Then what's happened will suddenly catch up with them.

We already know we won't be able to rehouse everyone within the boundaries of Southwark. There's too much pressure on our limited housing supply. So our neighbouring local authorities – Lewisham, Lambeth, Croydon, Tower Hamlets and multiple housing associations – help us out. Many of the people we are dealing with are in desperate need. Some of them have lost everything they own, then what wasn't burned has been soaked by the fire brigade's hoses so that most of it is unsalvageable. They'll all need home starter packs once they've found a new place.

The council will get this money back in the end when the insurance on the building site where the fire started pays up. But it's not about the cost – it's the sheer human misery that somebody's carelessness at work has caused. This can't just be entered in a spreadsheet. As I look around the emergency centre, I know that no payout by a company, however generous they're being, is ever going to make up for it.

• • •

'Is there a bag yet from No. 28?' asks Mrs Johnson.

She's a resident who's been assigned to me, a lovely lady who was widowed not so long ago. She lives on the ground floor of Meadowbrook, in the part of the building that took the full fury of the fire. I speak to all my residents daily, and each day they ask me when anything will be brought out from the properties. How soon will they know if any of their possessions have been saved? I tell them that as soon as it's safe, the clean teams will go into the buildings to search. They use numbered bags, and when everything that they can rescue from each flat has been gathered together, the bag will be given to its owners.

Everyone is desperate for their bags. But it's grim when they arrive because they all smell of burning, bringing the stench of the disaster right into the emergency centre. Not every flat is badly damaged, so there's joy and relief when a bag turns up full of possessions. But some residents are presented with a very small bag and realise this is all they have left. They're resigned to the fact that not a lot is saved, but what I also see is that they're glad to be alive.

'I'm not sure, Mrs Johnson,' I say to her. 'Would you like to wait here while I find out for you?'

She nods. She knows that everyone is working as quickly as they can. But for people who are scared that they've lost everything they own, each hour can seem like days. Some residents have broken down in tears, begging me to go up to their flat and look for family photos, jewellery, toys their children love. But I'm not allowed inside the building either. Mrs Johnson seems stoical and quiet and hasn't asked us for any extra help, but these long days of waiting are taking their toll. There's no clear emotion in her eyes and she's holding it together – so maybe that's a good thing. I don't know. Perhaps she has what we'd now call post-traumatic stress. It's obvious that she's in shock.

I go and look at the inventory list to see if No. 28 has been brought to us yet. Nothing is listed. 'I'm sorry,' I tell her. 'It's not here yet. It won't be much longer. It's just that they have to take their time going through each property, to make sure they don't miss anything.'

'Of course,' she says. 'I understand. But, Charmain, there's only one thing I want.'

'What's that?'

'I'm not holding out for all my things to survive. I know how bad the fire was. And they're just things, ain't they?

I'm not silly. I know it's all gone. But it's Brian's – my husband's – wedding ring. I hope I've not lost that. I left it in a drawer in the kitchen. Ever since he passed, I've been meaning to put it on my neck chain.'

I suddenly realise what she's making me think of: those old war films where the husband goes to fight and the wife knows in her heart that she might never see him again, but she's still trying to be brave. He's right in front of her, but somehow she knows she's going to lose him. I squeeze Mrs Johnson's hand. I feel so helpless.

'I hope so too,' I say to her. 'I hope that very much. As soon as the bag from your flat arrives, we'll let you know.'

• • •

'It was the screaming,' Sarah tells me. 'That's what woke me up.'

She's standing by my temporary desk in the Cator Street centre. Her one-year-old daughter is sitting in a buggy. When I smile at the family, the baby beams back at me. But Sarah's other two little girls are pressed very closely to their mother and I notice immediately that they don't smile. They're both silent and pale, gripping tightly to the handles of the buggy. Sarah shakes her head and runs her hands through her hair.

'And the banging,' she goes on. 'The neighbours were all shouting. They woke everybody up. We heard them saying that we had to get out. So I went to the window and straightaway I saw the fire – it was ever so close. I ran into the girls' room and I grabbed them. I couldn't think; I just had to get my kids out.'

I can see she needs to talk, but I stop for a moment. I'm wondering if the girls should be hearing all of this. 'Sarah, can you hold on just a minute?' I head across to where all the donations have been placed and ask where the toys are. There are piles and piles of boxes. I quickly scoop up some dolls and Lego bricks, all of them brand new.

'Here you are, ladies! Look what I've got for you! Would you like to play with these?' I lead the girls to a space at the side of the room, and hand them their new toys. They can't speak, but they begin to investigate. I've also grabbed a soft toy for the baby. As I hand it over, she gives me a huge smile and squeezes it against her chest.

'Thanks so much,' Sarah says.

'No worries. That's much better. Sorry, Sarah. Please carry on. What happened next?'

'So we all ran outside. Just like that. In our nighties. I didn't even think to pick up their shoes. Who does that?' She shakes her head and looks up at the ceiling.

'I'm not surprised,' I say. 'It was an emergency.'

'I'd heard people shouting fire and there was banging on my door yelling for us to get out, and I – I just felt like I was on autopilot. I jumped out of bed and ran into the girls' room and when I looked out of the window, there were flames. Oh my God, they were so high. There were people out there running, they were shouting, helping the oldies out, rushing all over. I just thought, *Get out get out get out* and I got the girls and we picked up coats on our way out the front door. It was like I wasn't even thinking, just, *Get out, deal with everything else later*.'

'Wow,' was all I could manage. What else can you say about something so traumatic?

'And I could see the fire getting closer to the only stair-well we could get to and then my neighbour ran up and grabbed the girls. He just picked them both up while I had the baby and he screamed for me to get down the stairs. It was like we flew. Believe me when I say this: we flew. I mean like Concorde.'

She's staring through me while she's reliving her ordeal. I'm just listening. I'm not a trained counsellor, but I know that she really needs to vent the way she feels.

'Everything just – went just like slow motion. But then suddenly, we were on the pavement, like it only took a second. I don't know, it's hard to explain. But I was still petrified. I was more scared then than when we were still inside. Does that make sense? I couldn't stop shaking, my whole body, even while I was holding my kids. I just kept saying, "Thank God thank God thank God," but then I started thinking, *Oh Jesus, what if?* I mean, how do firemen even go into buildings? How do you make yourself do that? How do you not run?'

I look across at her two older daughters. They're not talking, just watching their mum while they're holding their new dolls.

'And it was really windy.' Sarah squeezes her eyes tightly shut as though she's trying to push the pictures in her mind away. 'They said the fire started because the sparks blew over the road. But they were still blowing! There were sparks all over, just falling from the sky. I thought it was going to go on spreading and set fire to everything.'

'You're safe now,' I say to her. 'You and the girls. You did exactly the right thing. You did great.'

She nods. 'Yeah. We're okay and that's all that matters. But my God, Charmain, I keep seeing it. I just see it again and again. How do I stop thinking about it?'

I don't know what to say. This trauma will stay with her for a very long time. I breathe a prayer of thanks for her neighbours who responded so quickly, woke the whole building and gave everyone a chance. I advise her that she might need counselling, for her and for the girls, and she nods. I let her know that I'll make an appointment for her to speak to the counsellor who's on site.

A few weeks after the fire, as we're trying to cope with all the problems and rehousing issues and the distress of so many of our residents, one of the fire officers asks me if I'd like to visit the burned-out part of Meadowbrook. To start with, I'm not sure. But my tenants keep on asking me questions, and I think that if I've seen what it's like inside the building then perhaps I can answer them better. I agree that I'll do it. A few days later, along with a couple of other housing officers, we meet two members of the fire brigade and head over to the gutted ground floor together. We walk past the shells of flats, no windows, no doors, torn open to the elements. We look through one of the properties into an unrecognisable hallway. Then we step inside.

It's totally silent, freezing cold. The smell hits me first;

it's overpowering. I can even taste it in my mouth. I breathe slowly and look round. It's like a black and white photo – the colour has been burned out of every single inch of every room. I see the springs of a gutted sofa crouched on a living-room floor – no seats, nothing else recognisable at all. The rest of the furniture's a heap of rippled, broken sticks. And everywhere there's dripping as water from the hoses that put out the flames trickles endlessly down from what's left of the ceilings. Somebody's whole life has been reduced to this in minutes.

Despite the suffering and sadness in Cator Street, up until now I've mostly been relieved – that no one died, that people were so on the ball. I know how much worse it could have been. But now as I look, my positive thoughts get overtaken by my horror. I'm struggling not to imagine the heat here, not to hear the terrifying roar of the blaze that's torn these rooms apart. Now I understand how Sarah must feel.

I know I'll never forget being inside these flats. And if – God forbid – there's some awful future fire in a council block, I'll smell and taste the air in this devastated place all over again. I won't need to imagine what it's like. I'll know.

• • •

'No. 28 Meadowbrook's arrived, Charmain. Mrs Johnson's bag. It's here.' A member of the clean team is bringing down a delivery from Meadowbrook House. They know that I've been asking for this one. I hurry over to where the latest arrivals are piled in the meeting room.

'Which is it?'

The cleaner moves a couple from the top of the pile. 'This one,' he says.

The bags are transparent, so I can see straightaway that there's almost nothing in No. 28. But the clean team was told about the wedding ring. They've gone in there to try as hard as they can to find it. There must be a chance. 'It's really hard to find anything. Everything is black,' the cleaner tells me. 'Bad smoke damage. The bedrooms were gutted.'

'I'll phone Mrs Johnson,' I say. She hurries into Cator Street as quickly as she can.

'You were right,' I tell her. 'The ground floor was badly affected. They've not been able to save very much. I'm sorry.'

She hardly seems to hear. She takes the bag from my fingers and reaches into it. I know what she's searching for. I'm holding my breath.

When Mrs Johnson pulls her hand out of the bag, she's clutching something tightly. She peers at it more closely. Then, right in the middle of all this stress and sorrow, her face lights up. She holds out her hand towards me, and now I see it lying on her palm – a wide gold band. It's blackened and a bit bent from the heat, but as she rubs at it gently, a yellow gleam shines through. I realise there are tears on my cheeks – and a big smile on my face.

'Yaay!' I say. 'You got it! You found your husband's ring!'

I'm suddenly so happy. I'm ecstatic. After all the weeks of misery and grief, it's incredible to have this burst of joy.

'Thank God,' smiles Mrs Johnson. She cups the ring between both palms. 'And please say thank you to the people who brought it to me.'

Southwark Council clean team, I think to myself. *What a bunch of unsung heroes. Bless all of you for doing this.* 'I'll pass it on to them,' I tell her.

• • •

'What do I do if there's a fire?' In the weeks and months that follow Lakanal and Meadowbrook, my tenants keep on asking me this question. I know how vulnerable some of them are feeling.

Southwark Council works hard to update its risk assessments. Fire-risk assessment teams are introduced. We do walk-rounds on all our estates, checking that every fire door is modern and fully compliant with the latest safety regulations. These doors must be kept closed at all times, so some of them have to be repaired to make sure that they slam shut. Too many have been damaged by being wedged open over and over again – a few minutes' convenience for someone in a hurry casually swapped for saving lives.

We review all past repair work, making sure that nothing that's been done has affected fire safety. Every building must have a safe area where residents can shelter from fire in an emergency. We check hundreds of draft excluders, which can get worn away with use and allow smoke to pass through. Finally, we give all our residents detailed advice about escape routes, fire safety and exactly what to do if they become trapped. The London Fire Brigade continually works with us, monitoring everything we do.

Communal walkways turn out to be a very big problem. They have to be kept clear of obstructions at all times, so anything that might be a trip hazard in an emergency, or could block emergency services from getting access, is going to have to go. But even after everything that's happened, some residents are struggling to take the new rules seriously. They leave their children's buggies and bikes on their landings, or use the space for storage. I'm even finding statues and shrubs out there. I have to tell it straight: inside your property is for you to decorate, but the communal walkways are for the council to keep clear.

'Can you move those flowerpots!' I instruct one disgruntled resident. She's made a colourful display along the landing outside her front door. 'Twenty geraniums round your door might look pretty, but believe me, it won't look so pretty when they're carrying out a body. You have twenty-four hours, thank you!'

She'll also be reminded of the deadline in a letter. As housing officers, we're forever writing estate and block letters informing residents about what they are and are not allowed to do or not do, reciting their condition of tenancy. We need our tenants to work with us – to help us to help them. Council rules might seem a waste of time to them, but what if Sarah had been running with her daughters out of their flat in Meadowbrook and the hallway had been blocked with flowerpots? What if there'd been bikes in their way? Would she have got out then?

• • •

'Mr Ali,' I say, 'we're doing fire safety checks in this building. It's very important that everybody follows the rules, and the conditions of your tenancy state you must get permission from the council to install metal grilles. You have a multi-secure door fitted here, so this flat is very well protected. You can't get permission for a grille.'

Mr Ali looks suspicious and upset. He's in his late sixties and lives by himself in Shakespeare House. He's a quiet, anxious man, and I know that he worries a lot about his personal safety. That's why he's fitted these expensive metal grilles not just across on his front door but also on the windows of his first-floor flat. He's not the only resident who's done it. At least, I think to myself, Mr Ali's grille is on the outside and it's visible. Some tenants have had them put on the inside so there's no way to know that they're there. I know it makes them feel safe, but it's really very dangerous: the council's multi-secure doors are hard to break into, but imagine if the fire brigade was trying to get access to rescue the occupants and right behind the door there was another obstruction. That's life and death right there. So now I have to find them, and every single one has got to go.

'Mr Ali,' I say to him firmly, 'if there's a fire, you need to be able to escape. These extra gates and bars that you've put on, they could stop you leaving your flat quickly if you need to.'

'No, they wouldn't, Charmain,' he replies just as firmly. 'I can unlock this gate very easily.'

'I'm not sure you could. If there was a fire in the night, it would be dark. There could be a problem with the power, so the lights might not be working. There'd be smoke. You might just have woken up. You'd be confused.'

He gives a sigh, as though I'm being a bit stupid. 'No, no,' he says decisively. 'It would be quite easy for me to unlock the grille. I keep the key right by the door.'

'But, Mr Ali, you might not have very long to open it. It wouldn't be like unlocking it when you go out to the shops. A fire would be a very scary situation. You could easily drop the key, or lose it.'

He's still not persuaded. He goes on shaking his head. 'I am not going to lose the key, Charmain.'

I'll have to spell out the problem here. 'Mr Ali, if there was a fire, it would get very hot. The bars could melt, and it could stop them opening. You might find that you're locked in.'

He hesitates. He's frightened by that thought. I don't like scaring him, but he has to understand the reasons for this rule. And at least he's willing to talk about it. Mr Landesman, four floors above him, won't listen to anything I say. His wife stands just behind him, nodding her head and providing him with back-up.

'I'm not takin' this gate down!' Mr Landesman pronounces firmly.

'No, babe!' says Mrs Landesman heatedly. 'You tell her, babe!'

'It's our right!' He's raising his voice to a bellow. 'We paid for these gates! This is for our personal security! The council can't stop the burglars and druggies in the block!'

'No, they can't, babe!' says Mrs Landesman. 'The council don't do nothin'!'

'So our gate stays put!' Mr Landesman nods his head as though the matter is agreed. 'You can't force us to remove it!'

'Look,' I say, 'you and your wife could die if there's a fire and you can't get out. And your grandchildren come to see you sometimes, don't they? What if there was a fire while they were here?'

'We can open this gate! We can get out if we need to!'

''Course we can, babe!'

'Mr Landesman,' I say, 'you need to understand what a fire would really be like.'

That's when I get a memory – only for a second, like a weird mental shutter-flash. It's the image of the gutted, blackened living room at Meadowbrook House. I hear the drip of the water running down. It makes me shudder. I know what fire is like – what fire can do.

'Listen, both of you,' I say to them. 'In a fire, it would be dark. Very dark and very hot. Lots of smoke. You couldn't breathe, you'd be coughing, your eyes would be watering, you'd be panicking. It wouldn't be as easy to open the gate as you think.'

'Rubbish!' shouts Mr Landesman. 'Anyway, I'm a lease-holder, not a council tenant! This place is mine! I'm not takin' it down!'

By this time I'm losing my patience. Southwark Council is still the freeholder of all our blocks, even when units have been bought under Right to Buy. If you own the leasehold, that's your choice and you're certainly respon-sible for your flat, but the council still looks after the building. One of the conditions of your lease is that you have to ask the council for permission to make changes to the structure of the building. And if you're asking to install a dangerous obstruction that could prevent your escape in a fire, we're going to say no.

'Mr Landesman, did you at any time ask Southwark Council if you could install this security grille?'

He glares at me. We stand there in silence. Even his wife can't find a way to jump in. 'So, I guess you didn't. There's certainly nothing on your file. And if you acted without permission and something unfortunate were to happen, I'm afraid your leaseholders' insurance would be void.'

He hasn't thought of that. His face falls. 'You are a leasehold tenant, not a freeholder, Mr Landesman,' I tell him. 'And the council has a duty to keep you safe in this building, which it owns.'

'Anyway, I'm gettin' legal advice!' he mutters.

'Quite right, babe!' Mrs Landesman is looking daggers at me. 'We'll get a solicitor!'

'That's your prerogative,' I tell them. 'But when you go

to see them, make sure you take your lease. Then the solicitor can explain it to you in detail.'

The Landesmans are furious. But as housing officers we have a duty of care to protect our tenants – whether some of them want to be protected or not.

. . .

In the weeks following the Meadowbrook fire, the pressure of work gets to me sometimes. Since I've been working at Southwark, my daughter Indya has known that when I arrive home each night, I have to be left alone to decompress. 'Watch four cartoons, baby,' I used to tell her, 'and then I'm all yours.' I'd sit in the kitchen, smoke a fag, drink a cup of tea and empty my mind. Then, once I was feeling more like me, I could listen while she described her day at school.

As we're dealing with Meadowbrook, Indya's fifteen. She helps so much by just asking how my day's been. She's at an age to get it, although of course I can't tell her the exact issues I'm facing. She'll sit and chat about nothing in particular, and it diverts my thoughts and gets me back to me.

After all these years of working for the council, with everything we have to do and hear, I keep thinking that it's taken a long time for anyone to notice the effects on housing officers' mental health. Today there's more help available, but in the past this simply wasn't thought of. I've been told that members of the public think that all we do all day is drink tea and shuffle paper and tell jokes. If only that was true. In reality, whatever we go through, it's our families who get the fallout. I wish this was more widely understood.

• • •

In the early hours of 14 June 2017, a fire breaks out on the fourth floor of a council tower block in west London. It's caused by a malfunctioning fridge. I wake up around 6 a.m. to the sound of my phone ringing. 'Charmain?' I hear the voice of my friend Sharon. 'Turn the TV on.'

'Why?' I ask blearily. 'What's happened?'

She can't find words to answer. 'Just turn it on,' is all she says.

On the screen I see what looks like a *Die Hard* film. That's how unreal it is. Pure horror – an entire tower blazing, twenty-four storeys ground to roof.

'Oh my God,' I say. 'Oh my God.'

My phone keeps on ringing. I speak to friends. Sky, CNN, BBC, YouTube – we watch the clips of the Grenfell Tower disaster again and again. At first I'm hardly thinking, just staring in shock as the fire starts low down then shoots up the walls of the building, moving incredibly fast. I see people in the windows near the top waving and calling for help as flames roar all around. I see fire officers going into the inferno to try to reach them. I see chaos.

As my brain kicks in, all I can think is: *How could this happen? How has it spread so quickly? Oh my God.*

• • •

It was the cladding.

In the weeks that follow the Grenfell disaster, local authorities up and down the country have to assess their housing stock. In Southwark, we're no different. How many other homes in the UK are covered with dangerously flammable materials? Councils that own buildings like these are plunged into a financial and public-relations crisis.

What we do have in Southwark is expertise. We've dealt with the fires at Lakanal and Meadowbrook, so our emergency teams and our strategic head of service are invited to advise Kensington and Chelsea, the wealthy west London borough where Grenfell Tower stood. I hope their deep pockets can help them sort things out, although they didn't stop the fire from happening in the first place.

Gradually, I feel the ripples from Grenfell starting to spread. The blazing tower was a shocking sight for anyone, but for people living in council high-rises, it has brought fear. As the days pass, this fear seems to build. Southwark starts to look in more detail at our towers, responding to our residents' concerns. It does checks on our four high-rise buildings, which are all on the Hanbury estate in north Peckham: Broomhurst House, Sagefield House, Aberdeen House and Churchfield House.

A few days after Grenfell, I've booked some annual leave. I've nothing special planned – just some chilling out, laying on my settee watching old films. On the last day of my break, the phone rings. It's Denise.

'Hi, Charmain. I know you're still on leave, but can you get to the Hanbury, please.'

'What, now?'

'I said please. It's important.'

'Okay. But only because it's you,' I say to her. 'See you soon.'

What on earth's happened now? This better be good. I haven't even had dinner yet, Jeez…

• • •

When I get down to the Hanbury estate, I find commotion. The community centre is full of managers and plenty of other people I don't recognise. What's going on? I head inside and find Denise and my area manager.

'What's occurring, then?' I ask. Denise gets straight down to business.

'Issues have been identified in the four towers. We need to be on site while these issues are identified and appropriate resolutions are found. There has to be a 24-hour safety presence.'

Of course I get how serious this is, but what I'm thinking right now is, *I'm hungry*. 'And you called me here why?' I ask her. I probably sound flippant, but this place is packed with people who work for Southwark Council. Why do they need me? But Denise is not fazed.

'There's a need for housing officers who are acquainted with this area and you were the first that came to mind,' she replies.

'Okay,' I sigh. 'Okay.' There's clearly no way to get out of this even if I want to.

'Thanks, Ms B,' Denise says. 'Looks like it's going to be a long night.'

'No worries, Den. What do I need to do?'

· · ·

Southwark's four towers – Broomhurst, Sagefield, Aberdeen and Churchfield – aren't covered with the cladding that created that hell at Grenfell. They're sixties builds, more than half a century old, and in the next few days as I'm talking to residents, I keep hearing about the sixties and a disaster at a place called Ronan Point. I don't know anything about it and at first I find it odd that people are talking about it. Then I do some googling and learn that Ronan Point was a tower block in Canning Town, east London. One side of it collapsed following a gas explosion in 1968, when it had only been open for two months. There are some pretty shocking photos of the broken building on the internet.

Still, 1968 is a long time ago. Why, all of a sudden, do I have tenants talking and worrying about Ronan Point as if it was last week? What I'm learning is that the Ronan Point disaster triggered a lot of anxiety about living in tower blocks, and underneath the surface that anxiety's still there. When these buildings were planned, they were futuristic and exciting – new communities in the sky. But they were designed by architects and planners who were never going to live in them, never going to be victims of anti-social behaviour, who would never need to ask a cash-strapped council for ongoing repairs or become the victims of government cuts that the local authority takes the blame for. They were created by people who had choices in life. But for those who have no choice about living in the towers, the sky-cities dream has turned out more like a nightmare, and my tenants are caught in it.

Now everyone is talking about tower blocks and fires. I meet people who are so scared that they want to move right now. 'We're going to have another Grenfell!' they keep saying, and after all those pictures on TV, I really get how they're feeling. This rising panic throws us all into an emergency situation. Denise puts a strong team in place on the ground as quickly as she can. Four housing officers are seconded to be responsible for a tower each, and I get Broomhurst. Anyone who lives in the towers can drop by our temporary base any time for information and reassurance. We put security in place on site, with 24-hour-a-day fire marshals to do inspections on every floor. The buildings have hardwired smoke alarms, but they don't yet have fire alarms or sprinklers, so we knock on doors and patrol every hour on the hour, including through the night. Tenants are kept closely informed about everything we're doing. We send letters out to everyone asking when we can get access to carry out safety checks, and residents can leave their keys with us so that the inspectors can get in if there's nobody at home.

Grenfell Tower fills the news for weeks, keeping the tension very high. In Hanbury Community Centre, it's like working in the middle of a bubbling volcano, with intense emotions everywhere. To start with, we all do twelve-hour shifts, seven days a week. We're more and more exhausted, and I have a headache every day for a month. Gradually, as a better shift system is set up, our punishing hours on duty are reduced.

Most of our residents still don't really want to move, however. It's hard to abandon the place where you've lived for many years. They just need to know that we'll look after them and make it safe for them to stay.

• • •

The issue of safety in the four towers is starting to get political. An activist has arrived in the area. This guy is from east London, not a Southwark resident, but once he's parachuted in he puts himself about and starts asking lots of questions. Many of our residents don't like how he's playing on their fears. There's too much of a circus here already and some feel he's using their lives to make some political point. They also resent the way he's claiming to speak for them, because when our tenants don't agree with something, they have no problem telling us all about it themselves. This is their place and they're a strong and vocal community.

What I'd really like the activist to do is stop stirring up panic in Southwark and go to 10 Downing Street. That's where I see the source of all the problems we're having to deal with. Like all local councils, Southwark's facing round after round of budget cuts and still we keep trying to deliver our services to residents. When local authorities sold many of our homes under the 'Right to Buy' scheme, councils weren't given all the proceeds. We also weren't allowed to build more – and that's why a lot of our social housing stock was never replaced. Now there's not enough to keep up with demand and it's make-do-and-mend all the time.

Southwark is building more new homes, but with over 18,000 people on our waiting list, it still won't be enough. Local authorities have been left to take the public's anger about the housing crisis. The public-sector housing system is struggling and the government is failing us.

Rant over.

• • •

As the weeks go by, the arguments about high-rise safety continue to grow. By now I'm really feeling the pressure. As well as my duties at Broomhurst, I'm still managing my permanent patch. Some other officers have temps in place to cover their workload, but my temp left and he hasn't been replaced. I don't seem to have any choice apart from trying to do both jobs at once, and my backlog of work is piling up.

A big Southwark residents' meeting is held. The local MP comes along, and so does the council's strategic director of housing, Asset Management and the London Fire Brigade. We housing officers attend just as welcomers, to meet and greet our tenants in between covering the shift duties for our blocks. The idea is to keep residents updated with the action that's been taken. But the meeting is full of questions and deep frustration.

'Why did it take Grenfell for you to listen to us?' our residents demand. They thank their housing officers for trying their best to help, but they want to know why it's taken so long to respond to their concerns. I understand exactly why they're saying this – they've seen the images of Grenfell Tower burning and they're picturing themselves and their children caught up in a disaster like that one. In their place, I'd feel the same as they do. But I also think they're blaming Southwark's current housing team, which is trying to level with them and help them, for issues it's inherited from others long since gone. We're not making excuses – we're taking responsibility, involving our residents at every turn and being truthful with them. But in such a fraught atmosphere, it's difficult to bring people together.

The media's not helping. The presence of reporters ramps up the tension even more. They've been around for weeks and I've realised that they're thinking in headlines: what they're really up to is sniffing for the next big story. The housing team starts tensing up whenever we spot them clustering together outside our temporary offices. They come rushing towards anyone they think might stir things up, waving microphones. Some of our residents have them pushed into their faces at bad moments and get angry and defensive.

The second a reporter spots any of us, they dash over and pester us with questions, looking for an off-the-cuff reaction that might make a headline. We wear ID badges round our necks while we're working so that residents know who to talk to, but we decide to take these off when we're coming and going to avoid all the attention. It's impossible not to feel that the press want something bad to happen – a trauma, a tragedy, people's lives torn apart – just to increase their viewing figures. But the frustrated and frightened residents I work with aren't here to sell newspapers.

One day I go out to get lunch while some big story is breaking, and when I get back, I find my way completely blocked. The whole of the Old Kent Road end of Commercial Way is filled with vans with satellite dishes on the roof. *What the hell?* Everybody has to earn a living, but the frenzy of covering the news looks like madness. And at the end of the day, these journalists can all go back to their safe, comfortable homes. So can I, if it comes to that. All my attention and effort is concentrated on my tenants, who can't.

Two weeks after we set up our emergency centre on the Hanbury, somebody smells gas in Broomhurst House. The gas supply for the entire tower has to be shut down, followed immediately by precautionary shutdowns to the other three. Everyone's jittery already, and this makes things much worse. Eventually we replace all gas appliances in the building with electrical ones.

Then one afternoon as we're delivering letters with updated information through people's doors, we hear the smoke alarm going off in Sagefield. *Oh my God, what now?*

It turns out that one of the tenants went to work and left a slow cooker on in their kitchen without enough water in it. The cooker has started to smoke, and set off the tower's smoke alarms. This triggers an evacuation, with the fire brigade on site within minutes. More stress, more panic. The fire brigade, with the help of the housing officer in charge of Sagefield, quickly enters the property and shuts the slow cooker down. At least this shows us that our safety plans and fire alarms work properly!

Nevertheless, it's exhausting to stay in such a constant state of high alert. In my years working for Southwark Council, I've learned a lot about coping under pressure. I find that I have to detach: if you let yourself feel all the emotions that are swirling around you, you stop being able to function. But it still gets overwhelming at times, and I need to vent my feelings to colleagues who understand. The old Cedar office had a backyard which we used as a break-out area. The best thing we could do to handle stress when we worked there was to go outside and scream as loudly as we could. It sounds mad, but that was what we had at our disposal. You could sit there, have a fag, chat, or just decompress. There would be someone to talk to – someone understanding who would get how you were feeling and listen. When we'd let the tension out, we could get back to work and go on acting as though nothing fazed us. Right now, I really miss that yard.

• • •

It's around this time that I start to notice how my attitude to being a housing officer is changing. I used to love my job and take pride in it, in doing the very best I could for every resident. It was such a worthwhile role, making people's lives better, and it was satisfying too, because when I was responsible for something, I could usually see it through to the end. Southwark isn't perfect – because no local authority is – but everyone does their best and I've always been proud of the council and the knowledge and expertise we have within the organisation. Even though I've had my concerns at times, the whole place has felt like a team.

But so much has changed over the years, and it's really starting to show. Working practices have been altered so that housing officers have stopped being estate managers with practical responsibilities and have instead become just sign-posters. Nowadays, when someone asks for something to be done, I pass each request on, and that's all I'm officially expected to do.

Except it isn't. Every part of the council also uses housing officers to help them mediate between them and their service users or outside agencies. So they need us when things are going wrong, but when everything goes right, we're invisible. There's no acknowledgement for our efforts to deal with situations that other departments and council officials have created or are finding hard to control. We very seldom get call-outs or thanks at staff briefings – instead we're ignored, along with our colleagues on the clean team. Getting zero recognition demotivates even the most conscientious employee.

So when the tenant then complains that what they've asked for hasn't happened, what can I do? My power to see things through has been taken away. As housing officers, we still get all the complaints, mind you. We're there, our tenants can see us, they know our faces – and who else are they supposed to blame? Now add to that the abuse and aggression we receive from a minority of residents. A human being can only take so much. And sometimes, I feel that we're not looked at as human.

On safety duty in Broomhurst House, faced with frightened, angry people who don't want to live in an unsafe tower block or burn to death or die of smoke inhalation because the building can't stop it from spreading, my position starts to worry me. I'm not prepared to be a scapegoat after something has gone seriously wrong. I don't want someone's death on my hands. I think about how the residents of Grenfell Tower tried for years to raise the alarm over fire safety in their building. No one paid any attention. Councils need to listen and take action straightaway when their residents tell them that something isn't safe.

• • •

'So what do I do if there's a fire?' My tenants still ask me this, and when they do, I advise them to take the quickest and safest route out. It's only if you can't escape from the building that you should secure yourself – seal the doors with wet towels, open a window to scream for help, get yourself heard and seen. It would be a terrifying situation to be in, but try – if you can – not to panic.

We keep a constantly maintained database of vulnerable tenants in all our buildings who might need help to evacuate: wheelchair users, the sick, those with mental-health problems. If there's a fire, police and fire services use this list to know who they need to get to fast. But most vulnerable people live in safer locations now, not up in towers – unless it's what they prefer.

We also have residents who love their council flats up in the sky far too much to ever leave them. They've fallen in love with watching the clouds go by, and the sun rising and setting across the rooftops of London. I had a tenant with one leg who lived on the ninth floor of one of the four towers. He was offered transfers on many occasions, but he kept on refusing. He wanted to stay and he said that he felt safe. That's his right. We all want to love the place that we call home, and for him, it's his high-rise council flat in Southwark. After everything that's happened, even if it brings an extra risk, he can choose to remain in his tower.

CHAPTER TWELVE

PANDEMIC

2020

It's January, the start of another new year. I'm about to take my annual leave after working through Christmas. On the news, a story's coming through each day from some place called Wuhan in China.

On TV, they're showing us what looks like an abandoned city of skyscrapers out of a sci-fi movie, with all its people forced to stay at home. Everyone's talking about what's going on, but somehow it doesn't seem serious. There's no real feeling of alarm – it's happening somewhere else. I remember the scares about SARS and MERS – those diseases we all heard about a few years ago. *They didn't really go anywhere. It'll be the same this time. I can't see anyone taking this on.*

But this time, the new disease is moving. Slowly, this news story creeps around the world, getting closer and closer to England. It's in Iran, then North America, then

Europe. Italy's hit hard; so many people there are seriously sick that its hospitals can't cope. Suddenly we're hearing that the lockdowns might come here.

As a health and safety rep, I attend meetings with the director of resident services on a monthly basis, and at our January meeting the new virus is on the agenda. We have to ensure the safety of the frontline staff. It's agreed that Southwark will provide all its staff with protection: gloves, hand sanitiser, clothing, face masks. We're worried about our 'work through it' culture, which means people coming into the office when they're ill. A lot of our officers have huge workloads and are scared of being off because of what will be waiting for them when they return. But in a pandemic, 'working through it' could put us all at risk. So we get an agreement that staff with the virus won't have their time off counted as part of their annual sick leave.

Everyone in the council receives regular briefings via our internal information site and our team gets daily updates from our area manager. With all this information coming in, the pandemic starts to feel a bit more real. It's getting like *The War of the Worlds* – not 'if' this virus attacks, but 'when'. We have to be prepared.

In the middle of March, I wake up feeling a bit 'heady'. It's as though I'm coming down with a cold, but somehow it's not exactly like that. It's very strange. There are growing demands for a lockdown in Britain by this time, but the government hasn't announced one yet so I'm off to work as normal. I get ready and I think I'm going to be okay, but when I walk out to my car and the fresh air hits me, I start to get spaced out, like I've had a bit too much to drink. But all I had this morning was a cup of tea. I drive and find I'm having to concentrate hard on what I'm doing. Perhaps it's just that foggy morning feeling when you haven't woken up properly, I tell myself, convinced I'll be better when I get to my desk. Work is just ten minutes away but it feels like the journey's taken an hour when I finally arrive.

One of my colleagues notices straightaway that I'm not my usual self.

'Charmain, you okay?'

'Nah,' I say. 'You know what? I don't feel right. I don't feel like I'm really here. Perhaps I'm getting flu.'

Everyone backs off. If the situation wasn't so serious, it would be funny. I feel like Moses parting the waters as everyone, in unison, takes four steps away from me. 'Go home,' my line manager says to me. 'We don't know what's going on but if you might be ill, I don't think you should be here. You need to go home.'

No one has to tell me twice. As I'm leaving, I hear my colleagues telling me they hope I'll soon be better and I don't have the virus. *Well, you and me both.* I wonder for a moment if I should ask someone to drive me. It's not safe to drive feeling spaced out at the wheel. But whoever takes me would have to be in the car with me, a confined space where the virus could easily spread. Perhaps that's not safe either. It's very early on in the pandemic and it's not mandatory to wear masks yet. So I get in the driving seat and shake my head to clear it. Concentrating hard, I travel slowly home.

The next day, while I'm resting, a friend rings. As we're chatting, he says to me worriedly, 'Charmain, what's wrong with your breathing?'

To be honest I'm not aware of anything, but then, I'm not really listening to myself. 'You sound like it's hard for you to talk. You keep stopping to take in air, haven't you noticed?' he asks me.

I hadn't, but now I do. *Could I have this new disease? Oh bloody hell.* For the first time, I start feeling a bit scared. If I do have it, there's no treatment. I could get really sick. My friend suggests that I call the NHS 111 advice line and I realise I don't want to – maybe I'd just rather not know. But avoiding the problem won't help, I say to myself sternly, so I dial 111 and speak to a nurse. She listens while I describe my symptoms and tells me I sound breathless. Then she says that although there are no tests for this coronavirus yet, I have probably got it. I need to rest, drink fluids, keep warm – and most importantly, isolate myself and see no one for fourteen days so that I don't pass it on.

I do as I'm told. Luckily, my symptoms don't get bad, and pretty soon I start to feel much better. But while I'm isolating in my flat, the news grows worse and worse. On 23 March 2020, Britain goes into full pandemic lockdown due to Covid-19. By the time I'm allowed back to work, the whole world has changed.

• • •

'Mary? Mary! Can you hear me! It's Charmain! *MARY!*'

I'm banging on the tenant's front door as hard as I can. Surely, if she was inside, she would answer. But there's no response, and I'm starting to get seriously worried. It's mid-April and I'm back on duty in Southwark. As much as possible, housing officers are working from home. Routine visits and repair work on our estates have been stopped, but there's no way that our entire job can be done through a computer. We have to keep a close eye on our vulnerable tenants.

The vulnerables lists have been updated and they are our priority. We've targeted those over sixty-five, especially the very elderly, people with medical problems, those with poor mental health and families with vulnerable household members. The ones we're most worried about get phone calls every day, and the rest are divided into groups – some get weekly calls, some fortnightly, some we're pretty sure will be okay and we can call them once a month. We follow up our calls with a visit for any vulnerable person we can't get hold of. We can't go into homes now, even with the masks and gloves and hand sanitiser that are suddenly part of our kit, but it's vital to see them face to face. Just about every day, we update our lists to ensure that no one who needs support is slipping through.

Mary is definitely one of our vulnerables. She's a lady in her seventies living on her own, extremely deaf and with a heart condition, and she's not been answering my calls. Two days ago, I dropped a letter through her door, explaining I was worried about her and asking her to let me know that she's okay, but I've still had no answer.

As I make my way to Mary's, the stillness is amazing. Normally on this estate I'd see the druggies and roadmen selling gear. They always chip the moment I appear. But they're gone now and all I can hear are birds singing really loudly in the silence. It took me about half a minute to get here in my car through the deserted streets of Southwark. It's as though there's been some kind of apocalypse. *And perhaps,* I think, *there has. Just not one that has zombies in it. Not like we've been shown in all those disaster movies. This one's real.* It's a beautiful spring morning with a cloudless blue sky, but the thought makes me wary. *This is just too weird.*

It has an upside, though. Every week through lockdown, all Southwark's housing officers conduct in-person estate inspections to pick up any issues – anti-social behaviour, fly-tipping, rough sleeping – that would normally get spotted while we're out and about. We call them visual audits. Right now, I've noticed such a big reduction in these kinds of problems that I find myself wondering why it can't always be like this.

As I turn the corner, I meet Alphonse from Southwark's clean team, removing some rubbish from the bottom of a staircase. It's a health-and-safety hazard – what if there was a fire and we had to evacuate the area? – and a tenant has reported it. Our clean teams can't work from their living rooms either – they still have to be out and about. I watch Alphonse hoisting the heavy bags onto his shoulder and slinging them into his van. When he sees me, he gives me a wave. 'Everything okay, Charmain?' he calls.

'I'm good, how are you?'

'Never seen the place like this, eh? It's a ghost town!'

'I can hardly believe it!' I answer truthfully.

I reach Mary's door and knock. No reply. I knock again, a lot louder. Finally I bang on it really hard, so that I'm sure she'd have heard me by now if she was in. *Which means that she's not there, or she's too ill to get to the door – or… nope. Not gonna go there.* I just need to get into her flat.

I call the emergency repairs manager to inform him that we may need to do a forced entry. Then I call the Safer Neighbourhoods Team to ask the police to meet me at the property. This is urgent, I tell them; it needs to happen today. The team arranges to meet me back at Mary's front door at 4 p.m. If there's still no answer then, the police and Southwark Council's chippy will break in and find out what's going on.

• • •

'Did you hear about Vincent?' asks Denise.

'No,' I say. 'How's he doing?'

The housing team is in a meeting on Zoom. We've had to get used to talking to each other through screens pretty quickly in the first few weeks of the pandemic. 'It's bad news, guys, I'm afraid,' she goes on. 'I'm sorry to tell you that Vincent passed last week.'

Vincent? I can hardly believe it. Every face in the boxes

on the screen just looks stunned. That lovely guy, a gentleman with real class about him, only in his fifties. Somehow finding out about it online makes his death even more of a shock. He was one of our security guards. I hear my colleagues over Zoom: 'Oh my God.' 'Vincent from Gilbert Street? Seriously?' 'Oh my God, that's awful.' 'How did it happen?'

Then someone asks, 'Den, was it Covid?', and I see Denise nodding her head.

'Any idea how he caught it?'

'Not really,' she says. 'But there's going to be a collection, and the council will be sending flowers.'

She's got to be joking, I think. *So this virus is here now, killing someone I know, someone I worked with.*

Up to this point, I've known there was a risk and that we have to take precautions, but I didn't really think that it could get us. Now it hits me that what's happened to Vincent could happen to anybody. I hadn't comprehended it before. Even when I caught Covid myself and I felt a bit nervous, I didn't believe that I might die. But this kind, polite, gentle man, who was only three years younger than I am, who worked out at the gym to keep himself in shape… this virus has killed him.

Vincent's is the first Covid death I hear about, but it's not the last. There are further announcements at work. Thabo in Repairs. Delroy in Environmental Services. Victorine in Social Services. And as I'm seeing the faces of the dead on national TV and hearing their names, I'm starting to notice something. Just like my colleagues in Southwark, almost all of them are people of colour.

Right at the start of the pandemic, when we saw pictures of doctors and nurses who had died, I was thinking, *Well, that's terrible, but it kind of makes sense. Medical staff are exposed to the virus all the time as they're caring for their patients.* But Vincent wasn't caring for patients. Neither was Thabo. Neither was Victorine. They were ordinary council workers, doing their jobs, dealing with members of the public. And that's how they caught Covid and died.

Although we've been told from the start of the pandemic that Covid is all about equal opportunities and anyone can get it, I don't think that's true. It's starting to become obvious that risk is all about the kind of job you do. If you sit behind a desk, if you can work through screens, if you live in a big house where you can distance easily from others, you'll be able to stay safe. People in jobs like that are usually white. But Southwark's cleaners, security guards, social workers, carers, nurses, housing officers and environmental officers can't set themselves apart to keep safe. As frontline workers, there's no way we can shelter from the virus. Dealing with residents of Southwark face to face every single day is putting us at risk. And these kinds of workers are usually Black.

As soon as we understand what's happening, we start to ramp up health and safety to protect our colleagues – and ourselves – as much as we possibly can. Southwark Council already has good pandemic policies which apply to all its staff, but we also need personal risk assessments, because not every job is equal in the risk that it brings. We review every role and give each one a High, Medium or

Low rating. Just about every Black frontliner is deemed to be high risk and must be provided with PPE, sanitiser, goggles and face shields. We draw up working practices to allow our staff to distance – which means keeping two metres away from other people in all circumstances. Wherever possible, people can work from home. Southwark is supportive and all of this is quickly put in place. I'm appreciative of that.

When it's done, we feel that we have as much protection as possible in the ongoing situation of being a vulnerable group. Our basic vulnerability, however, can't be changed. So we have peace of mind, but also not quite peace of mind. At least we know that we've done everything we can.

• • •

All this gets me thinking. Many of us are children of the *Windrush* – the famous ship that brought the first generation of West Indian workers to this country in 1948. They'd been invited by the British government to do vital jobs and help with post-war regeneration. But it's well-known now how the *Windrush* arrivals were made to feel. Instead of being welcomed, in many cases they were met with racism and discrimination.

As their descendants, we carry a contradiction within us. Our parents always told us that we were West Indians. They were proud of where they came from, but we still saw and felt the stress they lived under every day because of the way Britain acted towards them. Now, seventy years on, our own children never question that they're British. My generation is caught in the middle, in between those two, and some of us end up just feeling half and half. Others feel more West Indian or African than British because that's what we've been told that we are, over and over again. I mean – when we're always getting asked, 'Where are you from?' or 'No, but where are you *really* from?' – how are we supposed to feel, right? The people who are asking that question don't say: 'Where does your family originate?' That would be a very different matter.

Now this pandemic is shifting our sense of belonging yet again, making us uneasy. It shows us we're not safe here, even though – just like our parents came to be – we're the vital workers who keep the country going.

• • •

For tenants on low incomes, the start of the pandemic is a really scary time. When they try to do their weekly shop, they're faced with empty shelves. There's a national panic about toilet-paper shortages so everybody's talking about that, but other things are vanishing as well: staple foods like tinned tomatoes and dried pasta. The news is full of stories about panic-buying and stockpiling – but you can only do that if you have money in the first place. People who shop from week to week don't have a pile of stuff at home to live off if the supermarket runs out of food. Before the pandemic that was nothing to worry about, but now life feels much less secure. Then, when lockdown starts, many of our elderly residents are too frightened to go to the shops anyway.

'I don't understand those people stockpiling, Charmain,' says Babs. We're on her weekly phone call, discussing the pandemic madness that's suddenly everywhere. She's a vulnerable tenant in her seventies, lively and upfront. She wasn't born around here; she migrated from north London when she married Steven in her twenties, and they're a really lovely couple, devoted to each other. When I remind her that she's a Peckham girl now, she laughs at me, but I think she's resigned to it: most of her life has been in Southwark and I don't think she'd ever leave. These days she has mobility issues, arthritis in all her limbs, high blood pressure and diabetes; our joke is that she's held together with superglue. She tells me that she rattles with all the pills she's got to take. Really I'm in awe of her because she's so bloody strong.

'What's wrong with 'em?' she goes on. 'I mean, how much toilet paper can one butt use?'

I have to laugh at that, and she laughs too. 'But they're selfish, you know,' she goes on. 'Buyin' all that stuff. They're not thinkin' about people like me and Steve. It's so disheartenin' when he goes to the supermarket and all them shelves are empty. We're not in a war.' She lets out a long sigh.

'I get it,' I say. 'Loads of my elderly residents are scared when they see the empty shelves. And did you see the news with that nurse who finished her shift and then couldn't get her shopping? Oh my God, I felt for her. Trying to save people's lives and then she goes to the shops and she can't get any food.'

Babs and I usually try to put the world to rights on our calls. Right now, it feels like the world needs a lot of work doing to it. She confirms that she and her husband are fine and that their son who lives just outside London came up at the weekend with bags of shopping. Babs was sad that he couldn't come in, but at least he dropped the bags at the door.

'It was so nice to see him,' she says, 'but it was hard not to give him a hug.' I can hear the disappointment in her voice. There are so many people missing loved ones right now. But she shakes herself out of it and ends the conversation by telling me that I need to take care of myself.

I always enjoy our conversations. There's something heroic about the calm common sense of the older generation. I've noticed an interesting thing about the pandemic: the way that my most senior residents handle it is different. Although they're in more danger from the virus than the younger people around them, it's hard to make them scared. They face it with an old-school, 'let's just get on with it' attitude. It must have been like this in Southwark in the Second World War – air-raid sirens sounding in the night, people hurrying to take shelter, the feeling you get when everybody's in it together. Back then, its people were fighting against an enemy they could see and hear, while this one's invisible, silent, harder to understand. But their spirit of resistance still lives. It's as though it's become a part of Southwark.

'There ain't no bombs droppin'!' Steven says to me cheerfully when Babs hands over the phone. 'All we got to do is stay inside! We can stay in our house, can't we? What's the problem?'

. . .

I'm so worried about Mary that I get to her flat half an hour early. While I'm waiting for the other members of the Safer Neighbourhoods Team, I decide I'll do another welfare visit just around the corner. But as I start to walk away, something tells me to give Mary another try instead, and without being quite sure why, I change my mind and go back.

I stand on her front doorstep, really stressing out by now, imagining all sorts. *Please let her be okay. Let her open the door.* I don't really knock this time – it's more of a policeman's bang. Still no answer. I give it one last try, and this time, I hear 'Hold on, I'm coming.' The door slowly opens, and Mary peers out at me. She's pale and looks really out of sorts, but at least she's alive.

'Mary!' I exclaim. 'I've been trying to get hold of you!'

I realise that she can't hear what I'm saying. I wait for a minute while she struggles to turn her hearing aids up.

'I said, I've been trying to contact you. You know you're on our vulnerable list, don't you?'

'Oh,' she says. 'Yes, well. I am fine.'

'Didn't you hear me knocking on your door?'

'Did I hear what?'

'Me! I was knocking!'

'Oh. Well, I was in bed,' says Mary grumpily. 'I didn't

hear you. These –' she taps her hearing aids '– these aren't working good.'

'I've been trying to get hold of you. I was scared that you'd collapsed! Didn't you see my letter?'

'What letter?' Mary asks. She frowns. 'Oh, that! Yes, I think I did see it. I just thought, you know, another thing from Southwark.'

It's hard not to feel frustrated with her. In normal times, when she's got a complaint – and she's made quite a few in the past, about some pretty small things – she doesn't find it at all difficult to contact me. But not when it really matters.

'Have you been here on your own?' I ask her. 'Mary, you don't look so good. You're ever so pale. Come on, I'd better call your doctor.'

'No, no, no!' says Mary irritably. 'I've just got out of hospital – with my heart, you know. I've not been home long. I don't want to see any more doctors. My GP came here to do a check-up. The only problem is my hearing aid's not working.'

'Then you need to get new ones.'

'I have. It's all been sorted. I'm waiting for them.' So there's really nothing else that I can do.

'Anyway,' says Mary, 'my daughter's coming up tomorrow to stay with me.'

'Your daughter?' I'm surprised to hear this. As far as I know, she's been estranged from her daughter for years.

'She tracked me down at the start of the pandemic,' Mary explains. 'She said she was worried about me.' It's then that she smiles and I see her whole face change. It's as though the pandemic has helped in some ways. It's made people realise that family is what matters most, and when there's an emergency, they face it together. Mary and I talk for a few minutes and she tells me how much her life has changed since she and her daughter have been back in touch. She feels wanted and not alone any more. I've never seen her look this happy, and as I'm listening I'm so pleased for her that I've forgotten all about my irritation. Then I suddenly remember that I've arranged to break into her flat and the Safer Neighbourhoods Team will be arriving any minute to do it.

'Oh God! I've got to stop the forced entry!' I realise that I've said these words out loud.

'Huh? What forced entry?' Mary looks really surprised.

'Mary, we were worried when we couldn't contact you. We thought you might be seriously ill. When that happens, we go to force entry just in case there's someone needing help.'

'Oh. Well, I'm so sorry for putting you through that, Charmain,' she says.

'Don't you worry, my darlin'! It can be stopped. Better safe than sorry! Now you get inside. Just you remember to answer when I call or text, though, do you hear me? And please can you send me your daughter's phone number? I need your next-of-kin details.'

She promises she will and shuts the door. I quickly dial the repairs manager and call off the forced entry. Everybody understands and there's relief all round that she's okay.

All's well that ends well – that's another one of our vulnerable tenants safely accounted for.

• • •

Homeless people are one of the most vulnerable groups in the country, and as the pandemic arrives, local authorities across Britain are trying to get them off the streets. As lockdown begins, Southwark decides to use its four high-rise towers – Broomhurst House, Sagefield House, Aberdeen House and Churchfield House – to house them. That way we'll avoid putting them in close contact in hostels and other shared accommodation where they might spread the virus.

Everyone who lived in the towers has been decanted by now, and they've been standing nearly empty, waiting to be demolished. The only ones left in there are the residents who'd bought their leases: they're either hunting for new properties to move into or they can't leave just yet for one reason or another. So the fire watch has had to continue and the security guards have stayed on duty, and that means the towers are still safe for the homeless. That's another problem dealt with – yet another crisis we've managed to avoid. Best of all, that's some more lives that we've managed to save.

• • •

Throughout the lockdowns, the Safer Neighbourhoods Team has to carry out a number of forced entries in our area. Fortunately in most cases, the tenant isn't there because they've been rescued by relatives or friends. Nobody knows how long the restrictions will continue, and families have decided they'll be safer together. But we're also finding people on their own, seriously ill or just ever so confused about what's happening.

As lockdown goes on, we're getting more and more concerned about our vulnerable residents. The pandemic's making everybody anxious and those who already have mental-health difficulties are the most at risk. But without face-to-face contact, it's hard to monitor them. One thing I notice is my phone calls getting longer – sometimes I'm talking to a vulnerable resident for up to forty-five minutes. I'd never hang up on anyone who's obviously lonely and I can give these tenants my time because we're not doing our usual repairs at the moment and only responding to emergencies, just the same as all social landlords. There are also fewer people out and about causing mayhem.

To be truthful, I enjoy these conversations. Lockdown is affecting me too – I'm not out on my estates daily, not knocking on doors, not interacting with my residents or colleagues, not seeing people I've known for years. Even when the phone is always ringing or I'm seeing people's faces over Zoom, it gets lonely working from home. If *I* feel that way, then I know that for some of our residents, lockdown must feel like a black void of silence.

I'm just so over it. This thing can't stop quickly enough.

CHAPTER THIRTEEN

SOLACE

But it's not showing any sign of stopping. Next, I hear that one of the housing team is dealing with a resident who's experiencing domestic violence. But the team member is a man, and the resident is asking to speak to a woman. He asks me if I'll handle it. Of course – not a problem.

A lot of domestic violence cases land on housing officers first of all. Unless Social Services are aware of a problem already, it's often neighbours who hear noises or see something that concerns them. So they ring us; we're the first line of defence. Even in normal, non-pandemic times, we feel like an emergency service. But this is lockdown, and we know that domestic violence is getting worse. Too many women are trapped in their homes with their abusers – nowhere to go, no chance to take a break or talk to anyone, groomed through fear until they think they have no way to leave.

My colleague sends me the resident's contact details straightaway. Her name's Annette but I don't have a lot of background on her. Anyway, in cases like these it's much better to get the history of what's happened from the victim. I'll also have to complete her risk assessment.

Over the years, my colleagues and I have had to deal with countless issues of DV. It's not just abuse by men on women – DV can be carried out by women against men, by gay partners, by adult children against their elderly parents... you'd be amazed by the variety, unfortunately. In my early days as a housing officer, I received a phone call from a gentleman who sounded terribly nervous. He told me that he was a victim of domestic violence and he needed help. I arranged for him to come to the Cedar neighbourhood office and when he attended our interview I was taken aback when this big, burly man walked into the room. I already knew his partner, the legal tenant of the property. She was a tiny little thing – half his size at most. Surely she couldn't be physically abusing him?

But I very quickly realised I had a lot to learn, and not to judge by appearances was one of them. We helped the victim and got him referred to a male-only domestic violence refuge. As soon as he had somewhere to go, he left his partner and I never saw him again. I still wonder how he got on.

The voice that answers the phone is very soft and small. It's the third time I've called and by now I'm getting pretty worried. 'Hello? My name's Charmain. Can I speak to your mum?'

'Who's this?' the voice asks.

'I'm from Southwark Council. You're expecting my call.'

The voice immediately starts weeping. 'Oh! Oh! You have to help me! Please help me!'

I realise that it's Annette. 'Okay, my love,' I say, 'my name's Charmain. Your housing officer said I'd call. I'm going to try to assist you.'

'He told me!' She's sobbing really hard. They sound like tears she's been holding back for years. 'Forgive me!' she says. 'Forgive me!'

'Annette, it's okay. I'm here. I'm not going anywhere, okay?'

It must be ten minutes before she can speak to me properly. She keeps apologising, and I keep telling her there's nothing to apologise for. It's hard to describe what I'm hearing. I sit there on the phone just listening to her crying like it's coming from deep in her soul. I want to cry with her; it's sad beyond comprehension. I ask her where her kids are and she tells me that they're in their bedroom and she's in the bathroom where they can't hear her.

'Okay, and where's your husband now?'

'Ray? He's – he was arrested. He's on bail. He's not supposed to come back here, but—'

'Are you worried he will?'

More tears. 'I – I know he will,' she tells me. 'He won't stay away – he won't do anything they tell him, I know he won't!'

'Does he still have a key?'

'Yes. Every time I hear the lift, the kids and me all freeze. We're waiting for the front door to open.'

'Okay,' I say. 'I'm going to arrange a lock-change straight-away. Have the police given you an alarm?'

'Yes. They said I'm a priority case and if I call they'll come straightaway but – but – what if they don't get here quickly enough? How can they help me then?'

The urgency in her voice is really scary. I'm shocked by the level of her fear.

'What about my kids?' she cries. 'What am I going to do? Please, I need a new lock!'

I know I have to remain calm if I'm going to have any chance of calming her.

'Annette,' I say, 'let me sort out the lock change now and I'll call you back directly. Please don't worry.'

I put the phone down and take a deep breath. In my head I start listing exactly what I have to do and who to call first. I send an email to Repairs to get the lock change job raised, and then phone Martin, the repairs manager, to get him to escalate it. This needs to be prioritised – it's called an R1 – so that it's done ASAP. I'm typing as I'm calling him; I know that he always responds quickly. A few minutes later, he calls back.

'Charmain? Hi, what can I do for you?' I quickly explain what's going on and that I have to give Annette some reassurance.

'We've got a really big backlog,' he tells me. 'It's the lockdown; it's slowed down all the work. But I'll see what I can do.' He hangs up and I wait. Then the phone rings again.

'Right,' says Martin's voice. 'Okay. They can be there in two hours. Tell her not to go anywhere. The chippie will call her when he's on his way.'

'Thanks, Martin. You're a star.'

As quickly as I can, I call Annette back.

'Thank you!' she says. 'Thank you so much!'

'You need to let me know as soon as he's done the job, okay?' I tell her. I know she won't find any kind of relief until then. I do know one thing – that door is a multi-secured one. Even if her husband is dumb enough to try to get in after the lock-change, he won't be able to break it down. But getting Annette to truly feel secure is going to take more than just a door.

'Right,' I explain, 'I need to take down some details of what's been happening, so we can work out what we can do next. I have to do a risk assessment for you and refer you to victim support. There's an organisation called Solace – they help victims of domestic violence.'

'The police already told the victim support people,' she says. 'They called me. They're coming to my flat to help me make it safe.'

'Okay. Good. And I could try to get you into temporary accommodation,' I say.

'In Southwark?'

'Well, it can be anywhere.'

There's a silence. 'Annette?' I ask.

'Oh, I don't know. I don't know,' she replies. She sounds so exhausted, confused and overwhelmed. This is too much for her to think about.

'Okay, let's leave that for the moment. Can you tell me what's been happening?'

As she explains, I just listen. She's been married for ten years and at first things were okay, but after her first child was born, her husband changed. He seemed to be resentful of the time that Annette gave to their baby.

'How can you spend too much time with your own child?' she asks me. She can't comprehend that, and I don't think I can either. She has four children now, two sons and then twin daughters, and Ray has grown more and more selfish and intimidating after the birth of each of them. She keeps trying to make things better and keep him happy, but it's not working.

'Nothing I do is any good,' she tells me. 'I sit at night trying to understand what I've done, thinking maybe this, maybe that, until I'm too tired to think any more.'

Her husband's physical violence started after the birth of their second son. She tells me how she served him some food but he said that it was cold. She started to apologise, but then he lost his temper. He threw the plate at the wall and in the same movement he slapped her across the face with what seemed like the back of his hand. The blow came out of nowhere and she was too stunned to be sure exactly what happened.

'I put my hand to my face,' she whispers, 'but he grabbed my hand and he flung me to the floor and I landed on the broken plate and the food. I looked up and I saw his foot come down on me. I couldn't move. I froze. I just froze. I don't think I had any thoughts in my head.'

She pauses. In the background I can hear someone knocking on the bathroom door. 'Mummy?' a little voice calls. 'Can I come in?'

'Annette,' I say to her, 'if it's easier, I can call you back tomorrow.' I know how hard this is for her.

'No. It's okay. Let me just sort out Isla and then we can keep talking. Hold on, please.'

When she's back on the phone, I ask her as gently as I can to go over the most recent incidents: I need these for the risk assessment. She does that, but to me she still sounds as though her mind is in the past, reliving everything that's been happening. She manages to tell me about the previous evening when her husband lost his temper.

'He'd – he'd been drinking,' she whispers. 'He – he drinks a lot, sometimes.'

'Does that make things worse?' I ask her. She bursts out crying again, but then she takes a breath and goes on speaking.

'When he gets back from the pub – it's – it's terrible, then. But in the lockdowns, he's drinking more at home. His boss cut his hours and he says he has no money and I'm spending too much on the kids. It's the girls – it's having twins. I keep telling him it costs more. I only buy the things they need.'

She stops speaking and catches her breath. 'I don't know, really,' she says softly. 'I never know what I've done – what makes him so mad.'

'What did you do next?' I ask.

'I sent the kids into their room quickly and I stood in

front of their bedroom door, but Isla – she's always braver than her sister – she kept opening the door while Ray was shouting and walking up and down the hallway. I was trying to shush her and tell her to get back in the bedroom with Mia but he shoved me really hard and I fell on the floor and he stepped over me and took Isla from her room.'

I'm getting scared just listening to her.

'Annette,' I ask, 'does Ray ever hurt the children?'

'No. No, he never touches them. He doesn't even shout at them. But…' Her voice is faltering again.

'But what? It's okay. You can tell me.'

'He – he says horrible things to them about me. He uses really awful words. So – so last night he took Isla into the living room and he had her on his lap and started to whisper in her ears. Oh, my baby, her face looked frozen. She didn't move, she just sat there. I told him to let her go back into her bedroom and I held out my arms for her to come to me but he wouldn't let her. He – he just kept her on his lap and then he – he said to my baby, "You see your mummy? Yes, your mummy is a prostitute. A slut" – that's what he said to her. "Mummy is a piece of cheap trash."'

I'm glad the interview's over the phone because I can feel my blood boiling. This is an episode of pure sadism. But I can't let her know how I feel. I have to stay as calm as I can. 'What happened then?' I ask.

'So I tried – I tried to say to him, "Please don't – please don't talk to her like that, she's four years old." But he just said that maybe, that if children weren't here, I would please him more. And then my eldest one – Ryan – he came running out of the bedroom. I couldn't stop him, he shot past me like a bullet out of a gun and he stood in front of me and he said, "Get out, Dad, get out – let Isla go, we know what you do to Mum, so get out or I'll call the police."'

The memory is making Annette cry even more and she stops for a minute. I just keep listening in silence.

'So – so I was terrified of what Ray would do and I grabbed Ryan and then Ray got up and that's when I saw he had a knife in his hand. I – I didn't see it before. He let Isla go and she ran to me and he slowly walked to the front door and he was smiling. I was so scared because I thought he might – I thought – I don't know. I couldn't think straight. The children's bedroom was closed and I was praying they wouldn't come out – and then – then there was banging on the front door and I heard the police shouting for us to open it. And – then Ray had to let them in.'

'Who called the police? Was it the neighbours?'

'No,' Annette whispers. 'No. It was Dylan. My other son. He s–said to me, "Sorry, Mum, I had your mobile and Ryan told me to call the police."'

'It was very brave of them to do that,' I say.

'But – but – the police were holding Ray's arms – they were arresting him – and Dylan was crying and he kept saying, "Sorry, Daddy, sorry, Daddy."' Again Annette pauses. 'My babies, Charmain. They're not babies any more, are they? Not after this.' I know she's asking herself this question and not me. She feels she's failed to protect them and I don't know what to say. There's no answer – and no comfort – I can give her.

• • •

I've seen how women who suffer from domestic violence can take on the shame of it, even though it really isn't theirs. It should belong to their violent husbands. It's especially hard if they come from a cultural background where the good name of the family is what matters most. A woman who steps out of line – who complains, who involves the authorities – can be seen as bringing disgrace. I think of the fear Pleasant felt, when she thought that if she told anyone what was happening to her, she would be the one who would get into trouble.

Annette has shown an awful lot of courage. It turns out that she has family in Essex, and when they find out what's going on, they ask her to move out there. She's not sure at first because her children are settled in their schools in Southwark. This can be an issue with some victims of domestic violence, who feel that protecting themselves will disrupt the lives of their families. In some cases, it's incredibly difficult to get them to put themselves first and seek a place of safety. Others, however, will leave everything without a second's thought. Each person deals with their trauma differently and until you've been there, you've really got no right to comment. All I can do is be with them and help as best I can with the resources I have at my disposal.

As a victim of DV, the law allows Annette to present

herself to her new local authority as unintentionally home-less. There will be an investigation into her case, but once all the information has been gathered from the agencies that have helped her, the new authority will have a duty of care for her and her family and she can be placed in temporary accommodation. As soon as that's done, she can terminate her tenancy with Southwark and start a new life with her kids somewhere else. There's one more helpful thing too: the Southwark flat is in her name, which will speed everything up. If it had been in Ray's, we would have had to wait until he was convicted of DV before we could apply to a court for repossession.

Annette has escaped from his abuse, and I hope that her future is happier. But when lockdown closed her world, it left her trapped. It also put even more pressure on her family and made her husband's violence more likely. She's not the only person this is happening to right now. She's been able to reach out and ask for help – but so many other women won't have managed to do that. I'm horribly aware that they're still in the nightmare, still in danger, still in need of help. Between 2020 and 2021, in the first year of lockdowns, more than 2,000 cases of DV were reported to Southwark Council.

• • •

When the government's national Test and Trace scheme starts up in May 2020, Southwark's housing team is told that the government wants us to help them. We're going to be required to conduct welfare visits on residents that the trace teams can't contact.

'Wait a minute.' I'm talking to Lanre over Zoom, and he's telling me all about this new plan. 'They want housing officers to track people down and monitor them? What sort of people? Do they mean our residents?'

'Er, no,' he says uneasily. 'Not just our residents. All local people who have a contact who's got Covid.'

'Anyone in Southwark?'

'Well, *potentially* anyone.'

'There's over 300,000 people in Southwark! And we're supposed to do this as well as our jobs?'

Lanre doesn't look very happy. He understands as well as I do what the problem is. 'Yeah, well,' he says. 'That's what they're saying. They want us to be a sort of back-up. If Test and Trace can't get in touch with somebody, local housing officers will be called in to help.'

I get that it's important. All contacts of people who have Covid must be told to isolate themselves so that the virus won't keep spreading. They have to be followed up with phone calls and texts. If this system works, it will help to break transmission. But why us? It isn't our domain. We can't visit people we don't know, and as housing officers we certainly can't force anyone to contact the government's Covid trace teams. Southwark housing officers are already working flat out to support our vulnerable tenants, calling them every day, conducting welfare visits, recording that we've seen them and that they're okay, identifying their needs and their problems.

'Who exactly volunteered us to do this Test and Trace?' I ask. 'So they just put up their hands and expect us to say yes and give less time to our vulnerables and our tenants and everything else we got to do. I mean, *what?* Has the world gone friggin' mad?'

Lanre doesn't reply. I know he can't say much; he's a manager. But I'm not. I can vent. 'I mean,' I go on, 'do they have any idea how much we have to do already? So housing officers are only visible when they want something done. As usual. But when we need support, they can't see us! Jesus, this is just too much.'

Then I think of something else – something that makes me really angry. 'Anyway,' I say, 'Test and Trace has been given billions to set this thing up! For God's sake! Shouldn't they be employing their own people?'

In the end the whole idea just gets abandoned, and council housing officers don't add unpaid Covid monitoring to our list of duties. But Test and Trace was given a budget of £22 billion by the government when it started. Another £15 billion was allocated to it a few months later. £37 billion in eighteen months is quite impressive. I wonder what they spent it on? Meanwhile, Southwark Council's staff have just been offered a 1 per cent pay increase. We feel like the forgotten service. Who's gonna fight for us? But if the country's housing officers just downed tools and stopped doing their jobs, I'm telling you, all bets would be off.

• • •

Abigail rings me up from the Cedar estate. She sounds panicky. She's in her seventies and has a heart condition, so now she's been told to shield because she's vulnerable. 'I've got half a loaf left, Charmain, and two tins of macaroni cheese. My daughter in Epping always does my weekly shop but she can't get here now! I'm not allowed outside with the virus! I'm going to run out of food!'

I note down her details and reassure her that I'll do something to help very quickly. But what can I do? I can't get to her, so I call one of my tenants, Norma, who lives right opposite. 'Hi, Norma, can you do me a favour?'

'Sure, darling, what is it?'

I explain the position that Abigail is in.

'Can you just check up on her?' I say. 'She's panicking a bit and her daughter can't get to her.'

'Don't you worry. I'll go over there now and I'll call you back.'

Norma is one of those strong, no-nonsense women who will pull up her sleeves and get stuck in. I know I can count on her. What makes this even more moving is she's not too well herself. She has a problem with her spine and it seriously limits her movement. It's lucky that some of her family members still live at home with her – that way, at least she gets support.

An hour and a half later, she calls me back. 'Done and dusted, Charmain. I went over there and she told me what she needed, and I've got my car so I went round to Morrison's and did a bit of shopping for her. She's fine and I'll keep checking on her until her daughter can get there. You don't have to worry, okay?'

'You're a diamond,' I tell her, but she just shrugs it off.

'Yeah, well, you got to do it, innit?' she says in her matter-of-fact way. 'Oh, and she tried to give me money and I told her I didn't ask for it so I don't want it. She kept on trying, though. So if she talks about it, just let her know it's not about that. Please can you get her to understand? It's just what we do for each other.'

I tell her I'll try. When I said Norma's a diamond, I meant it. People become a community in a crisis, and I love it. I just love it. It's humanity at its best.

But when Abigail rings me again, she's practically in tears. 'Charmain, I wanted to say thank you for sorting out my shopping. It's amazing. Norma just brought me two bags of shopping, there was meat and everything, oh God bless her, but I tried to give her back the money and she won't take it!'

'I know, Abigail,' I tell her. 'But she doesn't want you to pay her. Honestly, she doesn't. She did it because it's the pandemic.'

But Abigail won't have it. 'So of course I told her I'm going to pay,' she says adamantly, 'and then she walked off and she said if I did, she'd only give it back to me.'

I have to smile at the two of them arguing because they're both trying to be nice to each other. *Gotta love the strength of this community.* 'Well, yes. I'm sure she would do that,' I tell Abigail. 'She really doesn't wan—'

'Look here!' Abigail says. 'She's not well with her back.

I'm going to give you the money and you have to give it to her.'

'Nuh-uh,' I answer. 'Not happening. I'm not getting in the middle of this one! Anyway, she'd be insulted, wouldn't she? It's not what she wants.'

'Oh,' Abigail says. Then she's quiet for a moment, thinking. 'God is good, Charmain,' she says finally.

'Maybe you could buy her flowers,' I suggest, 'when things get a bit more back to normal?'

'I will,' Abigail says. 'I definitely will. I have to do *something*.'

The next day, Norma calls me again. She tells me that the local Tenants' and Residents' Association has been out knocking on all the doors in the estate finding out who needs help. They know there must be other people feeling just as scared as Abigail, so they're doing their bit for their community. They'll do shopping for anyone who needs it and deliver the food to people's doors.

The community is brilliant, but Southwark Council also swings into action and sets up a Covid hub based from the Kingswood estate. The hub distributes food, and anybody who's struggling can be referred to it for help. We've been calling our vulnerables so we already know who needs assistance, and we're also getting calls from other residents who aren't yet on the list. Southwark Council is trying its level best to help everyone who needs it. The hub has another benefit too – it's staffed by council employees whose roles have had to change in the pandemic, so it's helping to keep people in work. Cleaners who can't do their usual jobs drive with food deliveries door to door.

The hub turns out to be a lifeline for so many in the borough. There's so much need out there. The virus has brought a great wave of anxiety that has left some people too anxious to step outside their homes, and even people who don't need help in normal times are suddenly in trouble. Perhaps they've lost their jobs – that happens to so many who do casual work or zero hours or are employed in hospitality. Thousands are facing pay cuts or have no work at all. There are also the elderly who usually go to the post office and get their cash, but who now can't go out because they have to shield. And how long will this pandemic last? None of us knows that, so there's no reassurance we can give. We just grit our teeth and carry on.

· · ·

By July 2020, life still doesn't feel normal – at least, not our old normal. We're still phoning our tenants who are shielding, and still checking up on our vulnerables. People are still standing in socially distanced lines to go into shops and there are no planes flying overhead. We're only dealing with emergency repairs and we have to try to spot problems during visual audits because the communal repairs officers aren't out and about. When this is over – whenever that might be – there's going to be a very big backlog. But there are more cars on the streets and a little bit more bustle. It feels like there's some breathing space, at least.

It's now we start to see how the lockdown has really impacted on people's mental health. We've all tried our best to give support, but it's clear that in some cases it hasn't been enough. One day I get phone call from one of my tenants.

'Afternoon, Charmain. Didn't you get my messages?'

'I'm sorry, Peter, no. Can you tell me what the problem is?'

'Well, I left two for you,' Peter says. He really sounds upset.

I've not got his messages because my phone's been playing up and I'm waiting for a new one to be delivered. It's taking much longer than it should. Everything seems to be on a pandemic go-slow these days, from getting the equipment we need to solving IT issues. I think I should explain this to Peter before he makes a complaint to Southwark Council. 'Look, I'm really sorry. My phone's not storing all my messages and it doesn't ring so I'm missing calls. All I can do is apologise. What can I do for you?'

'It's my girl next door,' he says. 'I think she's poorly.'

'Is she doing it again?' I ask him.

'Yes.'

'Really loudly?'

'The loudest ever, I'd say.'

I immediately know what he means. Peter's next-door neighbour is called Valerie. She suffers from paranoid schizophrenia, and when she's doing well, she is lovely. But when she doesn't take her medication, she hears voices.

That frightens her a lot, and the only way she can drown them out is to play loud music or turn the TV right up. I can't even imagine the mental torment she's enduring, but it's awful for her neighbours.

'And is she leaving the rubbish outside?' I ask Peter.

'Yeah,' he says. 'There's loads.'

When she's in crisis, Valerie locks herself away inside her flat. She'll take her rubbish bags out but only as far as her front door, so piles of them build up on the walkway. She certainly won't go near the cupboard where the big bins are kept. Right now it's July – we're in the middle of a heatwave. Those bin bags must be rancid.

'She's doing all of it again,' Peter tells me. 'We've got the radio and the TV on permanent loud coming through the wall 24/7. The rubbish is all over – you can smell it in my flat. There are flies everywhere, Charmain.'

'Right, Peter. Okay. We'll get something done.'

It's been eighteen months since poor Valerie's been in such a bad way. That time it was because of Brexit – the decision that Britain should leave the European Union. Her usual medication wasn't made in the UK and suddenly, it wasn't available. It took time for the right one to be found, and until then she and other patients like her were left to suffer. I don't think anyone saw things like that coming when Brexit was decided.

'I get that she's not well,' Peter says to me, 'and I know she's a decent lady, but why isn't anybody checking up on her?'

'They are, Peter,' I explain. 'I spoke to her last week and

272

she seemed to be okay. I've been phoning and she answers, so there's not been any reason to do a welfare check. I'll be round on a visual visit tomorrow so I'll keep an eye out for her then. If she seems to be getting out of hand, I think you need to call the police.'

'Okay,' he sighs. 'And I'm not grassing her, you know. I'm just worried.'

'I know you are, Peter. No worries. Thanks.'

He's not so much angry as fed up. He understands that she can't help herself. I imagine the smell of rotting rubbish and the flies that he's having to put up with as I add 'follow up with Valerie' into my Outlook. It's recorded along with all the other urgent things I have to do tomorrow.

I've told Peter to call the police because that can be a fast track to get someone who needs to be sectioned and in hospital for treatment. Police officers aren't mental-health workers, but if a person is distressed and their behaviour is impacting those around them, calling 999 can be the best route to take. It shifts police attention away from crime, but it's the only way to go sometimes, if there's no other source of help. And why is there no other help around? Because every single service – the police, mental-health care and housing – is under severe strain after years of cuts, but it seems that no one cares about what's happening. The people who hold the purse strings certainly don't.

Next day I go round to Valerie's flat, but there are no bags of rubbish to be seen. The cleaner must have taken them away, I think. I can't hear music either. All's quiet on the Western Front, in fact. I try to look in through her kitchen window but the lace curtain doesn't have any gaps. So what's happened? I'm puzzled and concerned. As I'm walking away from the flat, I take out my phone and I see a missed call. Damn this old handset. I don't recognise the number, but I call back straightaway.

'Hi,' I say, 'it's Charmain from Southwark Council. I got a missed call from you?'

'Oh yes, hi. My name's Malcolm. I'm Valerie Wallder's mental-health support worker.' He explains that she's not in her flat because she's been admitted to the Maudsley. He thinks that she's stopped taking her medication.

'Last time I spoke to her,' I tell him, 'she told me she was fine. She said she was enjoying the sunshine. Then the next thing I know, I've got her neighbour on the phone telling me that she's repeating all her most worrying behaviour.'

Malcolm explains that the same thing has happened with her mental-health care team. Valerie seemed well, and she told them she was doing okay. Then one day two weeks ago, he says, she was directly asked if she was still taking her medication and all she answered was that she feels better now. Malcolm immediately realised what was going on. She'd stopped taking her medicine because she thought she was better. It's difficult when mental-health patients think that they're doing so well that they are cured, but really it's the medication making them feel like that. If they stop their meds, they'll revert to a much worse mental state. That's why they need supervision, and right now, that's just not happening.

'What did you do?' I ask him.

'I told her that she needed to visit the hospital and she just hung up. After that, she wouldn't answer the phone. So they went round last night – the police and ambulance. There were bags of rubbish everywhere and music blaring out. They had to section her.'

'Right. Did they speak to her neighbour?'

'Yeah. He came outside and saw them. They were surprised he wasn't angry.'

'To be fair,' I say, 'her neighbours understand the problem. They do look out for her.'

Malcolm tells me he'll confirm what's happened in an email so that I can put it on Valerie's file, and we say goodbye. At least Peter will have peace and quiet in his flat now. That's one less person to worry about, and at least Valerie's in the right place.

She's definitely not the only one who hasn't been taking their medication during lockdown. There are people in crisis who we've missed no matter what we've done and however hard we've tried. Warning signs are going under the radar, and problems that might have been controlled are blowing up to crisis point. Even when this pandemic is over, it will leave a trail of chaos through so many lives. Too many people were only just coping before, like Valerie. They lived too close to the edge, and a little protein-spiked virus was all it took to push them over.

• • •

275

'You're a horrible person, Charmain. You're useless at your job. You're a rubbish housing officer. You're shit. All you lot are fuckin' rubbish. You don't do nothin' to help me.'

After I've been listening to the message from my tenant for a moment or so, I put my mobile down. Unfortunately, though, I can still hear his faint crackly voice. *'You never contact me. You never ring me. You're a real piece of shit.'*

I push the phone right across the table to get it out of earshot. It's not the first time he's left a message. I've got several other rants just like this one stored on that mobile. This is the long tail of the Covid-19 pandemic. I'm seeing it in the backlogs of repairs, in mental-health crises, in fraying services. There's so much frustration and anger and distress. Some of our tenants were vulnerable to begin with. Others have been pushed to breaking point by all the lockdowns and months of anxiety. Their housing officers are the faces and voices that they know, so they take it out on us.

For far too long, we've put up with it. For years, as officers of the council, we've accepted abuse, intimidation and sometimes violent threats as just part of the job. Now, very slowly, officers, contractors and operatives are becoming aware of incident reporting and the council is starting to take it seriously. We've had enough and we want to fight back. We're here to assist as best we can, and to provide a service, but we're also human beings. Yet the very small minority of residents which behaves like this somehow thinks they have a right to disrespect us. How dare they?

My phone's five feet away now, but I can still hear my tenant ranting on. It's totally unacceptable. My colleagues and I have reached a point where we just can't take any more. I'd like to press delete on these horrible messages, but it's important to keep them because these audio files can be uploaded to the housing department's computer. That means they can be used as evidence when we report abuse like this. But for now, I can still hear that voice.

'You're a nasty bitch, Charmain. I'm gonna take you to court to tell the court what's been going on and all the things you never done for me. You never contacted me. You're rubbish at your job. Wait and see what's coming for you, you fucking nasty bitch, you just wait…'

All this because I couldn't do exactly what he wanted. But we can only follow the official procedures and the law. What is it that these people don't get?

• • •

Tenants can also be extremely kind. They try to look out for their housing officers, and during the pandemic I actually start to get phone calls from them asking me how I'm doing. The same thing happens to many of my colleagues – a lovely surprise. I hear residents telling me that they know I'm working hard when they're safe in their houses, asking me if I'm eating properly, if my mental health's okay, and telling me to take time out to care for myself. I feel so moved and cared for. As I go round on my audits, I hear tapping on windows and see residents waving at me.

'Charmain! How's it going? What you doing out here? Why aren't you working from home? You take care now!'

Perhaps this might sound unprofessional, but there are many residents I care very deeply about. They are such lovely human beings. It makes all the difference in the world at a time like this.

• • •

My mum and dad live in Sydenham, south London. They're both over eighty, so of course they have to shield in the pandemic. I'm the only one of their three daughters who lives close enough to get to them quite easily, so I'm there whenever they need anything. They know to stay inside although I think it's made my dad a bit stir-crazy; he loves to be out and about. Mum doesn't mind so much, and of course both of them are really aware of their vulnerability.

Mum was really confused about why people had an issue about toilet paper right at the start. But she still didn't want to run out and I had to make sure they had a decent supply. She was shocked by what some people got up to and how shameless they were, publicising all the stuff they'd hoarded on YouTube. It's unthinkable to the older generation to just grab what you want like that and not even be ashamed of what you're doing. 'They've got more money than sense, those people. And what are they going to do when all that stuff goes off?' Mum would exclaim. 'Carrying on like it's the end of the world! That's why other people have to do without.'

I'm also a grandmother myself. My daughter Indya has a beautiful little boy, and I regularly help to look after him, especially after the nurseries are closed. Just as for lots of other families, Covid has thrown all our busy arrangements into chaos. So as well as making sure my parents are provided for, I've had to help her too, and there've been days when I've felt like a Sainsbury's delivery driver, covering half of south London on my food runs. (Now *that's* a job I don't think I could handle.) As I drive around looking after my family, I find I'm thinking of the thousands and thousands of other people up and down the country who must be doing exactly the same. That thought really helps.

There's no difference between me and my tenants – we're all just people and we cope with these situations in the best way we can. Everyone's been feeling so much stress and anxiety during the pandemic and we all need help from each other sometimes. The best thing I can say about my own family's situation is that it gives me deeper empathy and understanding for everything my residents are going through.

• • •

In August 2020, the Cedar estate holds a socially distanced Bank Holiday tea party for all the local kids. It's a warm sunny Sunday, the mayor of Southwark comes and there's a barbecue, tea and cakes, and lots of games. The tea party is sponsored by a local company, and they make sure every child gets a present. It's a really lovely day, and it feels like a celebration. It especially helps the elderly people, who've been locked up for so long, and reminds them that they aren't alone.

Our kids will be going back to school. We can stop worrying about our jobs. The fear of disease and death that's hung over us for months is losing its grip. Maybe the pandemic is over at last.

But it turns out that it isn't.

• • •

'Why can't they just make up their bloody minds?' my tenant Alf asks me. I agree with him. It's autumn 2020, and Southwark has been placed in Tier 3. This is part of the government's latest plan for managing the pandemic: to put different areas of the country into risk levels depending on how many cases of Covid each one has. Each level has rules and restrictions but the tiers keep on changing at short notice, and the explanations aren't very clear. So if you're living in Tier 2 and you want to visit someone in Tier 3... well, let's just say that no one really seems to understand what they should do.

Lockdowns feel harsher now the weather's getting cold. It's harder to meet friends out of doors, and indoors there are bans on different households mixing. There's a lot of confusion. Plus we all thought the pandemic would be over by now, and that makes the situation even more difficult to put up with. As housing officers, we're often regarded as an authority on Covid rules, so my tenants keep on asking me questions, but to be honest I'm completely at a loss. We're struggling to keep up just like everybody else, and we're certainly not being given any extra information.

'Do you understand what's goin' on, then?' Alf says.

'Nope,' I say frankly. 'I think the whole country doesn't understand. I'm the last person you should be asking. I watch those government briefings on the telly and I'm no wiser when they stop talking than I was when they started.'

Alf chuckles. At least he's managing to keep his sense of humour. 'So I think we can meet six people outside, two people inside... I dunno,' he says. 'And what about at Christmas?'

'Well, right now they're saying that if we keep the rules then Christmas can be normal,' I tell him. 'At least, that's what I think they said. D'you reckon that's right?'

'Huh,' answers Alf. 'I bet they change that too. But what I really want to know is, how many reindeer can I have in my garden?'

'As many as you like, so long as they're all from the same household,' I tell him. We both burst out laughing. What else can you do?

Alf turns out to be right. National lockdown No. 3 begins five days before Christmas 2020. Everybody's festive plans get cancelled and a lot of people are upset that they can't see their families. But they still struggle on, they greet their relatives on Zoom, they cope as best they can. There's so much resilience in Southwark.

And then it's the start of 2021. I think of this time last

year – how we watched all those TV pictures of silent, locked-down Wuhan. It all seemed so remote. If you'd told me that something like Covid was coming to south London, I would never have believed it. And now, when I try to imagine this crisis ending, I feel the same way. The idea seems distant and impossible. In these dark, cold days of winter, it seems as though the pandemic is never going to be over.

• • •

The first week into the new year, I wake up one morning with a stinging headache. It's captured the entire top of my head, going down into my eyes. After two days with this pain, which nothing really shifts, I notice that I'm starting to feel cold. No matter what I do, I can't get warm – the chill is deep in my bones. I start to wonder: is this flu? Or could it be that bloody virus again? By day four I've ordered a PCR test – and it turns out to be positive. Within twenty-four hours, my boiler gives out and my house is like a fridge. That's when my condition gets much worse – so bad that my friends start getting frightened and pretty soon I have paramedics at my door. 'Nuff said. Covid can happen to the best of us.

Very slowly, things get better and I start to feel stronger. I'm still signed off so I'm not supposed to work, but I find myself thinking about the office, and the pressure that everyone is under. I just can't help myself. Perhaps it's a housing officer thing. The cases I was dealing with before

I was ill keep on running through my mind. What if something important has been missed in my emails or my messages – something that I would have picked up on? Who else is going to know?

Just to be sure, I switch on my work mobile and listen to my messages. There don't seem to be any emergencies, so that's good. But then I hear a message left two days ago by my tenant Mr Bradley. I know him – he's in his seventies and he lives alone. He's got some serious health issues. His voice on the phone is quite polite and calm, but I can tell he's pretty scared underneath. 'Er, hello, Charmain. Um, please can you help me? I'm shielding and I'm running out of food. My daughter can't get to me. I've got a little milk and bread but that's all and I'm getting a bit worried. Please can someone get shopping for me?'

I put down the phone and think. Now here's a dilemma. Mr Bradley's turned to me and I don't want to let him down. Some of my tenants are like that; they won't contact anybody else. Even if I can't fix their problems, they trust me because they know I'll always try, and I have colleagues on the team whose residents feel just the same way about them. But I can't contact my line manager about this because I'm supposed to be off sick. She won't be happy if she finds out I'm working. My friends would be upset as well if they found out; they're worried about how bad I was with Covid and I know they'd be telling me to rest. But I can't just leave Mr Bradley. I have to do something.

I quickly text the chair of the Cedar Tenants' and Residents' Association and ask if she can arrange help for him. She's straight on it. She sets up a delivery later that day through the Covid hub and also gets him on the list for a weekly supply of groceries. I text Mr Bradley to tell him what I've done and he texts back: 'Thank you so much. The Lord will bless you.' I ask him to let me know when he's received his shopping.

I go through all my other messages just in case there's anyone else in the same situation. For now, everything's okay. I message the chair of the residents' association to thank her – she's pretty much an angel in disguise. And now I should switch off my phone before my line manager gets wind of the fact that I've kinda been at work... but before I do that, I wait for Mr Bradley's text. A couple of hours later, it comes through and I finally know that he's okay. *I got the food*, his message says. *I feel better. Thank you, Charmain. Blessings.*

CHAPTER FOURTEEN

A PLACE TO CALL HOME

2014

As I trudge up the stairs in Shakespeare House, all I'm thinking is, *Another flight to go. Weren't lifts invented when they built this block?* My to-do list is as long as your arm. Once I've done this tenancy check there are five more after that, then a home visit to sort out some damp issues. *I can't wait for this day to end.*

I'm also feeling worried about Mr Mehri, who's the first on my list. He lives alone, his hearing's really poor and his health's not great either, so I know it will take him a while to answer the door. I've already helped him in every way I can, arranging for special equipment to help him stay independent. Southwark Council has installed a flashing-light doorbell for him and a phone that prints out words on a screen to help him when he tries to take calls.

I get ready to smile when I see him, but when he opens the door it's hard to hide my shock. He's in his early fifties but he's starting to look older than his years and he seems to have shrunk since I last saw him. He's of Arabic descent, but his face looks grey and ashen. He's not shaved, which is unusual for him; he likes to be smart and well-groomed.

'Morning. And how are we doing, then?' I ask him, and he nods to me and gestures that I should come in. His flat is sparsely furnished but always very clean. There's a rug in the middle of the living room and two small tapestries on the walls with Arabic text beautifully stitched on them. We sit down in two armchairs and although the day is warm, I notice there's a blanket on his seat and he wraps it carefully around him.

I'm doing my best to be chirpy and I beam at him with the biggest smile I can muster. 'So, how are you?' I ask him again. Usually I get a smile back, and then he'll say – very loudly, because he can't hear well enough to judge the volume of his own voice – 'you like I make you a cup of tea?' With his hearing aids turned up, we can manage to have a conversation, but today I can't see the brown devices that are usually attached to his ears. I'm sensing already that the answer to my question won't be good. He looks as though he's carrying the weight of the world. The invitation for tea is not forthcoming and he just shakes his head. I don't feel I can go on smiling any more.

Mr Mehri is a refugee from the civil war in Iraq. Because he'd been involved in resistance to the country's oppressive government, his life was in danger and he was forced to flee. Somehow he managed to get on a ship to Spain, then spent many weeks crossing Europe. It was a desperate struggle, but back then it all seemed worth it: he was young and strong and full of hope for a better future. His plan was to save money then pay for his wife and two young sons to join him.

Mr Mehri was treated as a single man, so it took a long time for him to get a flat from Southwark Council. He started working as a cleaner and put aside as much money as he could. He was desperate to keep in touch with his family but he couldn't afford a phone, so he wrote them letters and made calls from a friend's flat to a shop in Basrah, close to where his wife and children live. The shop-keeper allowed them to come and take the calls, and – some of the time – their contact system worked.

But that was back in the early 1990s. Slowly the dream of reuniting his family and living together in safety began to slip away. His biggest problem was money: after paying his rent and covering basic expenses, Mr Mehri hardly had anything left to save. He hasn't seen his wife in fifteen years and the two little boys he left behind are young men now. His hearing was damaged during the fighting in Iraq, and it's grown worse and worse over time, to the point where he's almost deaf. He doesn't find it easy to take care of himself, and sometimes he misses his medical appointments. If his wife was with him, I'm sure she wouldn't have let that happen.

Over the last few years, his health problems have got serious: he's developed diabetes and high blood pressure. He used to have wide, strong shoulders and stood tall, but now he's slightly stooped and has a permanent frown. It's getting harder for him to work, so he's had to give in to claiming benefits: 'give in' is how he sees it and he believes that he's scrounging, although he has paid his national insurance and tax. There comes a time when you just have to accept help, but he finds it shameful and never wants anyone to think that it's his choice.

What breaks my heart about Mr Mehri is how upbeat he usually is despite all this. He knows that if he'd stayed in Iraq he would probably have been killed, and he always manages to find something positive to say. But not today. I'm getting worried. 'What's been happening?' I ask him again. 'You taking your medication?'

He still doesn't speak, so I go on. It's as though I don't want to give him time to answer. For a moment I'm not sure why, and then I realise: *I'm scared that he's going to tell me something serious is wrong. Oh boy.* 'Medicine not working?' I ask. 'Okay, you'll have to see the doctor. D'you want me to make an appointment for you? I can do that. It's no problem, you know.'

'It's more things now,' says Mr Mehri at last, very slowly. 'I've got prostate cancer.'

I don't want to burden him with my reaction, so I try not to look shocked at the news. As he slowly slumps forward in his chair, I notice again how skinny he's getting. He's completely alone and very far from home. 'What more?' he asks suddenly. 'What more?'

He's not asking me. It's as though he expects an answer from another source. I have the same question in my head too: how much more does this poor guy have to take? I move forward and place both my hands on his. The moment I touch him, Mr Mehri lowers his head and I see his shoulders shaking. He's crying but making no sound.

'Why is this happening?' he asks me. 'What have I done? All the things I've tried to do, but I have nothing but sickness. And more sickness! And now this – the worst of all!'

All I can do is sit with him and listen, trying to offer him support. He starts to talk about his past and I let him continue for as long as he wants to. He tells me about his parents and the secure and happy upbringing he had in Iraq before all the problems there began. When his mother died five years ago, he wasn't able to go home for her burial. He couldn't give his own boys the family childhood memories he had himself: he hasn't seen them for so long. He wanted to offer them something better, a life of opportunity, but he feels that he's failed them and he's afraid he's going to die without ever seeing them again. He's alone in this flat with no one to bring him soup when he is sick. He lifts his head and I can see his wet face as he tells me all of this, but there's no anger or self-pity in his voice, just exhausted acceptance.

There are tears in my eyes too as I listen. I feel helpless. He holds such an agony of mind. *Mr Mehri says his prayers*, I think to myself. I know that he's a devoutly religious man. 'All I can say to you,' I tell him gently, 'is that you could find solace in Allah.'

'I always pray to him,' Mr Mehri whispers. 'And I do find solace.'

'I know he will be there for you. Try to be positive,' I

say. My heart is with him. I'd love to alleviate the sorrow that he feels. But I know that when I leave, he will still be here alone. 'How can I assist you right now?' I ask him.

'You're listening to me,' he says, 'and that's enough.' But for me, it definitely isn't enough. I start mentally drawing up a plan. There are practical steps that I can take to make things better.

'Well,' I say, 'it's time to get you more support. I'm going to speak to Social Services. With your diagnosis, I think you need a carer now, someone to come in and help. Make you some soup when you're not well. And if you have a problem, you can speak to the carer and they'll come and tell me straightaway.'

'Yes. Thank you for your kindness, Charmain.'

'As soon as the care package is organised,' I tell him, 'I'll request that the support worker can speak your language.' His eyes light up when he hears this. He's so deeply lonely.

'And I'll keep checking up on you, okay?'

I stay with him far longer than our scheduled appointment, which isn't unusual. I manage 700 properties where over 3,000 people live, but right now this desperate human being needs whatever time I can give him.

While we're talking, he tells me something else. He says that people in England don't always understand how life was for people like him in Iraq, fighting for injustice and a democratic way of life and the freedom to think for themselves. He sees the suspicious looks from those who think that he shouldn't be here, that refugees like him don't have the right to be helped. And it's not just looks and stares. Sometimes they whisper past him: *What are you doing here? Why are people like you here?* He had to flee from his home, but when he reached a country he thought of as full of opportunity, he was treated as less than fully human.

I can empathise with that. I remember my childhood, the words I heard, the things my parents and relatives told us when we were growing up. *Go back where you came from*, people would say to us. *Go back to your homeland.* Nothing much has changed. But England *is* his homeland now – there's no other home that he can go to.

• • •

'Morning. Is that Charmain?' I know the voice on the phone.

'Yeah, Ali, hiya. What's occurring, hon?' It's Alison, housing officer at the Howden Road Sheltered Housing Unit where Mr Sweet now resides. I hope there's nothing wrong, but pretty quickly I'm disappointed.

'Well, I'm afraid I have a problem,' Ali tells me. 'It's with a recent arrival – a Mr Sweet. I believe that you were his housing officer before he came to us.'

'Yeah, yeah, I was. How's he doing?'

'Look, Charmain, I'm sorry, I know you're not responsible for him any more, but we've got serious complaints and we need your help, please!'

I lay my forehead down on my desk for a moment, really glad that Ali can't see me. *Jesus*, I think, *what has he done now?* I'm almost too scared to ask her.

'Charmain? You there?'

'Yep, I'm here. But why're you doing this to me today?'

'I'm so sorry, love.'

'Oh boy,' I say. 'You better tell me. What kind of complaints? What did he do?'

'Well,' Ali says, 'so first of all he opens his front door every morning and puts a speaker in the doorway playing revival reggae music on full volume. I've got all the other residents complaining every single day.'

I know it sounds bad, but I start to laugh. 'What you laughing for?' Ali's a bit dismayed at my reaction.

'Nah, sorry, Ali.' I straighten out my face. 'It's just that, this is anti-social behaviour from a guy who's eighty. What else is he doing?'

'So when I go to him and I say, "Look, this is unacceptable behaviour," he just goes "Fuck off!" and "Go about your fucking business." He refuses to cooperate. Now I'm hearing he's been abusing the nurses and the carers who have to attend to him. This is getting out of hand, Charmain.'

It's worse than I'd expected.

'What kind of abuse?' I ask her.

'When the nurses attend, they have to dress the sores on his legs and make sure he is taking his regulated medication. He has this lovely Nigerian lady and as soon as she comes in it's 'fucking' this and 'fucking' that and 'don't touch me' and questioning everything she's doing. He's just being so nasty to her and he isn't much different with the carers. It's getting to the point when they're refusing to deal with him.'

'Oh my God.'

'Look, I know you have a way with him. You persuaded him to come here in the first place. So you're my last resort before I'm going to be forced to serve him with a notice. I don't want to go that far. Can you help?'

I have an instinct that I can. This behaviour of Mr Sweet's just isn't like him. Sure, he has his ways and he can be indignant and stubborn, but he always knows not to be abusive or rude. I can only guess that he's finding it hard to be reliant on others and also very hard to adjust. That can sometimes be the case when people go into sheltered accommodation. But there've been times when I've felt that he and I had a kind of understanding, so maybe I can use that to talk to him. And honestly, you've still got to laugh: Mr Sweet, this little old man, with anti-social behaviour and loud music. *He going back to his youth now, for true.*

'Okay,' I say. 'No worries.' I ask Ali to write a formal letter setting out all his anti-social and abusive behaviour. It will be given to him as a formal warning and placed on his file. Even though this is a sheltered unit, its vulnerable residents are still tenants, and any infraction of their tenancy agreements can be enforced: you don't get immunity from rules just because you're elderly.

'What time will the nurse be there tomorrow?' I ask. Ali tells me 10 a.m.

'Right, then,' I say. 'I'll meet you in your office in Howden Road at ten and we'll take it from there.'

'Thanks, Charmain.'

'One thing, though: don't you dare tell him I'm turning up!'

'Hell no!' Ali says. I can hear the sigh of relief as she puts down the receiver.

• • •

I arrive at Howden Road bang on 10 a.m. Alison lets me into the building and we go to her office. I notice that she's looking at me sternly. 'Judging by your expression, he's at it again?' I ask her. She just nods.

'Is the nurse in his flat?' Again she nods.

'Okay, then, let's go. You got the letter?'

She puts it in my hand and I quickly scan through it. It lays out his unacceptable behaviour and how this contravenes his tenancy conditions, with all the evidence attached. It also informs him that if he continues with his ASB he will be placing his tenancy at risk, which could ultimately result in action for repossession. In other words, he'll get himself evicted.

We leave her office and as we walk towards Mr Sweet's landing, true to Alison's description I can hear at full volume a John Holt classic revival tune. It gets louder and louder as we approach and we pass other residents in their doorways looking really annoyed and shaking their heads. His front door's open, and a speaker is sitting on the threshold. We stand there for a moment. Over the strains of John Holt, I can make out Mr Sweet's voice inside.

'An' wha' mi say? Nah buda me! Go 'way!'

I step inside.

'Excuse me! And who are you talking to in that fashion?'

I call out as I walk into the living room. Mr Sweet is sitting on a small green settee, dressed in his boxers with bandages around both his calves. The bandages have blood stains and what looks like a clear dry outer ring around each stain. The nurse is sitting next to him with a swab in her hands. He instantly freezes. The expression on his face is like a kid who's been caught stealing sweets. He doesn't utter another word. I catch the nurse's eye and she gives me a quick smile. *Poor woman*, I think to myself.

'Hello, Mr Sweet,' I say, without any warmth in my voice. 'Can you kindly turn off the music at once?' He picks up his remote control and does as he's been asked straight-away. *Ah, silence.*

'Mr Sweet,' I say, 'I was looking forward to coming to see how you're settling in. But now I'm hearing that you're creating havoc in here! What's going on?'

I notice him giving the nurse a pretty sharp look. He must know she's complained about him. 'Um...' he says, 'well – um...'

'Is there a problem with your new flat?' I ask him. 'Has anybody here been unpleasant to you?'

'Er, no.' He looks worriedly at Alison, who's standing next to me.

'Now before you moved here, Mr Sweet,' I go on, 'you were living in what can only be described as a very nasty environment. Everything was brown, you hadn't cleaned the flat in years, you even agreed your mother would have been horrified as she didn't raise you in somewhere that looked like that – innit?'

'Yes,' he mutters.

'So now you tell me,' I say – and I switch into Jamaican patois – 'how you a gonna disrespect somewhere like this? How you a start disrespecting de people dem who try fe look after you, you a play music no one else wanna hear like you a sound man inna dance!'

Mr Sweet hangs his head.

'The lovely nurse here sah –' I point in her direction '– she a come every day to nurse your leg dem, clean dem sores, so dem don't get infected! She try and keep you alive by mekin sure you take your pills and what tanks she get? You call her names! You abuse her wid foul language, like your muddah raise you so! Nah, man! You have to fix up, disgraceful!'

Mr Sweet now looks really embarrassed.

'Come on, now,' I say. 'You tell me why?'

He clears his throat. 'Well,' he says, 'dem people dem ah come all de time, ah push mi pull mi, tell mi! Mi haf fe do dis an' mi cyan ave dis and mi cyan ave dat. Mi nah mi own man nah more.'

I get it. I thought this was going to be the problem. He feels like he's lost his independence. He's not had so many people involved in his life for a very long time and he's become overwhelmed. I soften my voice. 'Mr Sweet, these ladies, your housing officer, this nurse and your carers are all here to look after you and care for you and to get you back on the road so you can be independent again. But behaving like a rude teenager won't get you back to normal, will it? You have to work with them so that they can help you.'

He nods.

'And you have neighbours here. They'd love to get to know you. You like dominoes, and there are gentlemen here who meet to play. You could make friends. But playing music like you inna blues dance is not the way to go about it! Don't you agree?'

He nods again.

'Right, then. Now Alison has to inform you of the council's procedures due to your unacceptable behaviour. So listen, and whatever you don't understand, she'll explain, okay?'

He looks like a lost little boy now. When Alison has gone through the letter, he just asks her: 'So if mi don't behave, yuh can tek whey de flat?'

'In a nutshell, yes,' she replies.

'Mi nah whan dem fe evict mi,' he says sadly.

I can see from his reactions that he's taking it all in. She hands him the letter and without any coaxing, he turns to the nurse and apologises. 'So, Mr Sweet,' I say to him, 'I won't have to come here again, will I?'

'No, no, I promise yuh. Mi nah whan see yuh again in a dis here place!'

We smile at each other. The nurse is smiling too. 'Thanks for apologising,' I say. 'That was really courteous of you. It would be good if you would do the same thing to your carers.'

He nods again, and I can leave with a relieved Alison.

'Thanks so much, Charmain,' she says.

'No worries. I think the juvenile has left the building!' We both laugh as we walk along the corridor.

297

'He misses his old flat, you know,' I say to her. *It's difficult to imagine, but it was his home. It was the place where he felt safe and leaving made him frightened. None of us behaves at our best when we're frightened.* That's something I can understand.

Another job done and I've survived. My intervention works: from that point on, he's as good as gold and there are no more complaints. He's safe, he's well looked after and now he lives with dignity. Sometimes in my job, what I'm really doing is helping people to feel worthy of themselves, so that they believe they deserve something – a good home, a place of safety, a second chance. I try to lift them up, and with Mr Sweet, I manage it. It's the best feeling in the world. The good you do will follow you. I truly believe this. For me, it's what being a housing officer is really all about.

• • •

Back in 2007, the Wooddene is pulled down.

It was a massive early '70s concrete development and, to start with, its airy, spacious flats and maisonettes were a godsend to the people who moved in. They came from a close community, they were used to looking out for each other and they brought the same neighbourhood spirit to the block that they'd had in their old places down at ground level. For a while, their new home seemed to work.

But as the years went by, the Wooddene changed. Its layout once seemed inviting, but it turned out to be dangerous – too many dark corners and windy open land-ings. Its public spaces started to feel scary and residents stopped using them. Gangs moved in and problems began – vandalism, crime and antisocial behaviour. There was even a shooting in the community centre. Fashion, as they say, goes round in circles, and housing is no different: developments that are being built nowadays are reverting to low-rise. So was the Wooddene experiment worthwhile? I honestly don't think so. It's easy to say this with hindsight, but perhaps all those houses that were demolished to make room for it should have been regenerated instead.

Late one November afternoon a couple of years before the demolition, I had to serve Notices Seeking Possessions on a few properties on the block as part of a rent action campaign. I didn't mind going there in the daytime, but visiting in the evening or on a grey wintry day made me uneasy. I usually delivered NSPs on my own, but this time I wanted someone else to come along. Still, no one else was free, so off I went. The daylight was fading and it wasn't at all easy to follow the numbering of the properties. Whoever planned the lighting didn't do a good job as far as I was concerned. The only sound I could hear was my footsteps echoing off the concrete as I walked in the cold, trying to work out where on earth I was.

Each row of maisonettes is two floors high and the block's built on stilts, so that means level five is nine floors up, and the lift isn't working. I sighed and started to climb. As I came out of the stairwell onto the top landing, a cold blast of wind that definitely hadn't been blowing down on the ground smacked me in the face. It was strong enough to be scary – the sort of wind that can knock you off your feet. At the same time, I noted that the guard rail was very low indeed. I'm not tall, but it was well below my waist height. I looked around. The numbers on the doors weren't making sense. I was starting to get scared – yeah, me. *I just don't like this place. Gonna have to ring the office for directions.*

I heard Melanie's voice answer.

'Melanie? It's Charmain.'

'You okay, hon?'

'I'm at the Wooddene. I swear to God, it's creepy. I might as well be in a haunted house in Transylvania.'

Melanie laughed.

'I know!' she said. 'What's the issue?'

'I need someone to come and save me. I'm on the top floor. There's a gale-force wind up here, which nobody mentioned. It's so high I swear I can touch the bloody moon. I got to serve three NSPs. The guard rail's only waist high and you know how short I am! That's a safety concern. I don't feel like playing Superwoman right now because I ain't got a bloody cape!'

As I was reeling off this monologue, I could hear Melanie creasing up.

'How can little people live up here?' I demanded. 'You know how little I am! I'm going to get blown over the flippin' rail!'

'You'll be fine,' she laughed.

'It's all right for you! You're an Amazonian woman! I need you to save me!'

'You're strong enough to hold on!' I knew there was nothing she could really do, but I was in a scary situation and the sense of camaraderie was helping. She gave me directions and I managed to serve the NSPs by pressing myself against the wall like something out of a James Bond movie while the gale swirled around me. I was trying not to think of what would happen if a tenant who didn't like my letter came out and started raging at me. When I got back to work, I was greeted with 'Ha! You're alive then!' and the whole office was laughing. But that's what it was like. I never wanted to go up the Wooddene again.

• • •

'Charmain? It's Jeff Tomlinson speaking.'

He's an ex-Wooddene resident and I know at once what he's ringing me about. I get a sinking feeling. It's going to be another one of those calls. 'Good morning, Mr Tomlinson. How can I help you?' I say as cheerfully as I can manage. The Tomlinsons have been rehoused in an outer London borough ever since they were decanted.

'Well, now.' He sounds really annoyed. 'I was chatting with my mate and he told me he's going back to Peckham because of his right to return. He's moving into that new block that got built on the Wooddene.' There's a pause, as though he's waiting for me to respond. 'What about me, then?' he demands.

'Right,' I say. 'So when you were decanted, you had to fill in a transfer form. There was a right-of-return form along with it. You would have been given both of them. Did you fill it in?'

There's silence down the line. Then he says, 'I must have done, innit?'

'Well, I wouldn't know, Mr Tomlinson. But all this would have been explained to you at the time. And if you *did* fill out a right-of-return form, I'm sure you would have been contacted already. So I'm guessing that you didn't.'

'But I must have!'

'Can you remember doing it?'

'I dunno! There must be a record confirming that I did!'

I've had this conversation before. Sadly, it just goes round in circles. Even though I explain that we've got all the records, Mr Tomlinson is adamant that we either didn't tell him about his right of return, or else that he filled out the form and we've lost it.

'Housing Options has the forms now, Mr Tomlinson.'

'What's Housing Options?'

'It's part of Southwark Council. Another department.'

'So what am I supposed to do now? 'Cos I want to come back!'

I give him the contact details for Housing Options and tell him they'll assist him if they can. But he's shouting at the wrong person. That form was the only chance he had and he didn't take it. I'm not able to deal with an agitated man who's trying to blame Southwark Council for something he should have considered properly at the time.

But I also understand how Mr Tomlinson feels. It had its problems, but some of Wooddene's residents grew up there. Their parents and grandparents lived in North Peckham before the estate existed. Their friends were all round there and so were their family support networks. It's where they belonged and it's hard to have to start all over again somewhere else. As we moved these people out, we knew that we were breaking up a tightly knit community that couldn't just be recreated at the click of a property developer's fingers.

And who's taken their place in Peckham? A new community of high-fliers, people who can afford the prices. They don't involve themselves with locals. Some of the homes in the new development where Wooddene used to be are described as 'affordable', but all that word means is that rents are set at 80 per cent of their market value. But when a two-bedroom flat costs £625,000... well – is 80 per cent of that 'affordable', really?

I often walk past the new buildings and I can see how many of the flats are standing empty. It's at least a quarter, I'd say. Meanwhile, Southwark Council has 18,000 people on its waiting lists for housing. We're under huge pressure, building new homes as quickly as we can, but it's nothing like fast enough to meet the demand. Who benefits from these empty properties? Certainly not our residents. Not our communities.

Will we ever house those 18,000 people? I don't see it happening. As their children reach adulthood, demand will increase still further, and even more people will be forced to move out of the area, away from their families and the areas where they want to live. The support from having their kin around them will dwindle, making life harder and more expensive for them.

So what do we think we're doing? We've taken an area that once had a thriving community, and replaced it with empty space. Why not rent out that space that no one wants to locals at council rates? That way we could give people homes who need them and the developers would still be paid some rent. Or could having these buildings standing there just be some kind of tax benefit for those very developers?

• • •

When I was growing up, we often went shopping in Peckham. In those days it was full of working-class families like ours. There were no obvious differences between us other than the colour of our skin – you'd maybe see the odd person whose clothes may not have been as good as yours, or who had physical or mental-health issues, but as a kid it was just part and parcel of your life. I don't think anyone back then had the time to observe as much as they do now. I remember seeing a man in very threadbare clothes begging for money once: his skin looked like olive leather, his hair was matted and he had a tin cup in his hand. When my mum dropped what looked like two shillings in his cup, he smiled at her and said, 'Thank you, missus.'

Mum would meet her friends in Peckham market, like all the other mums, and they'd stand around chatting in awkward places while we kids were expected to wait silently next to them, bumped sideways by every passer-by and their aunt. There were women there from all different backgrounds trailing their kids along with them to carry shopping bags or pull the trolley, and every trolley-puller had a face just like me – one that said I'd rather be watching Saturday-morning telly or playing run-outs on the estate. Still, I knew I'd get a beef patty if I went shopping with Mum. *Wicked…*

The best place in the market was the pet shop. It had a big green parrot perched on a stand, like something from a zoo or off the telly. We were allowed to go and have a look at it and although you could see it had a lead attaching it to the perch, you always had the feeling it could go for you, so we stood at least five feet away. I was enthralled by this huge, bright, exotic creature right there in the middle of Peckham.

Afterwards we'd walk to Jones and Higgins – Peckham's very own version of Harrods – where Mum would buy her threads and laces for edging. That store had everything, from the restaurant to make-up and perfume counters, a toy department and fashion floors. It was *the* place to shop. And there was C&A, Woolworths… even Trueform, where we bought the 'granny shoes' that suddenly became a fashion statement for us '70s kids. All those establishments are long gone now, but they'll always be fondly remembered by us.

The Peckham of my youth has disappeared now. I'm all for change and modernisation – that's the progress of life. But we did feel like part of a community back then. I don't think our children or grandchildren will have what my generation grew up with – that sense of belonging. Above all, I think it's unacceptable for rich people to force out the poor. We have to try to keep the place affordable. If we don't do that, everything else will be lost to gentrification.

• • •

I've been a council housing officer for more than twenty years, and quite often I've seen changes for the better. Health and safety awareness is one of them: some front-line council employees have personal alarms, which are really effective. I wish I'd had one of those when my aggressive applicant Michael was blocking my exit from his flat. When things go wrong, there's counselling and support for staff who have difficult or frightening experiences. Housing officers are certainly safer these days, although we know that there will always be risks in the work that we do.

But not all the changes are so positive. Small local housing teams that were responsible for everything that happened on their patch have been replaced by centralised management systems. Tenants don't like it. Once, they could speak to a person who knew their situation, but now they get referred to many different departments. The new structure feels cold and remote. And housing officers don't like it either. Once, we took responsibility ourselves, and saw matters through to their conclusion; nowadays we're often just gatekeepers to other services.

Another big change is the way that council services are funded. As an old-school housing officer, I had my own budget and I was responsible for residents' repairs and voids on my patch. Of course, I had to justify my spending. But now the funds are centralised, each area is allotted their own amount and everything we want to do comes out of that. If anything needs doing on our estates that's not been budgeted for, we can apply for grants – with no guarantee that we'll be successful, of course – but as housing officers, we try. This competition for funding has introduced a lot of tension between the departments and agencies. Everybody's looking for someone else to pay, or trying to make the case that the money should come from somewhere else. And every year the pot gets smaller, so we're fighting over less.

I'm old school, I know, but everything feels corporate now, not personal. My colleagues and I often feel like glorified admin assistants. We went into this profession to help people, but now we're tied to Key Performance Indicators instead of being tied to our tenants. We don't blame the local authority, though – it isn't their fault.

Who really wants these changes? I don't know. But they still happen. It feels as though none of us can fight this. The council is focused on its strategic goals, but we remember the old ways of working and we feel a sense of loss. Digital gateways can't replace the right people working on the ground.

During the pandemic, the whole country clapped for our healthcare workers because we wanted to show our appreciation for all that they do – and they do go above and beyond, there's no doubt whatsoever. But no one acknowledged all the other frontline workers, out there every day because the nature of their jobs wouldn't let them work from home. We were never mentioned, and that does harm to your morale. We're a social service too.

• • •

We can't always make as much difference to our residents as we'd like. My tenant Mr Mehri is still living in his flat on the Shakespeare estate. I moved away from that patch and didn't see him for a while, but then I was moved back and it's been nice to have the chance to catch up with him again. He's needed some repairs and I've been sorting them out.

His cancer can't be cured but he's living with the disease; managing it. He probably won't see his family again, but his contact with them is easier than it was and he does get some news. I wonder how his sons are – perhaps they have children of their own by now. We chat but I don't ask him too many questions because I don't want to bring up things that will upset him. If he wants to talk, I'll listen. That's all I can offer him.

There can't always be a happy ending, and for some people there isn't an ending at all. Things just carry on. Sometimes as a housing officer, you have to help maintain a tenant in a situation that's not good. You know that what you are sustaining is only the unhappiness they feel. I can't comfort Mr Mehri and he's been left to endure his life, sadly and quietly. There's nothing anyone can do.

England is his home now. He knows it, but I'm not sure that he feels it. He's grateful to be looked after, but he also feels homesick and lonely. He misses the people he loves most. Home isn't just a place – it's a feeling, and it's many years now since he felt that he belongs. At least I can provide him with a safe place to live.

• • •

I'm walking back to my office in Meeting House Lane after an early morning visit, not taking much notice of anyone in particular, when I see a smartly dressed lady with a big smile on her face coming towards me. 'Charmain!' she calls. 'Charmain! It's Pleasant!' She can see I didn't recognise her at first.

'Pleasant! It's so great to see you! How are you doing?' We give each other the biggest and longest hug.

'I'm good,' she says. 'I'm on my way to work. Just stopped in Peckham to pick up some bits.'

'Oh my gosh, Pleasant – you look beautiful. So what are you doing now?'

'I'm a staff nurse.'

'Oh my God! But that's fantastic. The last time I saw you, you were still studying to be a nurse!'

'Yes, I know. I'm planning to do my masters now.' She smiles proudly.

'Wow! I knew you had it in you.'

Her face grows more serious. 'If I didn't have your help,' she says to me, 'I don't know where I'd be right now.'

I look her deep into her eyes. 'Pleasant, you did all of this, not me. I just pointed you to where you could get help, my love. Don't you ever praise me; praise yourself. You're a very strong woman.' I give her another huge hug. I'm just so proud. It feels a bit like she's my daughter and she's just graduated uni.

'And oh my God,' I ask, 'how are the kids doing?'

'Growing up!' She bursts out laughing. 'Ama's in primary school and Isaac's in secondary.'

'Get away! That little baby who used to sleep in the meeting room goes to school now?'

'I know. It's all so fast. But life is good, Charmain. It's changed from the way it used to be. You have to let me thank you properly. I am so grateful for all you did. I will never forget it.'

We look at each other, and both of us smile. 'And now,' Pleasant tells me, 'I am going to be late! I'm parked just round the corner.'

'You have a wonderful day,' I say to her.

'And you, Charmain.'

I stand there for a moment and watch her striding briskly along the pavement. I can almost see the energy and purpose flowing through her. It's another high-energy day in Southwark and all around us there's a buzz and whirl of motion. The area has its problems, sure, but it's still an amazing place to be.

I'd better get a move on, or I'm going to be late to work

myself. I've a busy day ahead of me: a referral to Social Services for a social worker to be assigned to a resident, a case conference with Children's Services, an appointment with one of my hoarders and… whatever else the day will bring. One thing you can say about being a housing officer: it's never boring.